Poverty and Health

Poverty and Health

Economic Causes
and Consequences
of Health Problems

Harold S. Luft

Ballinger Publishing Company • Cambridge, Massachusetts
A Subsidiary of J.B. Lippincott Company

This book is printed on recycled paper.

International Standard Book Number 0−88410−515−6

Library of Congress Catalog Card Number: 77−27913

Printed in the United States of America

Library of Congress Cataloging in Publication Data

Luft, Harold S.
   Poverty and health.

   1. Poor—Diseases—United States. 2. Poor—Medical care—United States. 3. Chronically ill—United States—Socioeconomic status. 4. Handicapped—United States—Socioeconomic status. I. Title.
RA418.5.P6L84   362.1'04'22   77−27913
ISBN 0−88410−515−6

Contents

Chapter 6
Disability and Social Welfare   171

List of Figures

List of Tables

Preface

This book reflects a concern about two major social problems—poverty and poor health. Each can be devastating alone; but they are often intertwined, compounding their effects. It is important for social policy, however, to try to determine what is cause and what is effect. In part, this desire stems from an oversimplified view of the world, one without simultaneous causes and feedback loops. More importantly, identifying causes can help suggest policies that can prevent problems, not just alleviate their effects. Prevention is critical because people are involved, not just nameless figures who get sick and then collect disability compensation or welfare payments.

A concern for the social implications of poverty and health problems leads to the design of policies and a call for action. The history of social policy, however, is replete with examples of well-intentioned policy initiatives based on incomplete data and an inadequate understanding of the problem. Sometimes such policies are merely expensive failures. Sometimes, however, the failure leads to a backlash that threatens not only the policy in question, but other initiatives as well. Thus, while we should still be daring in designing policy, we should first try to shed some light on the obstacles facing us.

This study attempts to provide some illumination of the interrelationships between poverty and health problems. At first glance, the two seem to be inextricably intertwined, yet closer examination reveals some rather clear unidirectional effects. Careful definitions of what is meant by "poverty" and "health problems" go a long way toward understanding their relationship. Well-designed data sets provide the second key ingredient to empirical estimation of causation.

While I have been fortunate to be able to use two such data sets, the Survey of Disabled Adults and the Survey of Economic Opportunity, I have also tried to show that much can be learned by careful examination of simple published data from the National Health Surveys. In fact, throughout this book I have attempted to develop each point in several ways, using several sources of data. The reasoning is that no single data source or method of analysis should be relied upon; only by developing a series of estimates that make logical as well as statistical sense can we place much faith on the results.

This investigation grew out of my training in public finance, human resources, and health economics at Harvard. The topic initially seemed to be a logical amalgam of those areas, but it also had to meet two other criteria—empirical rigor and policy relevance. I was fortunate in having two advisors, Martin Feldstein and Rashi Fein, who helped me meet those two criteria. Like many dissertations, it was completed under substantial time pressure. Unlike many dissertation writers, however, I then had a postdoctoral fellowship at the Harvard Center for Community Health and Medical Care to reflect upon and improve the work. Additional time thinking about the issues at Stanford University led me to add both empirical studies and policy analyses.

Whereas fine wines improve merely by ageing, this research improved with the help of many people who read and commented on parts or all of it. Especially important were Rodney Beard, John P. Bunker, Richard Caves, Victor Fuchs, John Hershey, Joel Kavet, Joan Morrell, and Kenneth Warner. Larry Casalino provided valuable research assistance in the rewriting of the entire manuscript. Natalie Fisher typed draft after draft with amazing speed and accuracy. Throughout the process, from the first glimmer of an idea to the final proofing, my wife Lorry not only reminded me about where I wanted to go with the project, but helped me get there. This book is the result of her gentle prods and substantive assistance.

Poverty and Health

※ *Chapter 1*

Discussion of the Issues

Major changes are currently taking place in both professional and public discussions of health problems. In the 1960s the major focus was on medical care and its provision. For many reasons, the emphasis is now beginning to shift to the causes and consequences of health problems. This book investigates the economic causes and consequences of health problems through empirical analyses of the magnitude of the issues and the causal relationships involved. Such analyses can serve as a foundation for rationally based policies to help reduce the prevalence of health problems and lessen their effects on people and society.

This book begins with the premise that health problems are widespread even among the under sixty-five, noninstitutionalized population. There is ample evidence of this in the National Health Interview Survey and other sources. Furthermore, these same data show a strong association between poverty and the presence of health problems. The question is, Does poverty cause poor health, or does poor health cause poverty? My first task is to unravel the lines of causation, at least for major, long-term health problems. The published data of the national health surveys and other, less well known, but more specific surveys, allow an identification of some key determinants of health problems. Low income, low education, and the occupations held by the poor *do* have an important *causal* role. But a "health problem" can be anything from controlled hypertension to totally disabling quadriplegia. Thus, my second task is to identify factors that lead a given level of functional limitation, such as a bad back, to be more or less disabling. As will be seen, people with less education, those initially in low paying jobs, blacks, and women are more likely to be adversely affected by a health problem and to suffer greater reductions in labor force participation and earnings. Those people who often begin with a greater chance of being in poverty tend to experience greater disabilities and become even more impoverished. This leads to my third task—measuring the individual and social effects of disabilities on personal earnings and the extent to which social welfare programs help alleviate the individual burdens. The costs of disability are large and account for a substantial fraction of poverty in America. While various programs help to shift some of these costs to those better able to bear the burden, much more needs to be done. Therefore, my final task in this book is to discuss some of the policy issues that must be addressed and to offer an approach for dealing with the problem.

This chapter will set the stage for the empirical work that follows. The first section briefly examines the shifting focus of health concern between the 1960s and 1970s and why such a shift has occurred. The second section outlines three broad areas of policy interest. The first involves factors that influence the incidence of health problems. The second is the role of socioeconomic variables in determining the severity of the effects of a given condition. The third focuses on the impact of a condition on a person and his or her family. The final section of this chapter provides a brief outline of the remainder of the book.

FROM MEDICAL CARE
TO HEALTH PROBLEMS

Social Policy and Access to Medical Care

The 1960s saw the culmination of several decades of effort on the part of advocates for social reform. The War on Poverty and the Great Society brought social action programs for the poor and, in the health arena, the establishment of Medicare, Medicaid, and Neighborhood Health Center programs. These programs marked the first major successes for the national health insurance advocates who had been maintaining the struggle for such social welfare legislation since the early 1900s (Corning, 1969; Harris, 1966). It was hoped that these programs would redistribute resources, remove the financial barriers to medical care, and make it accessible to all. Furthermore, the imminent passage of a national health insurance program promised to remove the last barriers to the perceived "wonders of modern medicine."

The causes for optimism in this period are not hard to discern.[1] The 1950s were a period of rapid innovation and dissemination of antibiotics and new vaccines for polio and other childhood diseases (Schifrin, 1978). New surgical techniques were making possible kidney transplants and open heart surgery. Other breakthroughs were occurring at a regular rate. It therefore appeared that the major social responsibility was to make the fruits of medical research available to everyone.

The underlying assumption was often a rather simple model of disease in which a single agent, such as a virus, bacterium, or genetic break, causes a lesion that then develops into what is recognized as disease (Powles, 1973). The goal of medicine is then relatively simple —find the causal agent, eradicate it in the patient, and repair the damage that the disease has done. Within this framework, people get sick and medical care cures them. Thus, it is particularly unfortunate if there are some people for whom medical care is inaccessible because of financial barriers or supply shortages within certain geographic areas. The new financing schemes of the 1960s, Medicare and Medicaid, were instituted to provide insurance coverage for the two major groups who could not afford private insurance coverage, the elderly and the very poor, respectively. Even if the poor had insurance to pay for medical care, the providers were often not available in the inner cities and rural areas. This led to the development of neighborhood health centers to bring the providers to the people, and medical schools were called upon and given support to train more physicians.

These programs were at least partially effective in meeting their goals. The proportion of the poor and elderly with insurance for medical care increased from about 30 percent in 1962–1963 to about 75 percent in 1970 (USNCHS, 1967: 10/42; USNCHS, *Health: United States, 1975*, 1976: 75).[2] There was also a redistribution of services toward those traditionally underserved groups. For instance,

---

1. Of course, not everyone was optimistic. In fact, the American Medical Association and much of the medical establishment bitterly fought Medicare. They saw (and still see) the involvement of the federal government as a fatal intrusion in the hallowed doctor-patient relationship and believed that it would lead to increasing bureaucratization of medicine. In some ways they were quite correct, but by the mid-1960s they no longer had the power to stop Medicare. (See, for instance, Kelman, 1971: 30–38.) The critical point, however, is that the pessimists did not argue against the efficacy of medical care, just that new financing schemes would encroach upon the traditional autonomy of the physician.

2. The *Vital and Health Statistics* publications of the U.S. National Center for Health Statistics will be frequently used throughout this book. References to individual publications in that collection will be identified by series and number, e.g., Series 10, no. 42 will be 10/42.

instead of the poor having the lowest number of physician visits per capita, the utilization rates have become comparable across income groups (Bice, Eichhorn, and Fox, 1972). Although these were impressive changes over a rather short period of time, not all the goals of equality of access have been met. Medicare and Medicaid reimbursement levels are sometimes so low that some practitioners will not accept such patients.[3] Existing programs have not been effective in attracting medical resources to the inner cities and the rural areas while, at the same time, federal funds for targeted programs such as the neighborhood health centers have dried up (Reynolds, 1976). Even the utilization data are misleading. Although per capita physician utilization is now about equal across income groups, those data show substantial differentials in terms of utilization patterns and utilization relative to "need." The poor are much more likely not to see a physician at all within the year, and if they do see one, it is much more likely to be in a clinic or emergency room (USNCHS, 1975: 10/97; Andersen, Lion, and Anderson, 1976). If one controls for medical need by the presence of chronic conditions or symptoms, the poor are still less likely than the nonpoor to receive care even if they are eligible for Medicare or Medicaid (Davis and Reynolds, 1976; Aday, 1975). Thus, more remains to be done in improving access to the medical care system.

Questioning the Value of Medical Care at the Margin

While there is still concern about access to care, in the 1970s some observers began to question whether more medical care for everyone is really an appropriate goal (Fuchs, 1974; Fogarty International Center, 1976). The emphasis, it seems, is beginning to shift from *medical care* to *health* and to the prevention of *health problems.* This shift is not anti-medical care. Instead, it recognizes the many true benefits of medicine while questioning whether the marginal (or incremental) gains of increased expenditures in medical care exceed the benefits that could be obtained by spending the extra resources on other means of improving health. It is still recognized that the poor are relatively underserved, and it may be appropriate to direct more medical resources toward them. Such resources, the argument goes, should be obtained by reallocating current expenditures for medical care, rather than from a further encroachment on nonmedical expenditures. (The share of gross national product

3. See, for instance, the report of a survey of California physicians in which 45 percent said they would not accept or are cutting back on Medicaid patients, largely because the fees were too low (California Medical Association, 1975).

allocated to medical care increased from 5.9 percent in 1965 to 8.3 percent in 1975 (Mueller and Gibson, 1976: 6)).

The increased expenditures on and utilization of medical care in the 1960s and 1970s are not associated with major improvements in health status as currently determinable. Of course, health status is a very elusive concept, and there are few agreed upon measures. One obvious partial measure is the age-adjusted mortality rate or some measure of life expectancy. Only in the last few years have there been improvements in the death rate. Some of the most significant reductions have been in automobile accidents following the 55 mph speed limit (USNCHS, 1977: 25/11, supplement). Furthermore, some of the recent reductions in major causes of death, such as heart disease, are not associated with any known changes in medical practice or service delivery (Walker, 1977; Stamler, 1975). Mortality, however, is a very limited measure of health status—its only advantage is simplicity. One measure of morbidity, the proportion of people describing themselves as being limited in their usual activities by health problems, has shown no observable improvement over the last decade or so.[4] Thus, the available aggregate measures do not indicate any substantial improvements attributable to the increased medical expenditure (Burger, 1974).

Questioning has also occurred at a more specific level. Substantial variations in surgical rates for specific conditions in various localities have been observed with little evidence of differences in outcomes (Bunker, 1970; Wennberg and Gittelsohn, 1973, 1975). Randomized controlled trials of certain popular procedures and drugs have often found few differences in outcome for specific groups of patients (Mather, et al., 1971; Cochrane, 1972; Braunwald, 1977; Murphy et al., 1977). Thus, the evidence is beginning to mount that, at the margin, more or less conventional medical care is unlikely to make much difference in health outcomes.

In part, this situation seems to have arisen because medical science has cured most of the easily curable or preventable diseases and is now left with the more intractable ones. The top three causes of death in 1900 were infectious or parasitic diseases such as influenza and pneumonia, tuberculosis, and gastritis, accounting for 31 percent of all deaths. By 1960 these three accounted for less than 5 percent of the deaths (Lerner and Anderson, 1963). Most of these conditions are treatable with antibiotics or are prevented by sanitation or innoculation. The major causes of death are now heart disease, cancer, and stroke, accounting for two-thirds of all deaths in 1975 (USNCHS,

4. See, for instance, Figure 6–1.

1977: 25/11, supplement). With some exceptions, there is little convincing evidence that modern medicine has been very effective against these conditions (Powles, 1973). In many cases, medical care merely briefly but expensively prolongs the final phases of the disease.

At the same time that people have been questioning the efficacy of medical care at the margin, they have also begun to think more about the quality of life. Lately there has been growing concern about environmental quality and the quality and safety of consumer products. In terms of health, people are beginning to question whether extreme measures should be taken to prolong life, if little can be said for the quality of that life. This issue has recently been raised in dramatic fashion by the case of Karen Ann Quinlan, and it will become more important as the population ages and the proportion of people with chronic health problems increases.

A New Model of Disease Causation

The emphasis seems to be shifting from the traditional medical orientation of "cure" to one of prevention and of adapting the environment to meet the needs of people with health problems. The new model of "disease" involves three broad groups of factors—heredity, external agents, and the host's resistance. Although some conditions are clearly hereditary, many more seem to have a hereditary factor in terms of predisposition to the disease. Some diseases are "caused" by an external factor such as virus or bacterium. Yet not everyone exposed to the agent develops the condition. The third factor is the individual's resistance to disease, which is often lowered by external stresses.[5]

This more complex view of the causes of health problems makes it necessary to place a greater emphasis on the environment and on lifestyle, areas not traditionally of major interest to medicine. Prevention now means not only vaccination, but also eliminating environmental and workplace hazards. It also involves changing behavior and lifestyles.

Although prevention may help reduce the incidence of certain conditions and extend the period of disability-free life, people will continue to develop health problems and become disabled. Thus, attention must also be paid to the needs of people with health prob-

5. A simple example of this has been demonstrated under laboratory conditions. A single strain of mice was randomly divided into two groups, both of which were exposed to the same cancer virus. One group was subjected to more stress than the other. The stressed group exhibited significantly more cancer within shorter periods of time than the nonstressed group (Riley, 1975).

lems and efforts be made to reduce the effects of their limitations. This is the easier task because it primarily involves policy changes of a much more traditional nature, rather than those that require new knowledge about the causes of disease and how to effect major behavioral changes.[6]

An Overview of the Extent and Impact of Disability

A brief preview of some of the results presented in subsequent chapters will help put these issues into perspective. These policies are addressed to major segments of the total population. For instance, if one limits the discussion to people who have chronic conditions that interfere with the amount or kind of work that they can do—a convenient definition of disability—then the focus is on people who still suffer a wide range of limitations but whose conditions are serious enough to warrant some public policy consideration. The social convention of retirement at age sixty-five makes it convenient to consider the elderly and nonelderly separately. A distinction must also be made between the institutionalized and noninstitutionalized populations; almost all of the former are severely disabled. About 40 percent of all noninstitutionalized people aged sixty-five or more are limited in their ability to perform their usual major activities. (This does not include those who have retired because of health problems but are not limited in their retirement activities [USNCHS, 1975: 10/100]). Among the working age population, aged eighteen to sixty-four, almost half a million, or 0.5 percent, are institutionalized and 17.2 percent of the noninstitutionalized are limited in the kind and/or amount of activity they can do (Frohlich, 1971: 1; Haber, 1968).

Most of the empirical analyses in this book will be restricted to this last subgroup, the eighteen to sixty-four year old, noninstitutionalized population with disabling health problems. Their health problems range widely in severity, from relatively minor problems that still allow a person to work full time, but at a different job, to conditions resulting in total incapacitation. Minor conditions are more common than severe ones—only about a third of the group is in the most severely disabled category. Even with this broad range of problems, the disabled lost at least $22 billion in earnings in 1967 relative to what they would have been expected to earn. More than half the loss was suffered by those who dropped out of the labor force for the whole year because of their disability. But health problems were

---

6. The next section will outline some of the policy questions relevant to these issues.

found to have an impact on every component of earnings, from weeks worked per year to the hourly wage rate.

The relationship between health problems and poverty is strong and can be measured in several ways. About 65 percent of poor families consisting of at least a husband and wife include a disabled adult. At least 30 percent of the disabled who are currently poor are poor *because* of their health problems; among white men this figure is close to 75 percent. Disability is responsible for at least 9 to 18 percent of *all* poverty among the nonaged. Similarly, at least 23 to 31 percent of all nonaged poor white men are poor because of their disability. Furthermore, the transfer payment programs do a very inadequate job. Payments total only about 40 percent of the lost earnings and remove from poverty only 40 percent of the disabled who were impoverished by health problems.

The probability of the average person in the eighteen to sixty-four age group becoming disabled within the year is 1.24 percent. Obviously, average incidence rates are misleading, since the probability increases substantially with age. More importantly, it varies with socioeconomic characteristics. The probability of an adult in a low (under $4,000) income family becoming disabled in a given year is about twice that of one in a family with $8,000 or more, after adjusting for age, race, sex, and education. Similarly, the likelihood of disability for someone with nine years or more of school is less than half that of someone with less than nine years, after adjusting for age, sex, race, and income. Furthermore, the twofold difference in disability incidence between black and white men is entirely explained by their differences in income and education.

Although these socioeconomic characteristics appear to be important causes of disability, they are, at least in part, serving to represent the influence of various occupational factors. Such factors play two rather different roles in disability. The first role is the traditional one of occupational hazards or conditions that lead to or exacerbate certain health problems. These are characteristics such as dust, fumes, stress, and the like. The second way that job characteristics influence disability is when specific activities are required, such as lifting or finger dexterity, that interact with a corresponding functional limitation. For instance, a back injury is likely to have more severe implications for a longshoreman than a watchmaker.

Other socioeconomic characteristics also have an influence on the severity of specific functional limitations. Education is particularly important in allowing job flexibility and in enabling people to shift to other jobs with a smaller loss in earnings. Education is also much more significant for those who "normally" have a smaller range of job opportunities—for example, the poor, blacks, and women—than for white men who had well-paying jobs before the onset of their condition. These differences lead to different behavioral responses to health problems. In general, white males are better able to obtain alternative jobs, although at a substantial reduction in weekly earnings, while blacks are more likely to be forced out of the labor force because of health problems.

This review has highlighted a number of points. Perspectives on health and medical are in the process of undergoing substantial changes. In the 1960s and early 1970s the focus was on assuring equity in access to medical care and on making more care available. Increasing costs and insufficient evidence that more medical care produces benefits worth the cost has led to a shift in focus. There is now a growing concern for the prevention of health problems and care for those with disabilities. The evidence to be presented in the following chapters suggests that this new emphasis is most appropriate. Disabling health problems impose substantial economic costs. They are also more likely to occur among and to severely affect certain already disadvantaged subgroups.

POLICY QUESTIONS CONCERNING HEALTH PROBLEMS

This background discussion leads to a consideration of policy issues in three broad areas: efforts at reducing the incidence of health problems, activities to reduce the severity of a given health problem, and programs to reduce the impact of disability on the person and his or her family's socioeconomic status. These three areas will be discussed in turn.

Reducing the Incidence of Health Problems

It appears to many that reducing the incidence of health problems is primarily a medical issue. However, by far the major emphasis of medical research is on the treatment of disease, not its prevention. Those studies that are concerned with the causes of disease usually focus on a single factor, not multiple, interactive causes (Powles, 1973). Thus, one major policy question is how to begin to shift the research interests of the medical community to broaden our understanding of what to do in terms of prevention.

Prevention, itself, involves two rather different foci. Primary prevention focuses on reducing or eliminating the causes of health problems. Secondary prevention focuses on the early detection and treatment of disease (Louria, et al., 1976). Screening and automated multiphasic testing programs have been suggested for various conditions. Some studies, however, indicate that many such programs are very expensive and may not be worthwhile (Cochrane and Elwood, 1969). The costs go beyond simple financial expenses; in some situations, errors may lead to unnecessary surgery and disfigurement (*Wall Street Journal*, 1977). In others, such as mammography, the test itself is hazardous enough so as to be recommended only for high risk people (Swartz and Reichling, 1977; U.S. National Cancer Institute, 1977).

The policy questions related to the socioeconomic and environmental issues in prevention touch upon almost the whole range of human endeavor. One in five disabilities are caused on the job. Thus, the importance of reducing occupational health and safety hazards should be given high priority. Government agencies currently set standards for workplaces and make some effort at enforcement, while Workers' Compensation programs are designed to make the costs of occupationally caused disabilities part of the cost of production. How effective are such programs, what incentives do they provide, and how can they be improved upon? In a broader social sense, who should bear the costs of disability or hazard reduction—the employer, the employee, the consumer, or society at large? Hazard reduction consumes resources that may be used for other purposes—how safe a society do we really want? Similar questions arise with respect to nonoccupational hazards, such as the safety of various consumer products. Probably more important are various types of individual behavior like smoking, drinking, and overeating. To what extent should people be encouraged, allowed, or discouraged from partaking in such individual vices and, if the current situation is nonoptimal, how should it be changed? Still other questions relate to broad social policies that may be supported for many different reasons. For instance, pure income support programs like a guaranteed annual income are likely to reduce the various stresses of poverty, allow people to have better housing and food, and safer products. But, at the same time, cigarette consumption may increase.

Reducing the Severity of Health Problems

A second group of policy questions focuses on what can be done to reduce the severity of health problems. Obviously, the individual's medical status is of major importance, and advances in treatment and physical rehabilitation are vital. But there are many areas in which broader policy activities may have a substantial influence on the extent to which a health problem results in job changes and unemployment. For instance, should vocational rehabilitation programs be expanded along present lines or changed substantially? What is the role of racial and sexual discrimination in the labor market, and would the reduction of such discrimination differentially affect the disabled? Can educational programs be established to provide people job skills and flexibility that can serve as implicit insurance in case they develop a health problem? Can employers be given effective incentives to hire the disabled; should they be required to do so? Do business cycle swings differentially affect the disabled?

Reducing the Impact of Health Problems

The third area of policy concern is alleviating the effects of disability on the individual and his or her family. How large are such effects and what do they involve in terms of income loss, extraordinary medical and other costs, anxiety, stigma, and so forth? Are insurance schemes possible to compensate for the income losses? What are the incentives implicit in such schemes and do they encourage or discourage efforts to rehabilitate the individual? How feasible is it to provide medical care "insurance" for someone with a known health problem?[7] Who should bear the extra costs that may be involved? When designing policies in all of these areas, attention should be paid to the problems of feedback loops. Is it feasible to develop a scheme whereby linkages are created between the causes of health problems and their consequences so that the incentives exist to encourage the reduction of hazards, where possible, and the payment of equitable compensation where hazard reduction is not possible? Such a system might then develop its own dynamic toward improving the health and well-being of the population. The remaining chapters develop at least partial answers to these and other questions.

OUTLINE OF THE BOOK

Chapter 2 sets the stage for the empirical analyses that follow by outlining a series of methodological considerations. This first requires a careful definition of various aspects of health problems. With these definitions in mind, it is possible to outline a causal model of the

---

7. A minor semantic difficulty arises because of my distinction between medical care and the new focus on health problems and health care. The latter is obviously a broader concept and includes the whole range of preventive actions such as hazard reduction, diet, and behavior changes. It is apparent, therefore, that the current forms of insurance that are called "health insurance" (such as Blue Cross/Blue Shield) are really medical care insurance. In Chapter 7 I will introduce an insurance scheme that could more appropriately be called health insurance.

relationships between various socioeconomic factors and different types of health problems. Various types of health problems, such as pathology, illness, sickness, impairment, functional limitations, and disability are introduced and distinguished. The approach to empirically estimating this model is then developed through a discussion of types of data and the specific sources used in the following chapters. The primary data sources are the 1966 Survey of Disabled Adults, a sample of noninstitutionalized disabled adults aged eighteen to sixty-four, and the 1967 Survey of Economic Opportunity, a random household survey of the entire noninstitutionalized population. The secondary sources are the various Health Interview and Health Examination Surveys conducted by the National Center for Health Statistics.

Chapter 3 presents a broad overview of the available national data relating to socioeconomic factors as causes of health problems. To provide consistent results on a national base, most of the data are drawn from the National Health Examination Survey and the National Health Interview Survey. The first section of the chapter provides a discussion of the problems in comparing acute and chronic conditions and argues that the exclusion of acute conditions is not a major problem. The bulk of the chapter is then split into six subsections. The first outlines a number of methodological considerations in interpreting the data. The remaining five discuss, in turn, pathologies identified by medical examination, impairments, chronic conditions, functional limitations and disabilities, and perceived health status.

Chapter 4 examines factors related to the incidence of disability. Two approaches are taken, one that considers all disabilities and one that focuses on occupational factors. The first approach develops a fivefold table of the probability (or incidence) of disability with respect to the person's age, race, sex, education, and income at the time of the onset of the condition. This rather simple technique suggests that either income and education, or things correlated with income and education, have a substantial causal role in the probability of disability. But, these variables may be serving as proxies for the effects of various occupational factors, both in causing specific pathologies or impairments and in interacting with functional limitations to cause work disabilities. The second approach, therefore, examines the influence of occupational factors in the causes of disabilities among men. It allows a richer set of variables, but at the expense of fewer observations and more approximations.

Chapter 5 emphasizes the factors that influence the various outcomes of disability: job changes, altered labor force participation, hours worked per week, and the like. Three approaches are taken in the examination of the influence of socioeconomic factors. The first investigates the importance of the interactions between functional limitations and job requirements in determining whether a worker continues to do the same type of work, takes different work, or is unable to work at all. The second approach focuses on the factors that allow disabled persons to maintain a high ratio of current weekly earnings to earnings at the time of disability onset. Of course, because this section is restricted to data from people who are disabled, these measurements actually refer to the importance of certain variables in lessening the impact of disability, relative to the average disabled person. The third approach provides measures of the magnitudes of the impacts of disability on various components of earnings by comparing the disabled and nondisabled, controlling for other variables.

Chapter 6 explores the magnitudes of the effects of disability and shows that they are very substantial; thus, if appropriate policies can be designed to lessen the impact of disability, they should be carefully considered and implemented. A preliminary question is whether the effects of disability, and health problems more generally, should be evaluated with respect to the individual, the family, or some larger unit? The first section of the chapter briefly explores some of these issues. Unfortunately, there appears to be little consensus on the appropriate unit, and few data exist for anything other than the individual or household. The second section focuses on the magnitude of earnings losses from two extreme viewpoints—the individual and society as a whole. The former measures the implicit loss imposed upon the person who is disabled, while the latter provides an estimate of the gross loss to society attributable to disabilities. Of course, earnings losses are not necessarily the only variables of interest. Policymakers may well be more interested in the income and poverty status of the disabled person's family, thus allowing for the effects both of other potential workers and of transfer payments. The third section provides this analysis of earnings, transfers, income, and poverty status and concludes that, while things are not as bad as is implied by the effects on earnings, disability still is responsible for a substantial fraction of poverty in the United States. The fourth section offers a brief discussion of the potential problems arising from the cross-sectional nature of these analyses. The key question concerns the importance of macroeconomic variables such as the unemployment rate in the overall analysis of the causes and consequences of health problems.

The concluding chapter leaves the descriptive and empirical discussion of the problem and offers some policy proposals. These proposals go substantially beyond most policy statements. They are not a blueprint for action but a means to promote more fruitful discussion of comprehensive policy. The primary emphasis of the proposed policies is on improving the chances for a healthy life, with a secondary concern for disability compensation schemes. Such schemes, however, are important and must be designed to offer the appropriate incentives and feedback so that they are not counter-productive. The first section of the chapter briefly reviews the evidence concerning the magnitude of the problems under discussion. The second section sets the stage for the policy discussion by outlining my assumptions about the major types of health problems and their causes. The third section reviews the appropriate role for public policy by focusing on two polar approaches—the interventionist approach and the pure market solution. Problems with both approaches will be discussed and then the general philosophy behind my choices will be outlined. The fourth section offers specific issues in designing policy. It includes subsections on reducing the incidence of health problems, reducing the severity of the effects of disability and reducing the impact of disability on family income. A final section outlines a scheme that applies economic incentives to try to integrate these policy issues.

✳ *Chapter 2*

Unraveling the Vicious
Circle: A Discussion
About Methodology

The relationship between low socioeconomic status and
poor health is often pictured as a vicious cycle that is
difficult or impossible to untangle. This is particularly
evident when one observes poor and sick people and asks: Are they
poor because they are sick, or sick because they are poor? Much of
the data presented in this investigation include temporally different
measures of economic and health status. This permits an evaluation
of the "cycle" in nearly unidirectional terms. First, we will examine
the effects of low income, education, and the occupations held by
lower class people on the incidence of health problems. Then we
will measure the effects of chronic health problems on changes in
labor force behavior and income.

As outlined in the previous chapter, one of the major findings of
this study is that the emphasis in the conventional wisdom of the
1960s and early 1970s should be revised. Although there is some
causal relationship from poverty to illness, it is much more subtle
than generally described. The effects of poor health on income,
however, are pervasive and account for a substantial fraction of
poverty in the United States. In other words, many people who
would otherwise not be poor are poor *simply because they are sick*,
but relatively few poeple who would otherwise be healthy are sick
simply because they are poor.

The mistaken emphasis in discussions of socioeconomic status and
health is not surprising given the difficulty in interpreting most of
the available data. Almost any crosstabulation comparing health status and income levels will show many low income people who

are sick and many sick people who are poor. From such a table alone nothing can be said about causation. The problem, of course, is that many of those people who are poor *and* sick were not poor *before* they became sick. Thus, a study that reports the health status and income levels of a group of individuals can demonstrate the presence or absence of a *correlation* between the two but says nothing about the *causation*. Some investigators note this problem and respond that the vicious cycle of income and health (the poor get sick, then because they are ill, they work less or lose their jobs and become still poorer) essentially makes it impossible to determine causation and that thus we must be satisfied with correlation (see, for instance, Antonovsky, 1967A; Kadushin, 1964). Others tend to ignore the circular relationship and concentrate on only one aspect, generally the effects of poverty on health status (e.g., Lerner, 1975).

Haunting pictures of the inner city slums of the nineteenth century, with their recurrent epidemics of tuberculosis, pneumonia, influenza, and other contagious diseases, have contributed much to the belief that poverty causes illness. At that time, overcrowding, horrendous working conditions, and the absence of any reasonable sanitation system almost certainly led to much higher illness rates among the poor than among the rich. For instance, Antonovsky (1967B) reviews a broad range of mortality studies supporting this image dating back to 1276. At least until the present century, the data indicate that mortality rates among the poor are at least twice those for higher socioeconomic classes. The next chapter will review existing studies of the effects of economic status on health, but the general findings indicate a lessening of the effect over time. This is probably attributable both to the alleviation of the extreme destitution that occurred fifty years ago and to medical advances that have all but eliminated most of the deadly infectious diseases.[1]

The emphasis on the causality from poverty to poor health (rather than the reverse) may also have been fostered by the general thrust of the social welfare programs of the 1960s. Not only would they reduce poverty, but in doing so, they would also keep people from getting sick. The reverse causality, from health problems to income, is less amenable to public policy. It is, however, one of the arguments used in favor of national health insurance proposals. In reality, such proposals have the primary effect of reducing the losses in wealth

1. Poverty in the United States is mainly a situation of relative deprivation. This does not make it any less real or important that steps be taken to eliminate it. It does imply, however, that certain diseases that can be prevented by adequate or even minimal sanitation and nutritional levels will not be a major factor in the United States. This is not the situation in many of the less developed countries (see Graham and Reeder, 1972).

associated with medical expenses, rather than affecting the earning capacity (or income) of the family.

There is some truth to the circular descriptions of the relationship between poverty and health, but it is more appropriate in some instances than others. For instance, the description of the poor who become ill, lose a little income, become more severely ill, and so forth, is most applicable, at least in its initial phases, to acute conditions. On the other hand, accidents, chronic conditions, and long-term disabilities are much more likely to be seen as a discrete, major change in health status. The effects of such health problems are also more likely to be large and, thus, measurable as changes in occupation or labor force participation. Long-term conditions are the most important in terms of their effects on the individual and society. Concentrating on them allows the interactions between socioeconomic factors and health to be examined as a series of phases. Thus, a person is likely to be working at a certain job, to be earning a given income, and to have certain basic physiological predispositions to illness for several years before the onset of a particular illness. This medical condition can then be evaluated and its interaction with the person's job and lifestyle measured. Then, by continuing to monitor the individual, various changes in his income and family conditions can be examined. By comparing these changes with the life history of similar, but healthy, individuals, the impact of the condition may be estimated.[2]

The remainder of this chapter will focus on the methods by which this model of the causes and consequences of long-term health problems can be empirically estimated. The first section will develop the model. It will be seen that a "health problem" must be carefully defined; different investigators often focus on different aspects of health problems. This lack of precision in the literature is often the cause of apparently conflicting results. The second section will identify the specific aspects of the model addressed in this work and how they fit together. A final section discusses the difficulties in empirically implementing such a model and the actual data sources to be used.

DEFINITIONS OF HEALTH STATUS

Most studies concerning poverty and health are rather explicit about the socioeconomic variables that are considered, and it is usually

2. Of course, for any one person these changes might have occurred regardless of the change in health status; but by averaging the data over a large number of individuals with similar initial conditions and changes in health, it is possible to estimate the impact of health.

obvious what factors, if any, are omitted. The definition of health status is usually less explicit. More importantly, attention is rarely paid to the conceptual differences among various measures of morbidity.[3] Many of the differing reports in the literature can be reconciled if four aspects of health are considered separately: pathology, illness, impairment, and disability, (Nagi, 1969B: 10–12). Furthermore, the types of data necessary for evaluating the various aspects are different and using the wrong type of data can be misleading. The four aspects of health problems refer to different *dimensions*, rather than to stages of illness or levels of functioning. While in most cases various levels of pathology, impairment, illness, and disability are correlated, there are many instances of a severe problem on some "scales" and not others.

Pathology is identified by the mobilization of the body's defenses and coping mechanisms. It can be subdivided into the onset of the disease or injury and the simultaneous efforts of the organism to correct for the disruptive aspects of the disease. It is apparent from this definition that pathology is, at least in theory, objectively measurable in terms of abnormal cells, destroyed tissue, and the like. Thus, pathology can be determined by the examination of the person without relying upon the person's recognition of a problem.

Illness and *sickness* are two related but somewhat different concepts. Both are behavioral patterns influenced by (1) the characteristics of the pathological condition, (2) the definitions of, and reactions of, the afflicted, which in turn are influenced by (3) the definitions of, and reactions to, the situation by others. In this con-

---

3. Aside from morbidity, many studies focus on mortality and/or medical care. The former may be appropriately considered as a health status category, but is usually considered separately for several reasons. Death is a very special event in Western culture and people often react to it in ways qualitatively different than they do to very debilitating health outcomes that are functionally close to death (see, for instance, Bailey, 1970; Kubler-Ross, 1969; Zeckhauser, 1973; Morison, 1973). A second distinguishing characteristic of mortality is its objectivity. One need not worry about interrater reliability and self-reporting biases. (There are, however, substantial biases concerning the reported *causes* of death.) Studies that combine or compare mortality and morbidity have the problem that, once a person dies, he or she is dropped from the sample, in contrast to a person with lingering morbidity. Thus, arthritis causes a great deal of morbidity but little mortality. The reverse is true for cancer. Household surveys show a great deal of arthritis and little cancer. Mortality data rarely even identify arthritis. The development of indexes to combine mortality *and* morbidity data is being undertaken with varying degrees of success (see, for instance, USNCHS, 1977). Medical care utilization generally follows from a state of poor health (except for preventive care) and may change the course of the condition or otherwise alter health status. It is more appropriately considered as something that is purchased to maintain or improve health than an end in itself or a proxy for health status (see, for instance, Grossman, 1972).

text, illness may be synonomous with symptom recognition. Symptoms are obviously related to the underlying pathology, although it is common for people to exhibit symptoms without any medically detectable pathology. Pathologies may also exist without any recognized symptoms. This is not limited to presymptomatic or asymptomatic conditions, like early stages of cancer. Cultural expectations often influence what is recognized. For instance, signs indicating problems in one population may be ignored in another, either because they are so ubiquitous as not to be unusual or because of their "fit" with major values of the culture (Zola, 1966: 393—95). As examples of the first, Zola suggests diarrhea, sweating, and coughing among Mexican-Americans and low back pain among lower class women. An example of the second situation are students who see tiredness as an indication that they are working hard enough.

Sickness is even more obviously the result of cultural expectations and the reactions of others. Societies have certain general expectations concerning the obligations of the sick person and those who interact with him (King, 1972: 139). A sick person gains certain rights in terms of exemption from normal social obligations and a recognition that he is not at fault. At the same time, he accepts the responsibilities of a desire to get well and to seek help. Thus, the sick role is not an unambiguous benefit, and people with the same illnesses will differ in how they accept the sick role. For instance, upper socioeconomic groups use a wider range of conditions for the definition of sickness (King, 1972: 140).

An *impairment* is a physiological, anatomical, or psychological loss. Pathology usually implies some impairment, but an impairment can persist when the pathology is no longer active: for instance, pathology (gangrene) may result in the amputation of an arm. Again, there is some degree of cultural involvement in defining an impairment, because "loss" must be measured relative to some norm. Thus, color blindness is considered an impairment, while tone deafness is not. In general, impairments can be linked to *functional limitations*— the activity losses or restrictions resulting from the impairment. Thus, the muscle atrophy caused by the pathology of a stroke is an impairment. The resulting mobility loss (which may be different for people with the same degree of atrophy) is a functional limitation.

Finally, *disability* is a behavior pattern that evolves when functional limitations interfere with an individual's ordinary daily activities. Many pathologies and illnesses do not necessarily result in disability—diabetes, for example. Furthermore, it should be clear that the definition of disability crucially depends on the person's ordinary daily activities. Some functional limitations do more than restrict normal activities; they place the individual at a competitive disadvantage and thus may be classified as *handicaps* (Haber, 1967: 3—4).

As an example of the above concepts, consider a novelist who contracts polio and loses the use of her nonwriting arm. Her pathology is polio. It produced a recognizable illness and she was probably in one type of sick role when acutely ill and another when the acute phase was over. The impairment is recognizable as a paralyzed arm, and there are obvious functional limitations stemming from the paralysis. However, for this novelist there may be relatively little disability and no handicap. The situation is likely to be very different for an unskilled laborer with the same impairment. (Chapter 5 will focus on precisely this type of difference in severity of disability.)

A MODEL OF THE RELATIONSHIP
BETWEEN SOCIOECONOMIC FACTORS
AND HEALTH

These various aspects of health status, or more precisely, health problems, serve as the key points in a causal model linking socioeconomic factors and health. This model is summarized in Figure 2—1. At the first stage are those factors thought to influence the occurrence of various pathologies. Certain conditions are clearly related to the usual factors, such as sex, heredity, and the process of aging. There is increasing evidence that the environment in which people live and work can affect their health. Such environmental factors may be highly concentrated in the workplace or generally present in the home environment, often through air or water pollution. For instance, some cancers are linked to industrial pollution in the region (Mason et al., 1975, 1976). Other studies suggest that certain conditions may be caused or exacerbated by on the job stresses (Margolis, Kroes, and Quinn, 1974; Caplan et al., 1975).

Accidents will be strongly influenced by some of the environmental factors both at home and at work. Nutrition affects health at both ends of the spectrum. Malnutrition lowers the body's resistance to various diseases and reduces its recuperative powers (Wray, 1974). Furthermore, severe malnutrition may cause brain damage in children (Winick, 1969). At the other end, obesity appears to be a major factor in increasing the risk of hypertension and heart attacks. Proper diet is influenced by income and educational levels as well as by cultural factors. While it is likely that, on the margin, medical care makes less of a difference in health status than is usually thought to be the case, it is an important factor in both preventing

Figure 2–1. A Conceptual Framework of Health Status and Socioeconomic Factors

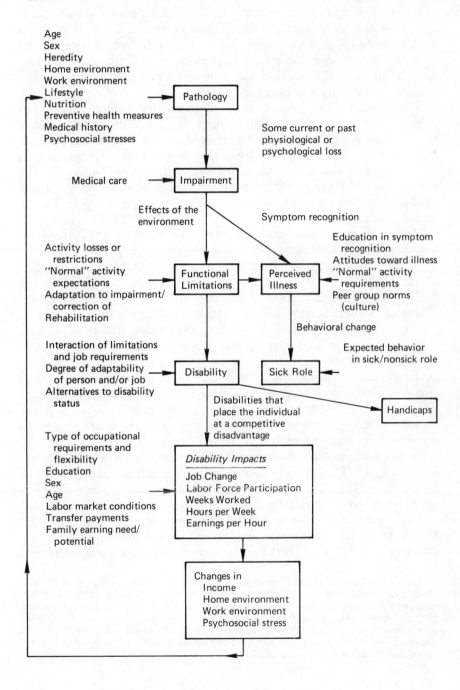

and arresting pathologies.[4] Finally, there is increasing evidence that psychosocial stresses can influence the development of pathologies (Dohrenwend and Dohrenwend, 1973). Such stresses are thought to influence not only such "logical" things as mental disorders, but even conditions such as cancer (Riley, 1975). In fact, it appears that at least three major factors are important in understanding disease: genetic predisposition, external pathogenic agents, and the functioning of the body's coping mechanisms.

The linkage from pathology to impairment is fairly direct, but may be altered by the extent of medical care. This is particularly true when the pathology can be arrested or removed with appropriate treatment. Receiving such treatment depends on perceived desires on the part of the individual, price and budget constraints, and the availability of services. Thus, socioeconomic factors that influence medical care utilization have an indirect impact on the permanency and extent of impairment.

Decisions to utilize medical care are strongly influenced by whether or not the person recognizes symptoms, perceives that he is ill, and is willing to accept the sick role (Graham and Reeder, 1972; McKinlay, 1972; Anderson, 1973). Various socioeconomic factors are important in perceptions of illness and sickness. As was discussed earlier, people must recognize a condition as being out of the ordinary to even think of it being a symptom, and their cultural attitudes must be such that illness is acceptable. Furthermore, specific problems are more likely to be noticed (and reported) if they interfere with "normal" activities—for example, more severe functional limitations. These factors lead to contradictory predictions concerning the behavior of the poor. On one hand, people in lower socioeconomic groups are thought by some to have a different body concept that leads them not to recognize problems or to "put up" with more physiological problems (Rosenblatt and Suchman, 1964; McKinlay, 1975). On the other hand, conditions are more likely to be recognized if they interfere with normal activities, and the poor tend to lead more physically demanding lives.

The "medical" aspects of the case only partly determine the extent to which an impairment results in a functional limitation. Obviously, functional limitation cannot be defined without reference

4. See Fuchs (1974) for a good discussion of the evidence that at the levels of medical care currently available to most people in the United States, environment and lifestyle are likely to be the primary methods of further improving health status. Fuchs is careful to point out that he does not believe that medicine is worthless, but rather that, at the current high levels, additional medical resources are unlikely to make a major impact on health status. See also Dubos, 1959; and McKeown and Loew, 1974.

to what normal functioning should be. Furthermore, people are often able to adapt to an impairment, correct it, or obtain rehabilitation services so that a given impairment is not limiting. For instance, people with sight in only one eye can learn certain cues to compensate for the lack of binocular depth perception. Eyeglasses and hearing aids are examples of devices to correct an impairment.

While the extent of functional impairment is influenced by relatively broad cultural definitions of normal activities, disability is defined by the more narrow interactions between limitations and rather specific job requirements. Thus, two people with exactly the same limitations may suffer different degrees of disability. A hearing limitation is likely to affect a musician more than a day laborer, while a foot injury would affect the laborer more than the musician. Furthermore, disability is not static. Aside from changes in a person's medical condition, it may be possible to either adapt the job to the person or the person to the job. Such flexibility is a function of not only the specific characteristics of the job, but also of the educational level of the individual, the ease with which he or she can be replaced, job alternatives, and other factors.[5] Thus, to continue the example, the suddenly tone deaf musician may be disabled in 1970. By 1975 he or she may have acquired new skills and taken a new job that does not require musical ability. A census of disabled persons in 1975 might not include the retrained musician.

Disability has several effects, including job changes, reduced labor force participation, weeks worked per year, hours worked per week, and the like. The options for change and the effects of a given disability are influenced by the person's initial (predisability) occupation, its work requirements, and their flexibility. Education may be very important in increasing a person's capacity to respond to the disruption caused by a disabling condition. Likewise, factors such as a person's age and sex influence the range of available alternative occupations. (One may argue that in a liberated society, sex will have little influence on job choice. Unfortunately, most occupations are still sextyped.) These factors will be further influenced by general labor market conditions and conditions for specific segments of the labor force. For instance, in a period of high demand for labor, less productive (disabled) workers are more likely to find employment. Finally, the individual's incentives to accept various outcomes will be influenced by the family's need for earnings, the earnings potential of other family members, and the availability of transfer payments. The impacts of disability bring the discussion full circle.

5. See, for instance, Schultz (1975) on the value of education in dealing with disruptions of normal situations.

They involve changes in income, occupation, home and work environment, lifestyle, and psychosocial stresses. But, while the vicious circle may still be present, it is more clearly defined and much more amenable to analysis.

The various parts of this model have often been studied separately. Epidemiological studies focus on the factors related to the incidence of various pathologies. Medically oriented studies examine the efficacy of specific treatments in preventing or controlling pathologies. Many sociologists focus on factors that explain how a person perceives an illness and what leads him or her to accept or reject the sick role. The people involved in vocational rehabilitation are, of course, primarily concerned with methods to reduce the impact of various impairments on functional limitations and disability. The public policy analyst emphasizes the effects of disability on labor force behavior and the design of the appropriate transfer payments to ease the burdens of job change and loss.

The primary focus of this study will be on the factors leading to a recognized disability and the effects of such disabilities. As such, the first part of the analysis will emphasize the interactions between the functional limitations of the individual and the requirements of the job. The origin of the impairment is important, but massive epidemiological studies with clinical evidence are required to firmly establish causation. It is possible, however, that much more modest studies can point toward factors that result in increased incidence of pathologies or impairments. For instance, a high incidence of disability among people in certain occupational or income groups can be explained in two ways: (1) there is something associated with being in such groups that *causes* the disability, or (2) people prone to disabilities happen to be overrepresented in such groups. In the following chapters it will be seen that the former interpretation is more likely.

The second part of the analysis concerns the different effects of disability and health limitations. It will identify those factors that make it more or less difficult for someone with a given problem to adapt to the change in health status with a minimum of disruption. In part, this adaptation depends on the type of impairment and its interaction with the requirements of the person's original job. Education, race, sex, and other labor market characteristics also influence the type of impact that a limitation will have.

The third part of the analysis will measure the effects of these adjustments to health problems in terms of earnings, total family income, and poverty status. In some cases, certain groups of the population are more severely affected than others. More importantly, an examination of the effects of disabilities suggests a number of specific desirable public policy actions.

IMPLEMENTING THE MODEL

The primary data sets used in this analysis are the 1967 Survey of Economic Opportunity (SEO) and the 1966 Survey of Disabled Adults (SDA). The SEO was conducted for the Office of Economic Opportunity by the Bureau of the Census in 1967. It consists of two parts: (1) a national sample of about 18,000 households drawn in the same manner as the Current Population Survey, and (2) a supplementary sample of about 12,000 households from areas where more than 30 percent of the population was nonwhite. Each observation is weighted by the inverse of the sampling ratio so that the total weighted population equals the civilian, noninstitutionalized population in 1967.[6] The SEO contains an extensive series of questions concerning labor force behavior, occupation and industry of workers, income of various types, and the usual sociodemographic variables.

The single respondent was also asked a series of health questions concerning all persons aged fourteen to sixty-four. The basic question was whether "health limits the kind or amount of work the person can do or prevents him or her from working." For women, an additional question was "whether health limits the kind or amount of housework they can do." Finally, for persons aged fourteen to nineteen, a question asked was whether health kept them from going to school. In all cases, only long-term illnesses were accepted as reasons. If a person was kept from work by influenza or pregnancy, the condition would be considered short-term and the person would not be counted as disabled. In general, these questions are rather similar to those used in screening the population included in the Survey of Disabled Adults.

In the spring of 1966, the Social Security Administration commissioned the Bureau of the Census to conduct the Survey of Disabled Adults to collect data on all noninstitutionalized disabled persons aged eighteen to sixty-four. The extent of work limitations (as evaluated by the individual) determined the classification of a person as disabled. Disability is defined in this survey as "a limitation in the kind or amount of work (or housework) resulting from a chronic health condition or impairment lasting three or more months." Although the initial population base is representative of all adults,

---

6. For a more technical discussion of some of the details concerning adjustments to the SEO, see Appendix A in Luft, 1972.

the interviews were only conducted with persons who were identified as being disabled (Haber, 1967: 6).

The survey was undertaken in two stages: first, a mailed questionnaire to determine which adults were disabled, and second, extensive household interviews with the persons so identified. Special sampling frames were chosen to "oversample" severely disabled adults with and without income from public income maintenance programs. (Each interviewee is, of course, weighted by the probability of his being chosen from the entire U.S. noninstitutionalized adult population.) These samples were drawn from lists of Old Age Survivors and Disability Insurance beneficiaries (OASDI), Aid to the Permanently and Totally Disabled, and Aid to the Blind recipients, and from denied applicants for OASDI benefits. Area population samples were obtained from the Current Population Survey and Monthly Labor Survey primary sampling units. The mail questionnaires were sent to about 30,000 households in February–March 1966. A subsample of these persons was selected and interviewed in April–May by census bureau enumerators. The final sample of 8,274 observations represents 17.8 million adults disabled for at least six months.

The questionnaire was administered to the disabled person (unless the person was unable to respond for him or herself). The range of questions was very broad, including education, current labor force and work experience, last full-time job, job at time of disability, effect of disability on labor force status, functional limitations, health insurance coverage and medical care costs in the previous year, rehabilitation services, assets, debts, income of all family members, assistance from relatives, and household and social activities before and after disability.

The SDA found 17.8 million disabled adults aged eighteen to sixty-four in 1966, in contrast to 15.4 million disabled adults identified by the SEO. The underestimate by the SEO can be attributed to a number of factors. First, the SDA was specifically designed to identify disabled persons. To this end, a series of pretests were conducted and various questions were used to eliminate confusion and the tendency to code disabled persons as having no limitation (Haber, 1967: 16–18). Second, the focus on disability in the questionnaire and screening form of the SDA was more likely to elicit positive responses from people who were only marginally limited than the single set of questions among the hundreds asked in the SEO. Third, the SEO used a single respondent for each household who reported data for each member of the family. A number of studies have indicated substantially lower estimated prevalence rates when a single respondent is used than when each person provides information about him or herself (Elinson and Trussell, 1957: 312). There is no way of accurately adjusting the SEO sample to reflect this undercount of the disabled. Because those who are omitted are probably less seriously disabled than the average, the estimated effects for disability are probably biased upward, indicating more severe effects. On the other hand, when estimating the overall impact of disability, the aggregate figures will omit some of the disabled and thus result in underestimates.

LIMITATIONS OF THE DATA

Aside from these issues of comparability between the two sources, there are some inherent limitations in the scope of both. The sample universe is restricted to the noninstitutionalized adult population aged eighteen to sixty-four in the mid-1960s, and health problems are restricted to impairments that affect work or housework.[7]

The major population groups not extensively discussed are (1) people with recurrent acute conditions that may have as much of an impact as long-term conditions, and (2) those who have died. While acute conditions account for more than half of the total number of restricted activity days (1,694,590 out of 2,996,059 in 1968), they are of relatively short duration—only 4.3 restricted activity days per acute condition (USNCHS, 1970: 10/60: 6, 7, 13, 20). This may be contrasted to an average of 61.0 restricted activity days experienced by persons with chronic conditions. Thus, it is unlikely that particular acute conditions have major, long-term effects on income and labor force behavior. Unfortunately, there are no data concerning the *distribution* of acute conditions. Thus, it is impossible to know how many people have recurrent acute problems that substantially affect their jobs and families. For mortality, the problem is the difficulty in followup. Large scale surveys concerning the effects upon the family of the death of one of its members have not been done.

The survey data used in this book are dependent on self-reported self-evaluations of health status and limitations. Two closely related aspects of this type of data are biases in evaluation and in reporting.

7. There are several reasons for these restrictions. The prevalence of serious illness among children is rather low, and what illnesses do occur cannot be expected to immediately affect family incomes. Among the elderly, illnesses are so common that determining causation is very difficult; in addition, retirement at about age sixty-five is so nearly uniform that the direct effects of health on earnings become very difficult to untangle. Institutionalized adults are excluded because data have only recently been collected from them, and that which is available is generally incompatible with data for the rest of the population. As all of the institutionalized are severely disabled, the effect of their health on income is quite obvious.

The dependency on self-evaluation may lead to the exclusion of conditions or limitations that the individual does not recognize. The previous discussion has pointed to some factors shown to influence differential recognition of health problems. Self-evaluation leads to including as "disabled" people who have no medically determinable impairment but think that they have a health problem and behave as if they do. Given the less than perfect diagnostic abilities of medicine, it is not clear that the analysis should be limited only to people with medically identified conditions.

One study that compares physician's and patient's evaluations of functional limitations indicates rather close congruency (Nagi, 1969A). Using a five point scale for the degree of limitation, there was exact congruency concerning general physical condition in 70 percent of the cases, and the evaluation of general work conditions was identical in 49 percent of the cases. Conversely, differences of 2+ degrees occurred in only 18 percent and 20 percent of the cases, respectively. Furthermore, the differences in evaluations support the assumption that the biases, if any, will not vitiate the analysis. Relative to the physicians' evaluations, individuals tend to underestimate their general physical condition and overestimate their ability to work. This comparison, of course, is limited to physical impairments. Evaluations of mental health status are likely to differ to a greater extent, particularly when part of the problem is that the person does not recognize that anything is "wrong."

Although some mental illness may be underreported because it is not recognized, the stigma attached to mental illness is probably much more important. This reporting problem is the second major source of bias in these data. Underreporting of "known" conditions arises from two reasons, the stigma or "sensitivity" problem and "general forgetfulness." For instance, not only is mental illness likely to be underreported because of its sensitivity, but so also are such chronic conditions as tuberculosis, hemorrhoids, epilepsy, and parasitic conditons. The "general forgetfulness" category is a catchall to describe those people who, for one reason or another, do not mention that they have a health problem about which they are aware. Various studies conducted by the National Center for Health Statistics strongly suggest that such underreporting (as measured by medical records) is inversely related to the degree to which the condition limits the normal activities of the person (USNCHS, 1965: 2/7; 1967: 2/23; 1972: 2/49; 1973: 2/57). Such a pattern is to be expected on the basis of what is likely to be important enough to people for them to be concerned about. The implication of such underreporting is that people with minor disabilities are excluded from the analysis.

This reduces the number of people considered disabled and increases the average severity of those counted as disabled. There are also some biases in underreporting by different socioeconomic groups that will be discussed in the next chapter.

SUMMARY

This chapter outlines the two prerequisites to unraveling the vicious circle between poverty and poor health—a carefully defined causal model and data sets that allow its estimation. The focus on disabilities further clarifies the empirical work. It allows us to concentrate on those health problems that are most likely to have both an identifiable onset and a substantial long-term impact. But disability is only one of the many aspects of health problems, each of which must be understood in relation to one another. Thus, the concepts of pathology, illness, sickness, impairment, functional limitation, and disability are related, but distinct. Various socioeconomic, occupational, and environmental factors affect each aspect of health, often in different ways. For instance, some jobs are both hazardous, leading to pathologies, and flexible, allowing workers with functional limitations to minimize their disabilities. The rest of this book will examine the three major aspects of this causal chain: (1) those factors related to an increased incidence of pathologies and impairments, (2) those factors that intervene to make a given functional limitation more or less of a disability, and (3) the effects of various levels of disabilities and how people adjust to them.

✳ *Chapter 3*

Socioeconomic Factors as
a Cause of Health Problems:
An Empirical Overview

The previous chapter developed a framework for discussing the linkages between various socioeconomic factors and health problems. The framework was designed to be very broad, so as to include the relationships between health problems considered by the clinician and those studied by the social scientist. This chapter will use this framework to present the available evidence concerning effects of socioeconomic factors on the various types of health problems.

Such an undertaking immediately encounters conceptual and empirical problems. With much of the available published data it is impossible to completely determine causation. Several techniques are used, and while there are problems with each, a generally consistent picture emerges. It reveals the increasing role of socioeconomic factors as one focuses first on pathologies, then on impairments, and finally on functional limitations and disabilities. The analysis also falls short of completeness because meaningful data are unavailable for acute conditions. Thus, most of the discussion is about chronic conditions and impairments.

The intent is to present a broad overview of the national data concerning pathologies, impairments, chronic conditions, functional limitations, and self-perceived health status; disabilities will be discussed in much more detail in subsequent chapters. To provide consistent results on a national base, most of the data are drawn from the National Health Examination Survey and the National Health Interview Survey. While for specific estimates other data may be better or more recent, these provide the best overall data base. Furthermore, they are readily available to others who wish to pursue specific points.

The first section provides a discussion of the problems in comparing acute and chronic conditions and argues that excluding the former will not substantially alter our findings. The bulk of the chapter is split into six subsections. The first outlines a number of methodological considerations. The remaining five discuss, in turn, pathologies identified by medical examination, impairments, chronic conditions, functional limitations and disabilities, and perceived health status. A final section provides a brief summary of the major findings.

ACUTE VERSUS CHRONIC CONDITIONS

Most of the health problems discussed in the remainder of this book are of a chronic nature for two reasons, one conceptual and one empirical. The conceptual argument is that chronic conditions are more likely to result in major effects upon the individual over an extended period of time. While acute conditions may be very severe, they are by definition brief. The sequelae of an acute episode can be roughly grouped into three categories. Some acute conditions result in death, obviously one of the most severe outcomes. But, as discussed in the previous chapter, it is very difficult to develop an approach to measuring the effects of a death on the survivors.[1] The second group of outcomes are those in which there is some permanent damage, such as impairments resulting from trauma or a stroke. While the cause was acute, and may have required extensive medical care, the effects upon the family are primarily the result of the residual disability. The third group are those in which there are no lasting health problems, but the acute episode itself may require varying amounts of medical care. Although substantial medical bills can reduce the family's wealth (if there is no insurance to cover them), their long-term economic and social position is unlikely to be affected.[2]

1. Economists are now well aware that the value of a life saved is not just the lost production of the individual in question. Schelling's 1968 article is the initial discussion of how one might begin to investigate the value of a life to family members and the community. Unfortunately, although there has been some additional work in this area, none of it completely resolves the problem (see, for instance, Acton, 1973).

2. While the focus of my language and data is on physical disabilities, psychological problems are perhaps an even more important problem. Obviously, if an automobile accident results in no physical trauma but leaves the driver with a phobia about driving, there is a substantial impairment resulting from the accident. Many health problems have a substantial emotional component but these are most difficult to measure. Furthermore, it is difficult to separate symptoms from root causes.

The empirical reason for focusing primarily on chronic conditions arises from the cross-sectional nature of the available data. Generally, household interviews are used that ask people about their current or recent health problems. Methodological studies indicate that recall falls rapidly with time for all but the most serious problems (USNCHS, 1972: 2/49; 1977: 2/69). For this reason, the National Health Interview Survey (NHIS) limits its questions about activity limitations and the prevalence of acute conditions to the two weeks preceding the interview. Because people are interviewed throughout the year, the NHIS can estimate the total number of acute episodes experienced by the population. There is, however, no way of estimating how many acute conditions are experienced by each person throughout the year. (This could be done if the same panel of people was reinterviewed every two weeks.) The long-term nature of chronic conditions allows the NHIS to ask questions concerning their presence during the preceding twelve months. Again the problem arises, but in a less severe form; there is no way of knowing how many people have the same (or different) chronic problems from one year to the next.

These difficulties in interpreting the data can be seen from the following figures drawn from July 1965 to June 1967.[3] Of the entire civilian, noninstitutionalized population in the United States, 94.9 million people, or 49.5 percent, had one or more chronic conditions. A total of 206.1 million conditions were reported, which averages out to a little more than one condition per person (USNCHS, 1971: 10/61: 2). There were also 385 million acute conditions per year, or 2.01 per person.[4] Does this mean that there were twice as many acute as chronic conditions? No; rather, the question is meaningless. Acute conditions are essentially measured as a flow, or incidence, within a (relatively short) time period, while the chronic conditions are a stock of health problems. By definition, all acute

3. The 1965–1967 data were chosen for several reasons. First, they cover a time period that approximates that of the other major data sources used in this study, the SDA and SEO. Second, June 1967 was the last time that the NHIS used an interview technique covering all the acute and chronic conditions of the respondent. Since July 1967, the NHIS has, in general, restricted its questions to those conditions that result in some activity limitation or medical care. There are additional, specific questions concerning the prevalence of certain conditions that are not restricted to those resulting in limitations or medical care (see USNCHS, 1972: 2/48 and USNCHS, 1975: 1/11). The third reason is that two years' worth of data provide more stable estimates, especially because of the sensitivity of the acute episodes data to the presence or absence of influenza epidemics.

4. This is an average of the 404 million reported in July 1965–June 1966 and the 366 million in July 1966–June 1967. In the latter period, there was no substantial influenza epidemic (USNCHS, 1967: 10/38: 16; 1968: 10/44: 15).

conditions occurred within the last three months and were present in the preceding two weeks. But, as will be seen in Table 3—1, only about 10 percent of the chronic conditions first occurred even within the preceding twelve months. If only a two week period is considered, there would be about 14.8 million acute conditions (385 million divided by twenty-six), or 0.077 per person, while most, if not all, of the chronic conditions would still be present.

Thus, it is impossible to compare the number of acute and chronic conditions, because the two are fundamentally different. It is, however, possible to compare the effects of acute and chronic conditions using similar units, such as restricted activity days (RADs). A restricted activity day is defined as "one on which a person substantially reduces the amount of activity normal for that day because of a specific illness or injury. The type of reduction varies with the age and occupation of the individual as well as with the day of the week or season of the year. Restricted activity covers the range from substantial reduction to complete inactivity for the entire day" (USNCHS, 1968: 10/44: 56).

Table 3—1 presents several measures of activity restrictions for acute and chronic conditions. The total of three billion RADs per year is split evenly between acute and chronic conditions. This is 7.7 days per year per person for each type of condition. On the average, there are 1.46 acute conditions that involve an activity restriction per person per year, implying 5.28 RADs per acute restricting condition.[5] Similar calculations for chronic conditions are shown in lines 7 and 8. On the average, there are 0.155 activity-limiting chronic conditions per person, with each resulting in 50.2 RADs per year, nearly ten times as much as per acute condition.[6]

It is possible that these average data may hide some important variations among types of acute conditions or the distribution of conditions across people. There may be a few acute conditions with a large number of RADs offset by many acute episodes having very few RADs, resulting in a low average. Alternatively, some people may have a great many acute episodes per year while many others have none, or just a few. Consider the following two polar cases that could account for the average of 7.7 RADs and 1.46 episodes per

5. This differs from the previously mentioned figure of 2.01 per person because the latter includes acute conditions that involved medical attention without an activity restriction.

6. In fact, these comparisons sharply underestimate the impact of chronic conditions, because they exclude people who have been forced to permanently reduce their "normal" activity—e.g., to retire. For such people, only *further* reductions in activity are counted as RADs.

Table 3–1. Measures of the Impacts of Acute and Chronic Conditions—U.S., July 1965–June 1967
(All figures are on a twelve month basis)

	All Conditions		Acute Conditions		Chronic Conditions	
	Total (000)	Per Person	Total (000)	Per Person	Total (000)	Per Person
(1) Restricted Activity Days (RADs)	2,961,257	15.50	1,470,632	7.70	1,490,625	7.8
(2) Bed Days	1,139,204	5.95	634,734	3.35	504,470	2.6
(3) Days of Work Loss, If Usually Employed	412,978	5.60	252,457	3.40	160,521	2.2
(4) Days Missed from School, Ages 6–16	207,636	4.85	183,567	4.25	24,069	0.6
(5) Incidence of Activity Restricting Acute Conditions	—	—	285,585	1.46	—	—
(6) RAD/Activity Restricting Acute Condition (1)/(5)	—	—	(5.28)	—	—	—
(7) Number of Chronic Conditions Named as the Cause of Activity Restrictions	—	—	—	—	29,700	0.155
(8) RAD/Chronic Condition (1)/(7)	—	—	—	—	(50.19)	—
(9) Persons with Activity Restricting Chronic Conditions	—	—	—	—	21,984	0.115
(10) RAD/Activity Restricted Person with Chronic Condition (1)/(9)	—	—	—	—	(67.80)	—

Sources: USNCHS, 1967: 10/37: 6, 7, 11, 17, 18; 1967: 10/38: 16; 1968: 10/43: 9, 10, 14, 20, 21; 1968: 10/44: 15; 1971: 10/61: 2.

person. In the first case, 5 percent of the population has 29.2 episodes per year and 95 percent has none. In the second case, everyone has 1.46 episodes per year, or about half the population has one episode a year and the remainder has two. There should be substantially more policy interest in acute conditions if the true situation is closer to the first extreme than the second.

Table 3−2 presents the available data concerning the incidence of RADs associated with detailed categories of acute conditions.[7] Only two of the twenty-five conditions have more than ten RADs per episode. Furthermore, these conditions—(1) pneumonia, and (2) fractures and dislocations—account for only 2 percent of all acute episodes, although they account for nearly 10 percent of all RADs associated with acute conditions. Of the remaining conditions, only sprains and strains and deliveries have activity restrictions that exceed a week. While an even more detailed breakdown of conditions may point out some others that have long periods of activity restriction, it appears that they would involve a very small number of people. Considering this list of acute conditions, it also appears unlikely that very many people have recurrent episodes without being listed as having a chronic condition such as chronic bronchitis.

SOCIOECONOMIC FACTORS
AND THE CAUSES OF VARIOUS
HEALTH PROBLEMS

This section reviews and interprets the available data concerning the influence of socioeconomic factors on various aspects of chronic health problems. The difficulty in interpreting any data on this question is the feedback from health problems to the socioeconomic variables. In some cases, it will be possible to eliminate these effects; in others, consistent patterns suggest underlying relationships. Two techniques are particularly valuable when using published data; one relies on comparing income and education relationships, while the other uses stratification by age. If the condition manifests itself after childhood, educational levels will not be affected by a subsequent health problem as might be the case with family income. Similarly, children's health problems are unlikely to affect family income.

The discussion will basically follow the framework outlined in Figure 2−1. Thus, the first focus will be on the presence or absence of specific pathologies as identified by a medical examination. Such

7. Data are only available for those conditions involving either RADs or medical attention. Thus, they include conditions that received medical attention without an activity reduction.

data eliminate problems of self-reporting biases and the requirement that the individual recognize the pathology. It does, however, limit the data to those conditions that can be easily measured and identified in an examination. The remaining measures must all be derived from self-reported health problems. These will include, in turn, impairments, perceived illnesses, functional limitations, and disabilities.

The Prevalence of Pathologies as Determined by Medical Examination

Physical examinations performed by medical personnel may be used to determine the "true" prevalence of certain pathologies. This eliminates the interview biases that may be correlated with various socioeconomic factors. Of course, the data from such physical examinations must be collected from a randomly selected population, not from people who come to physicians for either illness, preventive care, employment examinations, or other self-selected reasons.[8] The National Health Examination Survey (NHES) conducted by the National Center for Health Statistics comes the closest to meeting these requirements.[9] The NHES has had three cycles, each focusing on a different age group. The first, in 1960–1962, sampled adults aged eighteen to seventy-nine; the second, 1963–1965, sampled children aged six to eleven; and the third, 1966–1970, sampled youths aged twelve to seventeen. In each case, the target population is the civilian, noninstitutionalized population. The sample households were selected using a rather complicated cluster sampling technique. Eligible individuals were interviewed with a questionnaire similar to that used in the National Health Interview Survey. They were then asked to come for a free physical examination at their convenience. By using various followup techniques and being very flexible, the non-examination rates were kept very low. In the first cycle, the adults, it was 13.5 percent; in the second cycle it was only 4 percent; and in the third cycle it was less than 10 percent.

The nonexamination rate is important if those people who refuse exams differ from the rest of the population with respect to the variables with which we are concerned. For instance, if poor people with many health problems were more likely to refuse to participate than those with few problems, then the data would show relatively less

---

8. An outstanding example of such biased data are the results from Selective Service physicals, in which there is not only an income-education bias in who is called for the exam, but there were also strong incentives for certain groups to want to either pass or fail the exam.

9. The methodology used in the NHES is described in USNCHS, 1965: 1/4; 1967: 1/5; 1969: 1/8; 1965: 2/9; 1969: 2/36; 1973: 2/43; 1964: 11/1.

Table 3–2. Incidence and Restricted Activity Days per Year Associated with Acute Conditions—U.S., July 1965–June 1967

	RADs in Thousands	Incidence in Thousands	RADs per Episode	Percent Distribution	
				RADs	Incidence
All Acute Conditions	1,470,632	385,143	3.82	100.0	100.0
Infective and Parasitic Diseases	190,080	46,718	4.07	12.9	12.1
Common Childhood Diseases	68,748	11,912	5.77	4.7	3.1
The Virus, not Otherwise Specified	76,510	26,039	2.94	5.2	6.7
Other Infective and Parasitic	44,822	8,767	5.11	3.0	2.3
Respiratory Conditions	670,572	220,543	3.04	45.6	57.3
Common Cold	277,966	113,583	2.45	18.9	29.5
Other Acute Upper Respiratory	82,540	29,400	2.81	5.6	7.6
Influenza with Digestive Manifestations	25,460	9,486	2.68	1.7	2.5
Other Influenza	224,183	59,876	3.74	15.2	15.6
Pneumonia	31,636	2,230	14.19	2.2	0.6
Bronchitis	21,602	4,038	5.35	1.5	1.0
Other Acute Respiratory	7,187	1,928	3.73	0.5	0.5
Digestive System Conditions	65,456	18,602	3.52	4.5	4.8
Dental Conditions	16,583	7,300	2.27	1.1	1.9
Functional and Symptomatic Upper GI	8,651	3,899	2.22	0.6	1.0
Other Digestive	40,222	7,403	5.43	2.7	1.9
Injuries	323,744	51,242	6.32	22.0	13.3
Fractures and Dislocations	113,926	5,333	21.36	7.7	1.4
Sprains and Strains	67,501	9,441	7.15	4.6	2.5
Open Wounds and Lacerations	48,573	15,548	3.12	3.3	4.0
Contusions and Superficial Injuries	48,828	9,763	5.00	3.3	2.5
Other Current Injuries	44,917	11,158	4.03	3.1	2.9

All Other Acute Conditions	220,780	48,039	4.60	15.0	12.5
Diseases of the Ear	31,804	10,690	2.98	2.2	2.8
Headaches	4,493	4,225	1.06	0.3	1.1
Genitourinary Disorders	33,939	6,277	5.41	2.3	1.6
Deliveries and Disorders of Pregnancy and Puerperium	38,932	4,271	9.12	2.6	1.1
Diseases of the Skin	17,540	5,226	3.36	1.2	1.4
Diseases of the Musculoskeletal System	28,009	4,051	6.91	1.9	1.0
All Other Acute	66,063	13,300	4.97	4.5	3.5

Source: USNCHS, 1967: 10/38: 13, 14; 1967: 10/44: 12, 13.

pathology among the poor than is really the case. The available information suggest that this type of bias is not a problem. Table 3–3 is based on people interviewed at home prior to being asked to appear for the NHES physical examination. While examination rates are inversely related to family income (the poor being more interested in a free exam), they bear no relationship to self-appraised health status, controlling for income. The same conclusion appears to hold with respect to education and health status. These results suggest that there will be no substantial biases due to self-selection for examinations. The emphasis on searching out potential biases in these data is warranted by their use to represent the "true" prevalence of various pathologies without any reporting biases.[10]

Table 3–3. Examination Rate for Adults in the National Health Examination Survey, 1960–1962, by Self-Appraised Health Status, Income, and Education

		Self-Appraised Health Status			
	Total[a]	*Excellent*	*Good*	*Fair*	*Poor*
Family Income					
Under $2,000	89.3	89.9	89.3	88.3	90.9
$2,000–$3,999	86.6	83.2	88.6	90.0	82.2
$4,000–$6,999	88.6	87.1	89.9	92.1	80.8
$7,000–$9,999	86.8	86.7	87.7	86.7	(90.0)[b]
$10,000+	85.5	86.6	86.2	86.0	(80.0)
Unknown	77.2	80.2	82.6	77.6	78.6
All Incomes	86.5	86.1	88.1	88.3	85.7
Education of Individual					
Under 9 years	86.1	82.9	87.5	87.2	86.9
9–12 years	86.6	85.1	88.0	90.2	84.1
13 years and over	89.5	90.6	90.5	90.0	(76.9)
Unknown	72.1	69.7	82.8	81.8	(79.2)
All Levels of Education	86.5	86.1	88.1	88.3	85.7

Source: USNCHS, 1969: 2/36: 30, 44.
[a]Includes persons with unknown health status.
[b]( ) indicates base of less than thirty people.

10. Most of the effort to examine bias has been focused on the first cycle of the NHES, the adults. This is probably due to the very high examination rates in the second cycle, which allow little room for bias. The available data do indicate patterns in the second cycle similar to those of the first (USNCHS, 1967: 1/5: 31).

Before discussing the findings drawn from the NHES, there are two further methodological points. The first relates to the confounding of age with income and education, and the second deals with the method of interpreting the data. The "age" problem arises from the fact that the income and education distributions for the population vary by age, with disproportionately large numbers of the elderly being poor and having few years of school. Stated another way, if one only knows that a person is poorly educated, there is a better than average chance that he or she is elderly. Given the importance of the ageing process in health problems, unadjusted prevalence rates are almost guaranteed to show a negative relationship to income and education, even if there are *no* causal linkages. The NHES reports usually (but not always) recognize this problem and present age-adjusted figures. Usually an "expected" prevalence rate, say for an education category, is based on the national age-specific rates for all educational categories weighted by the age distribution within the category in question.[11] This expected rate is compared with the actual rate. Standard error tables are usually provided so that the differences can be tested for statistical significance.

This leads to the second point: What findings are of interest? The

---

11. Let x_{ij} be the observed prevalence rate in age category i and education category j. Let X_i be the observed, age-specific prevalence across all education categories. Let n_{ij} be the number of people in age category i and education cate-

gory j. By implication, then, $X_i = \dfrac{1}{\sum\limits_j n_{ij}} \sum\limits_j n_{ij} \, x_{ij}$ and the observed prevalence rate

for an education category j is $X_j = \dfrac{1}{\sum\limits_i n_{ij}} \sum\limits_i n_{ij} \, x_{ij}$. Then the "expected rate" for

education category j is $\dfrac{1}{\sum\limits_i n_{ij}} \sum\limits_i n_{ij} \, X_i$, which is compared to the observed rate for

the education category X_j. The "direct method" of age adjustment tends to be more common in publications other than the NHES series. In the direct method, the observed age-education rates are adjusted so that the prevalence rate in each education category is based on the same arbitrary age distribution, usually that of the total population. Using the above terminology, the direct age-adjusted

rate for category j is $\dfrac{1}{\sum\limits_i N_i} \sum\limits_i N_i \, x_{ij}$ where $N_i = \sum\limits_j n_{ij}$. Both types of adjustment

lead to substantially the same conclusions. The NHES often does not provide age-adjusted data for children, but this is not a problem because the relatively minor differences in the distribution of children by family income and education do not substantially affect the prevalence rates for children.

primary question is whether there are causal relationships between income and education on the one hand, and health problems on the other. Thus, it seems inappropriate to require that each difference between actual and expected prevalence rate be statistically significant. The procedure used here was to graph the actual and expected rates for each education (income) group and a band of one standard error about the expected rate. This allows a visual determination of whether there is a pattern in the relationship between the actual and expected rates. It takes into account the problems of varying sample size within categories and the expected random variations due to sampling error. It recognizes that consistent patterns of differences, each of which may be statistically insignificant, can be both highly significant and important when considered together.[12]

Tables 3–4 to 3–7 present the major findings with respect to income and education drawn from the complete set of NHES publications (through April 1976). Completeness, in this case, is important because a focus on only selected conditions can lead to inconsistent findings. In an earlier study, Lefcowitz (1973: 6) examined some of the NHES data and argued that there was *no* evidence of a linkage between poverty and health. A more complete examination tends to support the hypothesis that there *is* a negative association between high income and education and the prevalence of various health problems. Furthermore, the evidence is suggestive of a causal link from low socioeconomic status to some health problems. Table 3–8 provides a summary of the findings presented in the other four tables. Among adults, discernable relationships between income or education and prevalence are absent only for definite coronary heart disease and osteoarthritis. For the other major chronic conditions, such as angina pectoris, definite hypertension, definite hypertensive heart disease, rheumatoid arthritis, diabetes (glucose tolerance test), and symptoms of psychological diseases, there are clear or suspected negative relationships between income and/or education and observed prevalence rates. There are very strong negative relationships with respect to visual, hearing, and dental problems. Only for myocardial infarction and mean serum cholesterol levels are there any suggestions that prevalence may be *positively* associated with the socioeconomic measures.[13]

12. As this section is intended as background, the actual statistical tests were not performed, although they would not be too difficult to do. Tables 3–4 to 3–7 present the detailed interpretations of the NHES findings.

13. The findings from the serologic test for syphilis are included both for completeness and to demonstrate the need for examination data in contrast to reported prevalence. The general lack of relationship is in stark contrast to the general wisdom about the prevalence of syphilis as well as the findings of a number of studies (Covell, 1967: 15, 19). The reason behind the very sharp income

Table 3—4. Results from the National Health Examination Survey of Adults, 1960—1962 *(Age-Adjusted, Based on Actual and Expected Rates)*

Condition	*Major Findings with Respect to Income and Education*
Serologic Test for Syphilis[a]	For whites, no substantial patterns. Women show an insignificant *positive* gradient with respect to income. White men in the top income and education groups have lower than expected prevalence. For blacks, no discernable patterns, except for a negative pattern with respect to education for black women. Black women with 9—12 and 13+ years of school have significantly lower prevalence rates.
Definite Coronary Heart Disease[b,c]	No discernable patterns. Less than expected prevalence for men and women in $10,000+ income category.
Myocardial Infarction[b]	No discernable patterns for men. Men with less than five years of school have significantly lower prevalence, but no corresponding income findings. Slight *positive* gradient for women with respect to both income and education.
Angina Pectoris (Definite)[b]	No discernable patterns for men. Women exhibit a slight *negative* gradient with respect to income and education with the exception of women with less than five years of school, who have lower than expected prevalence.
Angina Pectoris (Suspect)[b]	Irregular *negative* gradient with respect to income and education for men and women.
Definite Hypertension[d]	For whites, *negative* gradients are clear with respect to education for men and especially for women. Possible *negative* gradient with respect to income for women, no discernable pattern for men. For blacks, slight *negative* gradient with respect to education for men and women; no patterns with respect to income.
Definite Hypertensive Heart Disease[d]	For whites, *negative* pattern with respect to education for women, possibly *negative* with respect to income. No discernable patterns for men. For blacks, *negative* gradient with respect to education for men and women (clearer for women). No clear patterns with respect to income.
Rheumatoid Arthritis[e]	*Negative* gradients are apparent for men, and for women (less clear). No discernable income pattern for women; for men, a significantly higher prevalence in the under $2,000 category.
Mean Glucose Levels[f] (if not previously diagnosed diabetic)[g]	*Negative* gradients are apparent for both men and women for income and education. The income gradients are clearer; the education patterns for both men and women show a relatively higher prevalence for those with 13+ years of school.
Osteoarthritis[h]	No discernable income or education gradients for men or women for (1) osteoarthritis (OA) of the hands and/or feet, (2) OA of the hands, (3) moderate or severe OA of the hands, or (4) moderate or severe OA of the feet. There are very weak *positive* income and education gradients for any OA of the feet. *(continued overleaf)*

Table 3–4. continued

Condition	Major Findings with Respect to Income and Education
Mean Blood Hematocrit[i]	For whites, there is no discernable income gradient for either men or women, while there is a slight *negative* education gradient for men and a slight *positive* education gradient for women. (None of the differences are very large.) For blacks, there are only three income and education categories, so trends are difficult to discern.
Binocular Visual Acuity[j]	For persons with uncorrected distance vision of 20/20 or better, there appear to be *positive* income and education gradients for both men and women with the exception of relatively lower proportions than would be expected in the 13+ years of schooling category for both sexes and in the $10,000+ income category for men. For corrected distance vision of 20/20 or better and corrected near vision of 14/14 or better, there are strong *positive* gradients for both sexes for both income and education. The greatest differences are in the lowest income and education categories. There are corresponding strong *negative* gradients for corrected distance vision of 20/100 or less and corrected near vision of 14/70 or less. Again, the greatest differences are in the lowest income and education categories.
Total Loss of Teeth[k]	For whites, there are substantial *negative* gradients for both men and women with respect to income and education. The gradient appears somewhat stronger for women. For blacks, there are only three categories of income and education, and there are no discernable trends.
Periodontal Disease[l]	Clear *negative* gradients for both men and women with respect to both income and education. The gradient with respect to income is still apparent when holding education constant.
Oral Hygiene[m]	Clear *negative* gradients for both men and women with respect to both income and education. The gradient with respect to income is still apparent when holding education constant. (The oral hygiene index is a measure of foreign matter adhering to the teeth.)
Decayed, Missing, and Filled Teeth[n]	The total number of decayed, missing, and filled (DMF) teeth show clear *positive* gradients for both men and women with respect to both income and education. The income gradient is still apparent when education is held constant. These *positive* gradients are the net effect of very strong *positive* gradients for filled teeth and clear, but less substantial, *negative* gradients for both decayed and missing teeth.

[a]USNCHS, 1965: 11/9: 17, 18, 27.

[b]USNCHS, 1965: 11/10: 23, 43.

[c]Defined as myocardial infarction on ECG, definite angina pectoris, or both, or certain other manifestations with history of myocardial infarction (see USNCHS, 1965: 11/10: 2, 3).

Table 3–4. (Notes continued)

[d]USNCHS, 1966: 11/13: 24, 25, 61.
[e]USNCHS, 1966: 11/17: 21, 22, 43.
[f]USNCHS, 1966: 11/18: 11, 12, 25.
[g] The glucose challenge test was not given to persons who had a clear history of diabetes with medical care (see USNCHS, 1966: 11/18: 1). The prevalence rate for persons diagnosed as diabetic shows no consistent pattern with respect to income. No data are presented with respect to education (see USNCHS, 1966: 11/18: 3, 12.
[h]USNCHS, 1966: 11/20: 25, and Tables 2, 3, 4, 5, 6, 7.
[i]USNCHS, 1967: 11/24: 22, 23, 36.
[j]USNCHS, 1967: 11/25: 11, 13.
[k]USNCHS, 1967: 11/27: 12, 13, 20.
[l]USNCHS, 1965: 11/12: pages 6–8, 16, 18, 19, 28.
[m]USNCHS, 1966: 11/16: 4–7, 14, 15, 28.
[n]USNCHS, 1967: 11/23: 4–8.

Table 3–5. Other Findings from the National Health Examination Survey of Adults, 1960–1962

Condition	Major Findings With Respect to Income and Education
Mean Serum Cholesterol Levels[a]	Age-adjusted levels suggest a small *positive* relationship with income for men, but no change for women. There are no data for education.
Hearing Levels[b]	Age-specific and age-adjusted hearing levels suggest *positive* associations between better than normal hearing and income and education for both men and women and correspondingly *negative* associations for impaired hearing.
Need for Dental Care at an Early Date[c]	Textual discussion of age-specific and age-adjusted rates suggests *negative* income and education gradients for both men and women. The only exception appears to be black men.
Selected Symptoms of Psychological Distress[d]	Age-adjusted rates for the four race-sex combinations and twelve symptoms suggest a *negative* gradient with respect to income and education, with the exception of black women and income. Individual symptoms show a less clear pattern. The gradients for nervousness were generally *positive*.

[a]USNCHS, 1967: 11/22: 6, 16.
[b]USNCHS, 1968: 11/31: 3–6.
[c]USNCHS, 1970: 11/36: 5–6.
[d]USNCHS, 1970: 11/37: pages 7–9, 28, 29. As part of the medical history section of the NHES, questions were asked about twelve symptoms of psychological distress: nervous breakdown, felt an impending nervous breakdown, nervousness, inertia, insomnia, trembling hands, nightmares, perspiring hands, fainting, frequent and/or severe headaches, frequent and/or severe dizziness, frequent and/or severe heart palpitations.

Table 3–6. Findings from the National Health Examination Survey of Children Aged Six to Eleven

Condition	*Major Findings with Respect to Family Income and Education of the Head of Household*
Decayed, Missing, and Filled Teeth[a]	Using actual and expected rates, weak *positive* income gradients are found for the DMF index for white boys and girls and a weak *negative* income gradient for blacks. There are no discernable gradients with respect to education. The DMF index is the net result of strong *negative* income and education gradients for decayed teeth and strong *positive* gradients for filled teeth. In general, the findings for black children are much less clear. There are no discernable trends for the very low rates of missing teeth.
Hearing Levels[b]	Hearing sensitivity shows clear *positive* gradients with respect to family income and parent's education at various frequencies, for both boys and girls. The relationships for income tend to be somewhat clearer than for education. At speech levels the correlations between sensitivity and income was $r = 0.12 \pm 0.018$; between sensitivity and education was $r = 0.14 \pm 0.025$; and between sensitivity and education, holding income constant, $r = 0.09$.
Binocular Visual Activity[c]	Defective uncorrected distance visual acuity of 20/40 or less was *positively* associated with income, with the exception of an insignificant, but lower than expected, rate in the $15,000+ category. The same holds for acuity of 20/100 or less. There are no discernable income patterns for defective near vision. This pattern is also observable, but is less clear, with respect to education of the head of family.
Periodontal Disease and Oral Hygiene[d]	Data for actual and expected levels of the Periodontal Index and Oral Hygiene Index indicate strong *negative* gradients with respect to income and education for both sexes and races.
Color Vision Deficiencies[e]	Data with respect to income are only available for red-green deficiencies in white boys. These data indicate a generally *positive* gradient.
Height and Weight[f]	Clear *positive* relationships for both height and weight are evident with respect to income and education of parent. The gradients are still discernable when controlling for one of the two factors (income or education).
Hearing and Related Medical Findings[g]	Medical history information concerning trouble hearing, earaches, and running ears indicate some differences by income and education of parent, but *no* discernable patterns. Otoscopic examination of the eardrum suggests a possible *negative* gradient with respect to both income and education of all abnormalities and three specific abnormalities. Complete or partial removal of the tonsils is strongly *positively* related to family income up to

Table 3-6. continued

Condition	Major Findings with Respect to Family Income and Education of the Head of Household
	the $7,000–$9,999 range and is *negatively* related thereafter. Correcting for those who have had tonsillectomies, there are no discernable patterns with respect to degree of enlargement. There are also no consistent income patterns for abnormality of the oral pharynx.
Occlusion of Teeth[h]	Use a Treatment Priority Index and actual versus expected levels. No discernable patterns in TPI with respect to either income or education. There are very strong *positive* income gradients for those who report having their teeth straightened.
Blood Pressure Levels[i]	Using three income categories ($< \$3,000$, $\$3,000–\$9,999$, $\$10,000+$), there are *no* discernable patterns for mean systolic pressure for white or black children. There is a *positive* gradient in mean diastolic pressure for black children but not for whites. There are weak *negative* education gradients for both black and white children for systolic pressure and a *negative* education gradient for white childrens' diastolic pressure.
Skeletal Maturity[j]	Mean skeletal age (hand-wrist) appears to be weakly, but *positively*, related to income for white boys and girls. The pattern is less consistent for black children. For both races combined, a positive education gradient is apparent. Similar, although less clear, findings are evident for individual hand-wrist bones. There are *no* discernable patterns with respect to the age of onset of ossification.

[a]USNCHS, 1971: 11/106: 44, 45, and Tables 7, 8.
[b]USNCHS, 1972: 11/111: 8–11, 35–40.
[c]USNCHS, 1972: 11/112: 10, 11, 28, 29.
[d]USNCHS, 1972: 11/117: 4, 5, 6, 7, 14, 17.
[e]USNCHS, 1972: 11/118: 8, 23.
[f]USNCHS, 1972: 11/119: 10–12.
[g]USNCHS, 1972: 11/122: 2–9, 15, 16, 21, 22.
[h]USNCHS, 1973: 11/130: 7, 14, 42.
[i]USNCHS, 1973: 11/135: 3, 5, 20.
[j]USNCHS, 1975: 11/149: 19, 20, 21, 22, 24, 30, 45, 48, 50, 52, 67–69, 71.

The two measures of socioeconomic status, family income and education, can test the importance of the causal link from health problems to reduced income. It is unlikely that the conditions in question manifest themselves early enough to affect the schooling

gradient for syphilis in the traditional data is that the information is based on cases reported to the local public health agencies. Poor people use the public clinics and are sure to be reported; high income people use private physicians who are likely not to report such cases.

Table 3−7. Findings from the National Health Examination Survey of
Youths Aged Twelve to Seventeen

Condition	Major Findings with Respect to Family Income and Education of Family Head
Visual Acuity[a]	Weak, but consistently *negative*, relationships between uncorrected acuity and income with a reversal in the pattern for the $15,000+ group. Stronger and more consistent *positive* relationship for acuity with usual correction.
Color Vision Deficiencies[b]	No consistent patterns for red-green deficiencies with respect to income, unlike the slight *positive* gradient for children aged 6−11. Other data are unavailable.
Periodontal Disease[c]	Comparison of actual and expected levels of the Periodontal Index show strong *negative* income and education gradients for white youths of both sexes. For blacks, the *negative* relationship with respect to income is clear for girls and less clear, but still discernable, for boys. The *negative* relationship with respect to parents' education is fairly clear for boys and *not* apparent for girls.
Decayed, Missing, and Filled Teeth[d]	For the total number of DMF teeth, the only consistent income gradient is for white females and it is *positive*. There are no discernable patterns with respect to education of the head of family. There are clear, strong, *negative* income gradients for all four race-sex groups for decayed teeth and missing teeth, and correspondingly strong *positive* gradients for filled teeth. These patterns are repeated for education. The relationships are somewhat clearer for whites than for blacks.
Hearing Levels[e]	There are clear and consistent *positive* gradients for hearing sensitivity for both boys and girls across nine test frequencies. (The worst hearing levels were consistently found among low income youths.) The same patterns are present, although not quite so clearly, with respect to parent's education. (This may be due to the use of eight education groups.)
Mean Hematocrit Values[f]	There are small, but consistent *positive* income and education gradients in hematocrit levels for white males and females in each age group. There are *no* discernable patterns for black youths of either sex although blacks consistently have lower values than whites.
Refraction Status[g]	There are consistent *positive* income gradients for the proportion of youths whose unaided acuity is brought up to 20/20 by simple trial lenses, both with and without their usual correction. This implies that poorer children tend to have more severe or complicated problems. There are no educational results.
Oral Hygiene[h]	The oral hygiene index of calculus and debris showed strong *negative* income and education gradients for both sexes and races. The following partial correlation coefficients for a six variable equation are indicative of the findings.

Table 3–7. continued

Conditions	Major Findings with Respect to Family Income and Education of Family Head
	Age = − 0.07, Sex = − 0.14, Race = 0.12, (0.017) (0.017) (0.050) Income = − 0.13, Education of Parent = − 0.16. (0.019) (0.017)
Serum Uric Acid Levels[i]	There appear to be very weak *positive* income and education gradients that are more apparent for males than for females.
Eye Examination Findings[j]	The proportion of youths with any eye abnormality exhibits clear *negative* income gradients for white boys and less clear but still discernable *negative* gradients for white girls. For four of the five specific conditions there are clear negative gradients for both sexes and no discernable gradients for tropia (manifest strobismus). For black youths the sampling errors are very high and there are no discernable patterns.

[a]USNCHS, 1973: 11/127: 18, 19.
[b]USNCHS, 1974: 11/134: 9, 25.
[c]USNCHS, 1974: 11/141: 3, 4, 8, 9.
[d]USNCHS, 1974: 11/144: 6– 7, 19– 24.
[e]USNCHS, 1975: 11/145: 15–19, 74–75.
[f]USNCHS, 1974: 11/146: 6–9, 28 – 31.
[g]USNCHS, 1974: 11/148: 15, 40– 43.
[h]USNCHS, 1975: 11/151: 5–9, 11, 20, 21, 25, 26.
[i]USNCHS, 1975: 11/152: 7, 8, 23, 24.
[j]USNCHS, 1975: 11/155: 9–11, 43, 46, 47.

process.[14] Thus, the education data are independent of subsequent income changes due to health problems. Education can also serve as a proxy measure of the family's normal, permanent, or expected level of income. If many people with the specific pathologies suffered income losses, then the negative gradients should be much stronger with respect to income than to education. Evidence supporting this hypothesis is found for myocardial infarction, and contrary to the hypothesis for definite hypertension and definite hypertensive heart disease. This overall lack of support for the effects of pathologies on income are in contrast to those of household surveys to be discussed below. The likely reason for this inconsistency is that the NHES findings focus on the presence or absence of specific conditions, while

14. The primary exceptions are hearing and vision problems, and perhaps psychological problems. See below for evidence with respect to hearing and vision problems of children.

Table 3-8.   Summary of Findings from the National Health Examination Surveys

Age Group and Condition	Family Income — All Races M[a]	Family Income — All Races F[b]	Family Income — Whites M	Family Income — Whites F	Family Income — Blacks M	Family Income — Blacks F	Education of Head of Family — All Races M	Education of Head of Family — All Races F	Education of Head of Family — Whites M	Education of Head of Family — Whites F	Education of Head of Family — Blacks M	Education of Head of Family — Blacks F
Adults 18-79												
Serologic Test for Syphilis	—	—	O[c]	P?[d,e]	O	O	—	—	O	O	O	N[f]
Definite Coronary Heart Disease	O	O	—	—	—	—	O	O	—	—	O	—
Myocardial Infarction	O	P?	—	—	—	—	P?	P?	—	—	—	—
Angina Pectoris (definite)	N?	N?	—	—	—	—	O	N?	—	—	—	—
Angina Pectoris (suspect)	N?	N?	O	N?	O	O	N?	N?	N	N	N?	N?
Definite Hypertension	—	—	—	—	O	O	—	—	O	N	N	N
Definite Hypertensive Heart Disease	—	—	O	N?	—	—	—	—	—	—	—	—
Rheumatoid Arthritis	N?	O	—	—	—	—	N	N?	—	N	—	—
Mean Glucose Levels	N	N	—	—	—	—	N?	N?	N?	N	O	O
Osteoarthritis	O	O	O	O	O	O	O	O	—	—	—	—
*Mean Blood Hematocrit[g]	P?	—	—	—	—	—	P?	P?	N?	P?	O	O
*Uncorrected Visual Acuity	P	P	N	—	O?	O?	P	P	—	—	—	—
*Corrected Visual Acuity	—	P	—	N	—	—	P	P	N	—	O?	O?
Total Loss of Teeth	N	—	—	—	—	—	—	—	—	N	—	—
Periodontal Disease	N	N	—	—	—	—	N	N	—	—	—	—
Oral Hygiene (problems)	N	N	—	—	—	—	N	N	—	—	—	—
Decayed Teeth	N	N	—	—	—	—	N	N	—	—	—	—
Missing Teeth	P	N	—	—	?	—	P	P	—	—	—	—
*Filled Teeth	P?	O	N	N	N	N	—	—	—	—	—	—
Mean Serum Cholesterol	P	P	—	—	—	—	P	P	N	N	N	N
*Hearing Levels	—	—	N	N	N	N	—	—	N	N	?	N
Need for Dental Care	N	—	N	N	N	O?	—	—	N	N	N	N
Twelve Symptoms of Psychological Distress (medical history)	—	—	N	N	N	—	—	—	N	N	N	N

Children 6-11

Health Problem												
Decayed Teeth	—	—	N	N	—	—	N	N	—	—	?	?
Missing Teeth	—	—	O?	O?	—	—	O?	O?	—	—	O?	O?
*Filled Teeth	P	P	P	P	P	P	P	P	—	—	P	P
*Hearing Sensitivity	N	N	—	—	—	—	—	—	P	P	—	—
*Uncorrected Visual Acuity (distance)	O	O	—	—	—	—	—	—	N?	N?	—	—
*Uncorrected Visual Acuity (near)	—	—	—	—	—	—	—	—	—	—	—	—
Periodontal Disease	—	—	N	N	—	—	N	N	—	—	N	N
Oral Hygiene (problems)	—	—	N	N	—	—	N	N	—	—	N	N
Red-Green Color Vision Deficiencies	—	—	P	P	P?	P	P	P	—	—	P	P
*Height	O	O	P	P	O	O	P	P	—	—	P	P
*Weight	O	O	P	P	O	O	P	P	—	—	P	P
Trouble Hearing (medical history)	—	—	—	—	—	—	—	—	—	—	—	—
Earaches (medical history)	N?	N?	—	—	—	—	—	—	—	—	—	—
Running Ears (medical history)	P/N	N?	—	—	—	—	—	—	—	—	—	—
Eardrum Abnormalities	O	O	O	O	O	O	O	O	O?	N?	—	—
Tonsillectomy	O	O	O	O	O	O	O	O	N?	N?	—	—
Enlarged Tonsils	O	O	O	O	—	—	—	—	—	—	—	—
Oral Pharynx Abnormalities	—	—	—	—	—	—	—	—	—	—	—	—
Occlusion of Teeth (treatment priority)	O	O	O	O	O	O	O	O	O	O	N	N
Blood Pressure (systolic)	—	—	P	P	P	P	—	—	—	—	O	O
Blood Pressure (diastolic)	—	—	P?	P?	O	O	—	—	P	P	O	O
*Skeletal Maturity	—	—	—	—	P	P	—	—	P	P	N	N
Age of Onset of Ossification	O	O	P	O	—	—	—	—	O	O	—	—

(Table 3-8. continued overleaf)

Table 3–8. continued

Age Group and Condition	Family Income — All Races M[a]	Family Income — All Races F[b]	Family Income — Whites M	Family Income — Whites F	Family Income — Blacks M	Family Income — Blacks F	Education of Head of Family — All Races M	Education of Head of Family — All Races F	Education of Head of Family — Whites M	Education of Head of Family — Whites F	Education of Head of Family — Blacks M	Education of Head of Family — Blacks F
Youths 12–17												
*Uncorrected Visual Acuity	N	N	—	—	—	—	—	—	—	—	—	—
*Visual Acuity, Usual Correction	P	P	—	—	—	—	—	—	—	—	—	—
Red-Green Color Deficiencies	—	—	O	O	N?	—	—	—	N	N	N	N
Periodontal Disease	—	—	N	N	N	N	—	—	N	N	N	N
Decayed Teeth	—	—	N	N	N	N	—	—	N	N	N	N
Missing Teeth	—	—	P	P	P	P	—	—	P	P	P	P
*Filled Teeth	P	P	P	P	P	P	—	P	P	P	P	P
*Hearing Sensitivity	—	—	P	—	—	—	P	—	P	P	O	O
Mean Hematocrit	P	P	P	P	O	O	—	—	—	—	—	—
*Visual Acuity Corrected in Trial	—	—	—	—	—	—	—	—	—	—	—	—
Oral Hygiene (problems)	P	P?	N	N	N	N	P	—	N	N	N	N
Serum Uric Acid Levels	P	—	—	—	—	—	P	P?	—	—	—	—
Eye Abnormalities	—	—	N	N?	O?	O?	—	—	—	—	N	—

[a] M   indicates males.
[b] F   indicates females.
[c] O   indicates no discernable pattern.
[d] P   indicates a positive gradient.
[e] ?   indicates a qualified or somewhat unclear pattern.
[f] N   indicates a negative gradient.
[g] *   indicates an inverse scale; that is, higher levels indicate fewer health problems, e.g., higher values of visual acuity are "good."

household survey data emphasize the more severe problems. Upper income people can also obtain medical care to correct or control their condition. This effect is most obvious for vision and dental problems. In the upper socioeconomic group, people are much more likely to have glasses to adequately correct their visual problems and to have fillings rather than decayed or missing teeth.

Data from the medical examinations of children and youths further support the hypothesis that there is some linkage from socioeconomic status to at least some health problems.[15] With the exception of uncorrected visual acuity and red-green color deficiencies for young white boys, none of the data indicate positive relationships between socioeconomic status of the children's families and their health problems. Very clear negative relationships are apparent for hearing and dental problems and there are positive relationships for height, weight, and skeletal maturity at given ages. Even the vision results indicate an advantage for children of higher socioeconomic groups. Not only are they more likely to have glasses to correct their vision defects, but the defects are more easily corrected with simple, low power lenses, and they have fewer eye abnormalities.

The lack of relationship between income-education and "trouble hearing," "earaches," and "running ears" runs counter to other evidence and to the NHES data on hearing sensitivity and eardrum abnormalities (Kessner and Kalk, 1973; Dutton, 1977). The first three conditions are identified through a medical history and may represent the combination of a true "negative prevalence gradient" and a positive reporting bias. Again, there is clear evidence concerning the importance of socioeconomic factors in the treatment and correction of problems such as decayed teeth and visual problems. The examination also indicates that the partial or complete removal of the tonsils is strongly related to income up to the $7,000−9,999 category and that it falls somewhat thereafter. Among those children who still have intact tonsils, there is no income pattern with respect to enlargement. This may imply that enlargement bears no relationship to income or that tonsillectomies have eliminated all the "ex-

15. There is, of course, the problem of separating genetic from environmental factors. These data cannot be used to determine whether the children of poor people have more health problems because their parents are poor (and thus feed, clothe, and shelter them less well) or because their parents passed on certain genetic traits, say poor vision, that account both for the family's income level and the children's health problems. Both factors are probably operating to some extent; but as long as there is reason to believe that the environmental factors are of some importance, policy measures may be directed toward reducing poverty.

cess" enlarged tonsils among the middle income groups. The former seems more likely.

The medical literature generally does not indicate the existence of any important relationship between income and the etiology of these diseases. Of course, income per se is not a factor. Rather, it is those things dependent on income, such as housing, nutrition, and preventive medical care. Occupation, however, *is* thought to relate to the incidence of certain chronic conditions. Heavy labor is often implicated as a cause of degenerative joint diseases or osteoarthritis (American Rheumatism Association, 1964: 441; Cobb, 1971: 71, 74–75). The NHES data tend to support the findings that occupational stress or trauma is implicated in osteoarthritis. For instance, men employed as clerical-sales and as service workers had substantially lower than expected rates of moderate or severe osteoarthritis of the hands, while craftsmen and foremen had higher than expected rates (USNCHS, 1966: 11/20: 2–5). For a number of the other diseases examined in the NHES, some specific occupations were found to have higher or lower than expected prevalence rates, but there is no discernible pattern either with respect to income or physical effort.[16] Only for corrected visual acuity was there any clear occupational gradient, and in this case it is probably a reflection of the income effects (USNCHS, 1967: 11/25: 12–14).[17]

In summary, the data from the three cycles of the National Health Examination Survey indicate that the relationships to socioeconomic status of the prevalence rates for the conditions studied range from no relation to strong negative relationships. There are very few cases of health problems being positively related to the socioeconomic variables. Furthermore, the data are suggestive of no strong relationship between the prevalence of *all* levels of severity of a condition and reductions in income.

The Prevalence of Impairments

Impairments are broadly defined as some current or past physiological or psychological loss. Operationally, impairments tend to be measured in terms of the loss or decrease of functional ability of the senses of vision, hearing, and speech, and of the musculoskeletal sys-

16. See USNCHS, 1965: 11/10: 8; 1966: 11/13: 9; 1966: 11/17: 13; and 1968: 11/31: 8.

17. A major problem in interpreting any of these findings is that they relate to current occupation. It is easy to see how an occupation could cause a health problem so severe that those who contract it must change their jobs. A cross-sectional study of such people classified by current occupation may even show a lower than expected prevalence rate.

tem. Impairment data are drawn from two sources, medical examinations and self-reported impairments. The data from the NHES concerning visual and hearing impairments were reported in the previous section. In general, there were clear negative gradients in the prevalence rates with respect to income and education.

The prevalence of self-reported impairments can be estimated from the National Health Interview Survey.[18] Figure 3–1 presents age-specific prevalence rates with respect to income and education for

Figure 3–1. Selected Impairments — 1971

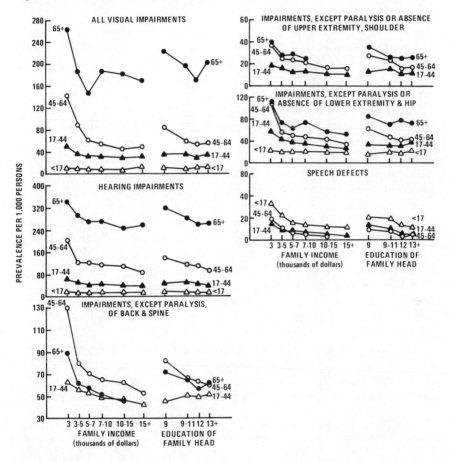

Source: USNCHS, 1975: 10/99.

18. While these data are based on household interviews and thus are subject to the biases mentioned above, they are probably more reliable than much of the data with respect to chronic conditions because they are more obvious to the interviewer and are more likely to bother the person in question.

the six impairments with prevalence rates in excess of 10 per 1000 persons (USNCHS, 1975: 10/99: 3).[19] In general, the age-specific prevalence rates show negative income and education gradients for hearing impairments, speech defects, and impairments (except paralysis or absence) of the back and spine, upper extremity and/or shoulder, and lower extremity and/or hip. The estimates for visual impairments are somewhat less clear.

There are two important sets of findings in these data. The first is that the income and education gradients tend to become steeper with increasing age of the population. In fact, for a number of the impairments there is no gradient or even a slightly positive relationship for the youngest age group. The increasing gradient with respect to age is easily understandable if the "disease" process is considered in terms of an annual *incidence* rate and a *prevalence* rate that is the cumulation of all people who had had the impairment occur in their lifetime. Suppose that *incidence* is unrelated to income or education. Then, if an impairment does reduce people's earnings potential, they will shift downward in the income distribution and make the *prevalence* gradient steeper. This effect is greater for older cohorts because a larger fraction is impaired. This hypothesis gains some support from the steadily increasing prevalence rates with respect to age for all conditions except speech defects and impairments of the back and spine. The latter exception is probably due to the exclusion of complete and partial paralysis data from the graph. The overall prevalence of this condition is 6.9 per 1000, ranging steadily from 4.6 for the seventeen to forty-four age group, to 10.7 for the forty-five to sixty-four age group, to 23.1 for the sixty-five and over age group. The inverse relationship between the prevalence of speech defects and age may be due to people's ability to overcome such problems with time, while most of the other impairments listed tend to be irreversible.

The second major finding is that the income gradient for any age group tends to be steeper than the education gradient. This is evidence that those who have a true impairment are at some disadvantage in the marketplace and do suffer an income loss. The education

19. The impairments are: *visual impairments; severe visual impairments; *other visual impairments; *hearing impairments; *speech defects; paralysis, complete or partial; absence of major extremeties; absence of entire finger(s) or toe(s) only; orthopedic impairment (except paralysis or absence): *back or spine; *upper extremity and shoulder; *lower extremity and hip; other and multiple, N.E.C. of limbs, back, and trunk. Asterisks indicate those impairments with prevalence rates of about 10 or more per 1000 persons. This cutoff was chosen so that the age-income and education-specific rates would be reasonably stable. Such cutoff estimates have a relative standard error of about 25 percent (USNCHS, 1975: 10/99: 41–44). Standard errors for the actual cells may be larger or smaller.

gradient is probably causal; with the exception of the small number of people impaired during childhood, there is no reverse effect. The difference in slopes between the income and education curves provides a rough indication of the effect of the impairments on income.

In addition to various chronic diseases, injuries are an important source of impairments. Nearly 25 percent of all the impairments in the 1971 survey were reported as having been caused by injury (USNCHS, 1973: 10/87: 1). With injuries, the date of onset is clearly defined and data concerning income and occupation prior to the injury can be obtained. The NHIS is limited to injuries that were medically attended or caused at least one day of restricted activity. While there are biases related to the differential likelihood of receiving medical care by income groups, they are probably only important for very minor injuries. Despite this flaw, these data are particularly attractive because they avoid the impact of health on income; the injury rates are based on the experience in the two weeks prior to the interview, while the income measure relates to the previous year. Table 3–9 presents estimates of the injury rate by age and family income. While the overall injury rates do not show any particular relationship with respect to income, the age-specific rates indicate rather striking differences. There is a very clear positive gradient for both groups of children, contrary to the usual expectations concerning the prevalence of hazards and degree of supervision given poor children. These data, however, are not a direct test of those factors because of the much greater likelihood that the upper income parent will seek treatment for relatively minor injuries and thus will report "acceptable" injuries. For the three working age groups, the injury rates exhibit a strong inverse gradient with only two minor exceptions. If there is an income-reporting bias, it is not likely to reverse itself with age, although it may become less pronounced. To the extent that the bias is still present, these data underestimate the effects of income and of factors related to income on injury rates.

But to what extent do these injury rates result from occupational, rather than pure income, factors? An examination of injury rates for July 1961 to June 1963 indicates that while male professional, technical, and kindred workers suffered 65.5 injuries at work per 1,000 employed persons, the comparable rates for operatives and laborers were 234.4 and 305.8, respectively.[20] More recent data indicate that injury rates vary with income even within the blue collar group of workers.[21] They are 349 per 1000 for those with family incomes

20. These are the most recent data from the NHIS concerning injury rates for all occupations (USNCHS, 1965: 10/21: 50).

21. This group includes craftsmen, foremen, operatives, and laborers, except farm and mine laborers.

Table 3–9.   Number of Persons Injured per 1,000 Persons per Year by Age and Family Income: U.S., July 1965–June 1967[a]

Age	All Incomes[b]	Family Income				
		< $3000	$3000–4999	$5000–6999	$7000–9999	$10,000+
All ages	253.1	222.4	263.1	255.6	261.3	264.2
Under 6 years	296.0	224.0	242.7	277.3	340.7	389.2
6–16 years	281.2	181.0	244.4	284.5	300.2	328.9
17–24 years	322.7	341.4	364.4	310.3	305.4	293.0
25–44 years	261.4	312.0	305.5	262.8	258.7	232.6
45–64 years	191.4	231.7	220.1	197.1	148.6	179.0
65+ years	152.3	140.9	203.8	100.2	—	166.4

[a]Includes only persons with injuries involving one or more days of restricted activity and/or some medical attention.
[b]Includes unknown incomes.
Source: USNCHS, 1970: 10/58: 16.

between $3,000 and $7,000; 291 for those in the $7,000 to $9,000 bracket; and 279 for those in the $10,000+ bracket (USNCHS, 1972: 10/68: 9). It is, however, very likely that working conditions vary with income within the blue collar group.

The Prevalence of Chronic Conditions

Chronic conditions do not fall neatly within any one of the categories outlined in Figure 2—1. They are often associated with an impairment and functional limitations, and yet, as was indicated at the beginning of this chapter, most chronic conditions do not cause an activity limitation. Similarly, while many chronic conditions are the cause of the perceived illness, many do not lead to such illness behavior as hospitalization, physician visits, or the taking of medication. Table 3—10 presents the effects of the major chronic conditions for which the NHIS has data. These conditions, and the impairments listed at the bottom of the table, account for most chronic conditions. It is apparent that many very common chronic conditions are rather minor. For twenty of the thirty-two conditions, fewer than 10 percent of the people with the condition report that it limits their participation in any usual activities; even fewer would be limited in their major activities.[22] People with these chronic conditions also tend to have fewer bed disability and restricted activity days than one would expect. There is also substantial variation across conditions with respect to the extent to which they bother people. For instance, while several of the circulatory conditions limit the activity of about half of the people who have them, they are a "bother" to a smaller fraction than are digestive conditions.

This discussion merely highlights the point that there tends to be a wide range of severity for most conditions. The question, of course, is whether the poor are more likely to have a disproportionate share of severe conditions, adjusting for the effects of their health problem on income. (The most likely cause for this disproportionate allocation is the intervention of medical care; upper income people are better able to afford treatment and thus to reduce the effects, or slow the debilitating progress, of the condition.[23]) One way to approach this question is by comparing the prevalence rates for all levels of severity to the rates for only those conditions causing activity limitations.

22. In this count it is assumed that those entries with asterisks have values of less than 10 percent. Given the sample sizes and the standard error tables, this is a reasonable assumption.
23. See, for instance, Kosa and Zola, 1975; Davis and Reynolds, 1976; and Aday, 1975.

Table 3–10. Selected Measures of the Impact of Specific Chronic Conditions[a]

Conditions and ICDA Numbers	Prevalence (1000s)	Number/ 1000 Persons	Percent Causing Activity Limitation	Percent Conditions With 1+ Bed Days in Year	Restricted Activity Days in Past Year/ Condition	Work Loss Days Per Condition Per Year
Chronic Circulatory Conditions, 1972[d]						
Heart Conditions (390–98, 402, 404, 410–29, 782.1, 782.2, 782.4)	10,291	50.4	41.6	21.6	30.2	2.2
Hypertensive Heart Disease (402, 404)	2,142	10.5	46.5	23.4	38.3	2.2
Coronary Heart Disease (410–14)	3,307	16.2	60.1	31.1	43.1	3.4
Unspecified Disorders of Heart Rhythm (427.9, 782.1, 782.2)	2,442	12.0	10.9	7.0	7.1	0.9
Hypertensive Disease NEC (400, 401, 403)	12,271	60.1	8.9	7.0	6.2	0.5
Cerebrovascular Disease (430–38)	1,534	7.5	51.0	28.0	51.0	1.8
Varicose Veins NEC (454, 456)	7,519	36.8	3.9	4.1	3.7	*
Hemorrhoids (455)	9,744	47.7	0.7	5.4	2.9	0.5
Chronic Respiratory Conditions, 1970[e]						
Chronic Bronchitis (490, 491)	6,526	32.7	4.0	47.1	7.5	0.4
Asthma w/ or w/o Hay Fever (493)	6,031	30.2	17.1	31.8	15.0	0.8
Hypertrophy of Tonsils and Adenoids (500)	4,359	21.8	1.2	60.6	8.2	0.7
Chronic Sinusitis (503)	20,582	103.0	0.7	10.5	2.1	0.3
Hay Fever w/o Asthma (507)	10,826	54.2	1.5	6.8	2.4	0.3
Chronic Digestive Conditions						
July–December 1968[f]						
Ulcer of Stomach and Duodenum (540–542)	3,360	17.2	10.9	24.6	18.0	2.2
Hernia of Abdominal Cavity (560–561)	3,191	16.3	16.0	24.3	16.9	1.9
Functional and Symptomatic Upper GI (544, 784.0–784.3, 784.5, 784.6, 784.8)	2,564	13.1	*	8.1	7.3	*
Gallbladder Condition (584–586)	2,013	10.3	7.1	36.7	19.8	1.2
Chronic Enteritis and Ulcerative Colitis (572)	1,827	9.3	6.4	20.0	13.2	1.2
Frequent Constipation (573.0)	4,654	23.8	*	2.6	2.5	*

Table 3-10. continued

Conditions and ICDA Numbers	Percent Ever Hospitalized	Percent Bother Often or All the Time [b]	If Bother, Percent Bother a Great Deal	Percent Occur in Past Twelve Months	Percent with 1+ Physician Visits [c]	Percent Taking Medicine/ Treatment
Chronic Circulatory Conditions, 1972 [d]						
Heart Conditions (390–98, 402, 404, 410–29, 782.1, 782.2, 782.4)	41.0	25.7	32.3	12.2	78.7	58.6
Hypertensive Heart Disease (402, 404)	32.3	34.5	37.1	7.8	90.0	78.1
Coronary Heart Disease (410–14)	66.6	35.2	35.6	8.6	89.2	79.0
Unspecified Disorders of Heart Rhythm (427.9, 782.1, 782.2)	10.6	7.9	21.3	20.8	60.3	21.5
Hypertensive Disease NEC (400, 401, 403)	7.1	11.0	18.6	14.7	83.1	59.5
Cerebrovascular Disease (430–38)	64.7	51.0	44.6	14.0	77.0	63.4
Varicose Veins NEC (454, 456)	13.5	18.7	17.4	4.7	39.8	16.1
Hemorrhoids (455)	8.8	12.2	19.9	11.0	43.6	19.2
Chronic Respiratory Conditions, 1970 [e]						
Chronic Bronchitis (490, 491)	14.3	18.4	40.9	21.5	79.9	19.9
Asthma w/ or w/o Hay Fever (493)	19.1	37.5	46.7	7.4	68.7	51.4
Hypertrophy of Tonsils and Adenoids (500)	18.0	18.6	49.7	20.4	86.4	12.0
Chronic Sinusitis (503)	3.4	26.9	22.6	6.0	48.4	21.9
Hay Fever w/o Asthma (507)	1.9	22.3	29.5	7.2	49.2	34.1
Chronic Digestive Conditions, July–December 1968 [f]						
Ulcer of Stomach and Duodenum (540–542)	40.6	83.1	34.2	NA	61.9	61.1
Hernia of Abdominal Cavity (560–561)	34.4	58.5	22.0	NA	63.6	18.6
Functional and Symptomatic Upper GI (544, 784.0–784.3, 784.5, 784.6, 784.8)	8.0	93.9	21.7	NA	45.1	31.7
Gallbladder Condition (584–586)	38.8	69.4	36.0	NA	67.3	37.3
Chronic Enteritis and Ulcerative Colitis (572)	27.4	78.9	29.9	NA	61.1	45.5
Frequent Constipation (573.0)	3.9	91.7	21.5	NA	49.6	38.2

(Table 3–10. continued overleaf)

Table 3-10. continued

Conditions and ICDA Numbers	Prevalence (1000s)	Number/1000 Persons	Percent Causing Activity Limitation	Percent Conditions With 1+ Bed Days in Year	Restricted Activity Days in Past Year/Condition	Work Loss Days Per Condition Per Year
Chronic Skin Conditions, 1969[g]						
Eczema, Dermatitis and Urticaria NEC (690–93, 708)	5,966	30.2	2.0	2.5	1.9	*
Corns and Callosities (700)	8,197	41.5	*	*	0.4	*
Diseases of Nail (703)	4,529	22.9	*	1.5	1.1	*
Diseases of Sebaceous Glands, (Acne) NEC (706)	3,889	19.7	*	3.0	1.4	*
Chronic Musculoskeletal, 1969[g]						
Arthritis, NEC (710–15)	18,339	92.9	17.6	8.1	12.4	0.7
Bunion (730)	2,420	12.3	*	*	1.9	*
Synovitis, Bursitis, and Tenosynovitis (731)	3,256	16.5	4.2	8.7	5.6	0.6
Selected Impairments, 1971[h]						
Visual Impairments (x00–x05)	9,596	47.5	12.5	2.3	6.0	0.4
Other Than Severe (x01–x05)	8,291	41.0	8.5	2.0	3.8	0.3
Hearing Impairments (x06–x09)	14,491	71.6	4.0	1.6	1.0	*
Speech Defects (x10–x11)	1,934	9.6	9.7	*	3.3	*
Impairments, except paralysis or absence of:						
Back or Spine (x70–x72, x80, x81)	8,018	39.6	24.5	15.3	13.8	1.4
Upper extremity/shoulder (x73, x74, x86–x88)	2,440	12.1	19.9	4.3	9.4	1.1
Lower extremity/hip (x75–x77, x82–x85)	7,387	36.5	23.4	5.0	12.9	1.2

* = More than 30 percent relative error.   NA = Not available.
[a] Conditions were selected for presentation on the basis of prevalences of 1.5 million or more.
[b] Adjusted for missing information.

Table 3–10. continued

Conditions and ICDA Numbers	Percent Ever Hospitalized	Percent Bother Often or All the Time[b]	If Bother, Percent Bother a Great Deal	Percent Occur in Past Twelve Months	Percent with 1+ Physician Visits[c]	Percent Taking Medicine/Treatment
Chronic Skin Conditions, 1969[g]						
Eczema, Dermatitis and Urticaria NEC (690–93, 708)	3.0	22.6	23.7	18.5	54.6	37.5
Corns and Callosities (700)	*	25.0	21.8	6.9	49.8	4.9
Diseases of Nail (703)	*	15.3	20.4	11.0	46.8	4.5
Diseases of Sebaceous Glands, (Acne) NEC (706)	3.2	28.3	10.9	23.1	64.1	21.7
Chronic Musculoskeletal, 1969[g]						
Arthritis, NEC (710–15)	7.6	41.8	31.3	9.4	53.2	36.4
Bunion (730)	2.7	28.4	23.4	4.7	36.4	4.2
Synovitis, Bursitis, and Tenosynovitis (731)	5.0	20.5	35.1	20.2	54.9	19.5
Selected Impairments, 1971[h]						
Visual Impairments (x00–x05)	NA	40.0	33.6	8.6	44.7	NA
Other Than Severe (x01–x05)	NA	40.1	27.5	8.9	44.9	NA
Hearing Impairments (x06–x09)	NA	46.1	20.9	5.5	22.2	NA
Speech Defects (x10–x11)	NA	35.9	23.8	7.0	18.1	NA
Impairments, except paralysis or absence of:						
Back or Spine (x70–x72, x80, x81)	NA	33.4	40.0	9.5	38.3	NA
Upper extremity/shoulder (x73, x74, x86–x88)	NA	30.0	26.2	11.6	25.1	NA
Lower extremity/hip (x75–x77, x82–x85)	NA	31.9	30.1	9.8	27.9	NA

[c] For conditions in past twelve months, adjusted for missing information.
[d] USNCHS, 1974: 10/94: 2, 3, 6, 8, 11, 12.
[e] USNCHS, 1973: 10/84: 4–9.
[f] USNCHS, 1973: 10/83: 2, 3, 5, 6, 7, 8, 9.
[g] USNCHS, 1974: 10/92: 4, 5, 7, 8, 9, 10, 11, 12, 13.
[h] USNCHS, 1975: 10/99: 3, 9, 10, 11, 12, 13.

Figures 3–2 to 3–5 present the age-specific prevalence rates by income and education for the conditions in Table 3–10. These data include all levels of severity; activity limiting conditions are addressed in the next section. The income and education gradients range from strongly positive to strongly negative. It is not surprising that those conditions with clear positive income and education gradients are the ones that appear to be least serious and most subject to differential reporting: hay fever without asthma; eczema, dermatitis, and urticaria; acne; and enteritis and colitis. While it is difficult to generalize from these data, a few patterns do emerge: (1) Negative gradients for both income and education appear to be somewhat more common than was the case when medical examinations with uniform definitions were used. (2) The patterns are much less consistent for these chronic conditions than for the impairments in Figure 3–1, probably

Figure 3–2. Chronic Circulatory Conditions–1972

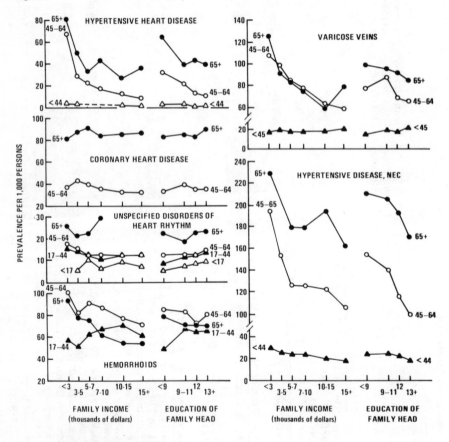

Source: USNCHS, 1974: 10/94.

Figure 3–3. Chronic Respiratory Conditions—1970

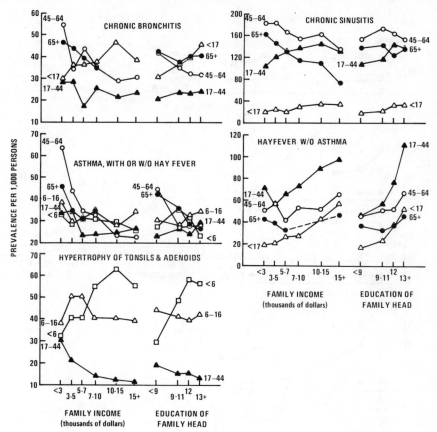

Source: USNCHS, 1973: 10/84.

due to greater consistency in definitions for the latter group. (3) It is difficult to discern consistent differences between the income and education patterns. In summary, then, the reported age-specific prevalence rates for the most common chronic conditions, with a few exceptions, appear to bear a general negative relationship to income and education. They do not exhibit marked effects on socioeconomic status. It is important to remember, however, that these prevalence rates include a great many people who report that the condition does not affect their usual activities or bother them much.

Functional Limitations that Affect Usual Activities and Disabilities

Restricting the analysis to people who report chronic conditions affecting their ability to perform their usual activities does two things. First, it eliminates a great many of the minor conditions for

Figure 3–4.   Chronic Digestive Conditions — July–December 1968

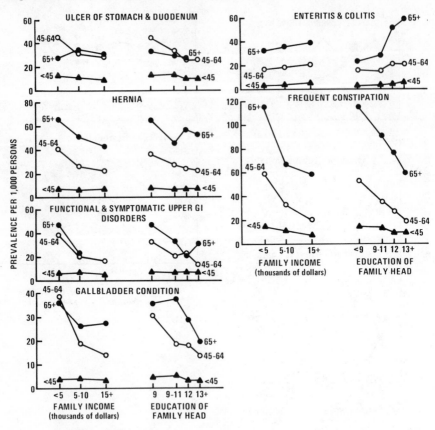

Source: USNCHS, 1973: 10/83

which the likelihood of reporting is most biased by greater knowledge or receipt of medical care among persons with higher incomes or more education. Second, the restriction to more severe conditions increases the importance of the effects that the condition has on income. Table 3–11 presents data concerning the proportion of people in each income and age group who have no chronic conditions, have one or more chronic conditions with an activity limitation, or have varying degrees of activity limitations.[24] The first section of the

24. Unfortunately, these data for 1963–1965 are the latest set with a complete breakdown by these categories. Much more recent data for 1972 show precisely the same patterns for people with chronic conditions causing activity limitations of varying degrees; but there are no data given for people with chronic conditions not causing limitations (see USNCHS, 1974: 10/96: 22).

Figure 3–5. Chronic Skin and Mucculosketal Conditions—1969

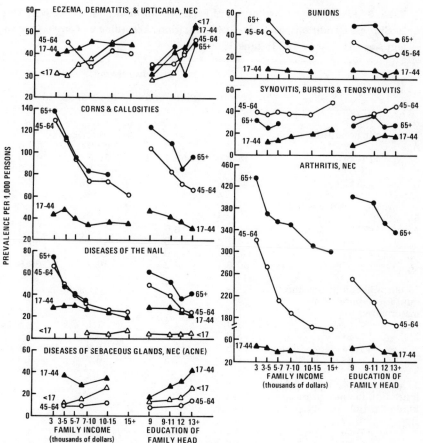

Source: USNCHS, 1974: 10/92.

table shows the proportion of people reporting no chronic conditions. For children and adults aged seventeen to forty-four, there is essentially no relationship between income and chronic illness, although there is a slightly higher prevalence rate among children in families with incomes over $7,000 (a smaller proportion with no chronic condition). For individuals aged forty-five and over, there is a clear positive gradient with respect to income for those with no conditions. There is some indication that this gradient is somewhat steeper below $7,000 for the forty-five to sixty-four age group.

The remainder of Table 3–11 indicates the distribution of those persons with chronic conditions by the extent of their activity lim-

Table 3–11. Percent Distribution of Persons with Limitation of Activity Due to Chronic Conditions, by Degree of Limitation, According to Family Income and Age—U.S., July 1963–June 1965[a]

	Family Income			
	< $2000	$2000–3999	$4000–6999	$7000+
	(1)	(2)	(3)	(4)
No chronic conditions				
Age < 17	80.2	80.9	80.0	76.6
17–44	48.1	52.4	50.6	49.0
45–64	22.7	29.4	35.3	37.0
65+	12.8	15.7	20.3	22.7
1+ chronic conditions but no activity limitations				
Age: < 17	16.6	16.6	17.9	21.5
17–44	37.7	36.8	41.9	44.8
45–64	36.5	43.0	46.9	50.1
65+	30.6	34.2	36.2	37.9
1+ chronic conditions and limitation, but not in major activity				
Age: < 17	1.4	1.3	1.1	1.1
17–44	3.8	3.2	3.1	3.0
45–64	6.8	6.3	5.2	5.1
65+	8.1	7.5	6.7	6.9
1+ chronic conditions and limitation in amount or kind of major activity				
Age: < 17	1.3	1.0	0.8	0.7
17–44	8.4	6.3	3.9	3.0
45–64	25.7	16.5	10.4	6.8
65+	31.6	27.8	24.5	20.1
1+ chronic conditions— unable to carry on major activity				
Age: < 17	b	b	0.2	0.2
17–44	2.0	1.3	0.5	0.2
45–64	8.4	4.8	2.1	0.9
65+	17.0	14.7	12.4	12.5

Source: Covell, 1967: 11, from unpublished NCHS data.

[a] Adding the values down for each income-age-limitation category will produce a total of 100 percent.

[b] Figure does not meet standards of reliability or precision.

itations. This substantially alters the relationship between income and illness. There does seem to be a negative relationship for children, one that becomes stronger when more severe limitations are considered. Of interest is the *positive* relationship for those with chronic conditions but no activity limitation. It is likely that this pattern is at least in part due to educational differences: the more highly educated are more likely to report these less serious—and therefore less obvious and less troubling—conditions because of more knowledge about symptoms.

The results for the adults are a composite of two effects: (1) the likelihood that a condition interacts with factors associated with different income levels (the impact of "income" on health); and (2) the likelihood that the limitations actually cause a reduction in various factors that determine the family income level (the impact of health on income). The impact of health status on income is probably most apparent in the two working age groups. There is a consistent, monotonic negative relationship across incomes for each level of limitation. For those with an activity limitation, but not one in the major activity, there is little difference by income groups: 3.8 percent of seventeen to forty-four year olds with incomes under $2,000, as opposed to 3.0 percent of those with incomes over $7,000, were so limited. But for those conditions for which we expect the most complete reporting—limitations in major activity—prevalence rates were approximately three times as high among those with incomes less than $2,000 than among those with incomes of $7,000 or more. Complete inability to carry on major activity was *ten times* as common among the lowest income group, compared with those of incomes over $7,000.

With these data we can speculate on the impacts of income on health and of health on income. The relationship for children should be nearly unidirectional: their illness will not substantially influence the family's income. Thus, the 25 to 30 percent greater prevalence of chronic conditions without limitation in major activity among the poorest group, relative to the richest, probably represents the impact of income. This is supported by nearly identical ratios for the two working age groups. If the limitation does not, in fact, affect major activity, then by definition it has little impact on income. If children are again used as the control group for the category with a limitation in major activity, then children in the lowest income group have a rate approximately 90 percent higher than those in the highest income group. The corresponding relationships for the seventeen to forty-four and the forty-five to sixty-four age groups are rates 180 percent and 280 percent higher, respectively. The higher rates (relative to the children) probably reflect the impact of poor health on income. Because the impact of income-related factors on health continues to hold after childhood, there will be a cumulative effect, possibly enough to explain the much larger differential in the older age group.[25] The impact of poverty (income-education-occupation) is also expected to be greater for working age adults because of the influence of occupation both in causing conditions and in interacting with them to make reporting more likely.

The NHIS data do not allow the clear identification of those people who are disabled in the sense that will be used in the remainder of this book. This definition of disability includes all persons who are limited in the amount or kind of work or housework that they can do. The NHIS definition of limitation in major activity is more narrow because it compares the person's current abilities with what he usually does. Consider someone with a back injury that keeps him from performing a heavy labor job. While that may have been his usual job a few years ago, if he now does clerical work, he would not be considered by the NHIS to have an activity limitation unless the impairment affects the clerical job. A similar case is a person who retires early because of health problems. While such people are legitimately identified as having some disability, the NHIS only counts limitations that restrict their retirement activities. Thus, the results from the NHIS with respect to activity limitations are an underestimate of the number of persons who are disabled and are likely to underestimate the effects of health problems on income.[26] Even with these underestimates, there are strong indications that low income and education are causally related to the prevalence of the more severe health problems and that such problems have a substantial effect on family income.

25. The cumulative process may not be obvious. (The table does refer to the proportion of the population with a given degree of impairment, not changes over time.) Consider a family with lower than average income, and thus a higher probability of impairment. If the head of household develops a health problem that affects his job, then the family income is lowered; if the change is sufficiently severe, the family is counted in the next lower income bracket and boosts the percentage of "limited" persons relative to the other brackets. The change in income may take time; thus, it is more likely for the older age groups to contain families who have completed this income adjustment. It should also be remembered that the spouse in the family may also be more subject to illness after the income change.

26. The NHIS definitions are more likely to omit those people with serious health problems who have to make major adjustments to their normal activity patterns, such as retiring or dropping out of the labor force to be full-time housewives. Health problems that cause short-term interruptions in behavior are more likely to be included in the definition.

Perceived Health Status

A summary measure of health problems is the person's overall perception of his or her health status without reference to specific conditions. While such a measure is very general and is subject to a great amount of variability in interpretation, it offers two substantial advantages. First, it is a single measure that avoids the problems of separating acute from chronic conditions, usual activity status, and the like. Second, it may well be the case that a person's self-evaluation relative to others is a better measure of well-being and ability to cope than any external measures. The latter point gains particular importance because psychological problems often manifest themselves in ill-defined conditions.

The 1973 NHIS included a summary question that asked how each person's health compared to other persons of the same age.[27] Figure 3-6 shows the proportion of people in each age-income group who rated their health as fair or poor. The inverse gradient with respect to income is familiar. Even when there can be little reverse effect from health problems to family income, as for children, there is a clear negative relationship.[28] As has also been the case with the other measures of health problems, the gradients become steeper with age up to the forty-five to sixty-four age group. For those who are sixty-five and over, the income gradient remains negative, but it is less steep than for the forty-five to sixty-four age group. This pattern is probably indicative of the influence that health problems have on income; people of working age with fair to poor health are more likely to suffer an income loss. People above retirement age are much less likely to depend upon earnings, so their current income should bear little relation to current health status.

SUMMARY

If careful distinctions are made among several aspects of poor health, and the income-social class data are recognized to include, in some cases, the effects of poor health, then some tentative conclusions can be drawn from the literature. It appears that for many of the currently important diseases in the U.S., there are relatively minor, but observable, negative income gradients with respect to the prevalence of medically determined pathologies. Such relationships can be found for both adults and children, and certainly in the latter group

27. The options given were excellent, good, fair, and poor (USNCHS, 1974: 10/95: 62; and USNCHS, 1976: 243, 377, 437, 439, 551).

28. These findings mirror the parental ratings of children's health as elicited during the NHES (see USNCHS, 1973: 11/129: 24-25.

Figure 3–6. Proportion of People with Health Rated as Fair or Poor Relative to Other Persons Their Age—U.S., 1973

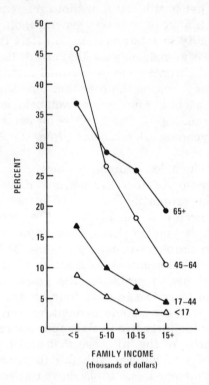

FAMILY INCOME
(thousands of dollars)

Source: USNCHS (1976), *Health: United States, 1975:* 377, 437, 439, 551.

there is little effect from the condition to family income. Comparisons of the income and education results for adults support the hypothesis of a causal linkage from factors associated with income and education to pathologies. There is very clear evidence from these data in the treatment patterns for specific conditions, with upper income groups obtaining more treatment for dental and visual problems.

Reported and clinically measured impairments give substantially the same results—rather clear inverse income and education gradients. A wide range of self-reported physical impairments also supports the view that observed prevalence varies inversely with income, but in a number of cases the curve is essentially a sideways J, with a high rate in the lowest income class with only a moderate gradient and much lower rates in the other classes. The income gradient tends to become steeper with increasing age and is generally more pronounced than the education gradient. Both findings suggest that the prevalence rates for impairments include the effects of health on income. Reported injury rates for adults show clear inverse income gradients, even within a relatively narrow range of occupations.

It is apparent that chronic conditions per se include a very broad range of health problems. Even specific diagnoses include many people for whom major problems, such as heart conditions, have relatively little impact or cause little trouble. Thus, it is not surprising that the income-education relationships for the prevalence for specific chronic conditions range from clearly positive to clearly negative. Those conditions that are positively related to the socioeconomic factors tend to be relatively minor, such as hay fever, eczema, and acne.

If one focuses only on those chronic conditions causing some activity limitation, then the interactions with income become much more apparent, especially for the middle age groups. Socioeconomic factors appear to be related both to the prevalence of more severe conditions and to the likelihood that a specific functional limitation becomes an activity restriction. Obviously, the more severe the problem, the greater its impact on income.

An overall measure of health status compared provides a useful summary of the general results. There are clear inverse income gradients for the proportion of people who think their health is fair or poor. This is true for both children and adults, with the relationship becoming increasingly strong with age during the working years, but it tends to flatten somewhat for people sixty-five and over. These findings suggest both an effect from low income to health problems and the reverse effect from health problems to lower income.

Chapter 4

Socioeconomic Factors and
the Probability of Disability

The preceding chapter has outlined the broadly based evidence linking various socioeconomic factors, in particular income and education, to health problems. While the evidence supports the hypothesis that factors associated with poverty have some role in *causing* health problems, the available data suffer from two major flaws—they are cross-sectional and they represent prevalence rates.

The cross-sectional nature of the data means that the findings of the NHES and NHIS are able to relate current pathology, impairment, limitation, and so forth to *current* family income, age, occupation, etc. Unfortunately, health problems are likely to have an effect on things like income, occupation, and life expectancy. Thus, knowing that a disproportionately large fraction of poor people have health problems tells us nothing about how many became unhealthy because they were poor and how many became poor because of their health problems. The analysis in the preceding chapter attempted to circumvent this difficulty by using age-adjusted data and by comparing the income and education results, the latter being relatively unaffected by postadolescent health problems. These adjustments, however, are rather crude and do not shed much light on the separate roles of income and education. Furthermore, there is no satisfactory way of investigating the causal role of occupational factors from these data.

The second problem involves the use of prevalence rates, rather than incidence rates. The latter measures the proportion of people in a group who develop a specific problem during a given period of time. It is essentially a measure of *flow.* The prevalence rate is the proportion of people at a given time who have the problem and thus is a stock measure. The prevalence of a health problem is obviously dependent both on the incidence rate and on how long people have the problem.[1] To assess the magnitude or importance of long-term conditions and disabilities, the prevalence rate is appropriate, but to examine the causal factors, the incidence rate is desirable.

This chapter presents two approaches to examining factors related to the incidence of disability. While cross-sectional data are used, the specific surveys involved allow the identification of income, occupation, and age at the time of the onset of the disability. Thus the empirical results will be free of the effects of health-caused changes in income and occupation. The data are also adjusted for the amount of time the person has had the problem, thus developing approximate incidence rates.

The first approach is the more general one. It develops a fivefold table of the probability (or incidence) of disability with respect to the person's age, race, sex, education, and income at the time of the onset of the condition. This rather simple technique suggests that income and education, or things correlated with income and education, have a substantial causal role in the probability of disability. The substantial difference in the likelihood of disability between black and white men can be explained by differences in the education and income distributions for each race. The same two factors account for much of the difference between black and white women. The income gradient, using predisability values and controlling for age, race, sex, and education, is still visible and important. Even with the other four factors held constant, education makes a difference in the likelihood of disability. In fact, age, education, and income account for 30 percent of the variation in disability rates.

As was suggested in the preceding two chapters, these variables may serve as proxies for the effects of various occupational factors. Such factors cause specific pathologies or impairments, and they interact with functional limitations to cause work disabilities. The second approach in this chapter examines the influence of occupational factors in the causes of disabilities among men. It allows a richer set of variables, but at the expense of fewer observations and more approximations.

---

1. The relationship can be easily seen with the analogy of a bathtub. The incidence rate is a flow, like the rate at which water is entering the tub. The prevalence is a measure of the depth of the water at any point in time. This is obviously also dependent on how fast water is leaving through the drain. With health problems, people leave the "prevalence pool" by being cured or by dying.

Both approaches utilize data from the Survey of Disabled Adults and the Survey of Economic Opportunity, which were described in Chapter 2. Specific calculations and adjustments to these data are discussed below in the methodology subsections of each of the major sections. A final section summarizes the results.

THE PROBABILITY OF DISABILITY: THE INFLUENCE OF AGE, RACE, SEX, EDUCATION, AND INCOME

The literature on the effects of poverty on health contains many studies showing the prevalence of disabilities among the poor, other studies indicating that factors such as education or occupation prior to disability might be related to health status, and a few very limited studies that use predisability income. There are, however, no investigations concerning the incidence (or probability within a year) of becoming disabled that include predisability income, education, age, race, and sex. This section provides such estimates for the United States.

The first subsection describes the data and methodology used in estimating the probability of disability. The second subsection presents the probabilities in a five way table so that age, race, sex, education, and income-specific disability rates can be examined. The various levels of this table are used to explore some of the relationships underlying the differences observed in more aggregate data. A third subsection provides the disability rates with respect to certain variables after they have been adjusted to account for differences in the remaining variables. The final subsection uses regression techniques to see how well these five variables explain the observed disability rates and presents the major conclusions.

Data and Methodology

To estimate the probability or incidence of disability, it is necessary to have the numerator represent the number of newly disabled persons for the time period and a denominator represent the population at risk. The denominator in this case can be fairly easily constructed from the U.S. Office of Economic Opportunity's Survey of Economic Opportunity (SEO). A series of questions were asked in the SEO to identify those people who had a long-term health problem that limited the kind or amount of work (or housework) that they could do. In developing the denominator for computing disability rates, only the nondisabled population was used. This reduces the bias caused by the effects of disability on income. The SEO has all the necessary information to classify individuals by age, race, sex, education, and current family income.

The data for the numerator must include comparable characteristics for individuals at the time they were disabled. Almost all previous studies investigating income and disability have had to rely on the current income of the disabled person and his family. As disability often results in a substantial reduction in earnings, the observed family income will be much lower after disability than before the onset of the condition. Estimates based on a current measure of income will be biased to suggest a very strong relationship between income and disability. Fortunately, the 1966 Survey of Disabled Adults (SDA) has data that allow the estimation of family income at the time of the onset of disability (see pages 25–26 for a description of the SDA).

The calculation of the disability rates and the estimation of family income require a number of demographic characteristics, such as race, sex, education, geographic region, urban or rural residence, and age. As the sample is specifically truncated to eliminate all childhood disabilities (those occurring before the age of eighteen), not much change can be expected in the education variable. It is assumed that the individual's residence did not change; and his or her age is adjusted to that at the time of disability. The critical variable to be estimated is family income at the onset of disability. This is made up of three components: the income of the disabled person, that of the other members of his or her immediate family, and that of other relatives in the household.

The first step is the estimation of the disabled individual's earnings. If he or she was working in a full-time job at the time of disability, the weekly earnings at that job are directly available in the SDA. These were inflated to 1966 values with an index of weekly wages (U.S. Bureau of Labor Statistics, 1971: 206). Given this value, an estimate of the number of weeks worked per year is required to approximate yearly earnings. The SEO data were used to estimate race-sex-specific equations for weeks worked per year by well adults.[2] The independent variables required by the regression for each individual are age, whether or not in school, years of school, marital status, number of adults, persons and children in the family, regional and urban location, income from assets, and other family income. The last two variables will be considered later; the others were read-

---

2. These regressions are comparable to the WKSWORK regressions discussed below in Chapter 5, page 153. The only difference is that the ones used for this chapter were based only on those people without a health-related work limitation.

ily obtained.[3] The coefficients from these regressions were then combined with the observed and adjusted values of the independent variables for each disabled person to obtain a prediction of the number of weeks worked. The product of the inflation-adjusted weekly wage and the estimated weeks worked per year is used as the estimate of the disabled person's earnings at the time of disability onset, adjusted to 1966 wage levels.

The other sources of actual family income in 1966 were examined to eliminate those that were obviously related to the disabled person's health status, such as Aid to the Blind or the earnings of any family member who claimed to have started work since the onset of the disabled person's problem.[4]

These calculations and adjustments are necessary because the sample size of the SDA is too small to allow direct estimates of incidence rates. The disability incidence rate in the population aged eighteen to sixty-four is 1.24 percent per year. Thus, only about 7 percent of the SDA sample became disabled in the preceding year. This results in too small a sample to provide useful estimates. Therefore, people who became disabled in the years 1955 to 1965 and whose conditions did not occur during childhood were used to provide an overall sample of about 4,100 cases.[5]

The number of persons in the SDA who were disabled in 1964 is less than would be expected on the basis of the 1965 experience. This is, in part, because the population at risk is somewhat smaller, but more importantly, because some of those who were disabled in 1964 either died, became better, or moved out of the age range before the survey was taken.[6] These factors can be lumped together

3. School attendance at the time of disability was approximated by comparing the number of years of school completed and the individual's age at the time of disability. If the difference was less than six years, the person was assumed to be in school at the time of disability onset.

4. For a complete discussion of the procedures used in evaluating other family income and the number of disabled persons, see Appendix C in Luft, 1972. In general, the procedures used are designed so that any biases will be in the direction of an overestimate of family income at the time of disability. Such a bias, if present, will reduce the estimated influence of income on disability.

5. The arbitrary cutoff date of 1955 was chosen as a compromise between (1) wanting to extend the period so as to enlarge the sample and (2) wanting a short period so as to reduce the effects of measurement errors due to faulty recall and changes in the variables used in the estimation process. The eleven-year period, 1955-1965, was chosen because it includes about one-half of the SDA sample.

6. The population growth aspect is less important than would be expected for the population as a whole because the sample is limited to those aged eighteen to sixty-four. Therefore, while the population base expands by about the number of seventeen year olds in the previous year, it contracts not only by

in what may be loosely termed a cohort survival rate. The inverse of this value, 1.055, was used to inflate each preceding year's disabled population.

The total population implicitly represented by these observations was then scaled twice. First, it was adjusted to represent the number of persons who would have been disabled in the population in any one year, 1.24 percent of the total.[7] Second, because the age used was that of the person at the time of disability, the age distribution was adjusted to that of individuals disabled in 1965. This is necessary because with each succeeding year of raw data (working backwards) there are fewer older persons.

The Probability of Disability by Age, Race, Sex, Education, and Income

The procedures outlined in the previous subsection make it possible to present the probabilities of disability shown in Table 4–1. These are based on predisability incomes, as well as on the usual variables such as age, race, sex, and education.[8] This presentation makes it possible to compare the estimated probabilities at various levels of aggregation, and thus not only to compare the results with a priori relationships, but also to examine whether the observed pattern is due to some underlying variable included in the table. In the discussions that follow, the importance of underlying variables will be emphasized with respect to income and race.

Prevalence rates have always indicated that much higher propor-

---

deaths among the eighteen to sixty-three year olds but also by the entire cohort of those aged sixty-four. It is also likely that more disabled individuals move out of the age group than move into it because of the much higher prevalence of disability among the elderly.

7. This estimate is derived from the number of persons in the SDA who became disabled in 1965. It is very close to the value obtained from the SEO data on disability.

8. As both the numerators and denominators for the values in this and other tables presented in this chapter are based on relatively small samples, care must be exercised in their interpretation. Mathematically, because of the ratio form of the data presented, the results are most sensitive to sampling error in the denominator. To serve as a guide in examining the data, those cells based on one to fifteen observations are underlined. (This represents a varying number of persons, but it is approximately 50,000 persons for the white population and 10,000 persons for the black population. The deliberate oversampling of non-white areas in the SEO tends to reduce this "small numbers" problem.) The SDA, on the other hand, did not attempt to increase the number of cases for blacks beyond their proportion in the population. Therefore, the numerator may be based on too few cases to be meaningful. As there are no data on what the disability rate should be, it is difficult to know when the small sample problem has seriously affected the results. It may be assumed, however, that no cell has a true zero probability of disability.

tions of the poor than the rich are disabled, but no evidence was available with respect to predisability income. The data in Table 4–1 indicate a clear income effect even when the "reverse" impact of health problems on income has been removed. For all persons, within each age group there is a substantial income gradient, although there are some minor deviations from monotonicity, especially at the extremes of the income and age categories.[9] In reviewing the income results, it is important to remember that there may be biases in the data that will tend to flatten the observed gradient and introduce some spurious values.[10]

The age-income results for the four race-sex categories in the right-hand section of the table make it possible to examine the income effect. For white men, the two younger groups exhibit a fairly clear income gradient, although the rates for those with family incomes below $2,000 are "out of line." These are probably the result of transitory income differences, and, for the youngest age group, represent the presence of low income but healthy students. The elder group of white men has an income gradient below $6,000, but the disability rate is essentially flat thereafter. The analysis of results for black men is clouded by the much smaller sample available. In spite of this, there is a generally negative gradient of disability rates with respect to income. The gradient is clearest for the middle age group in which the number of cases is large enough to provide confidence in the results.[11]

The situation for white women is comparable to that of white men, although the slight upturn at the upper end of the income distribution is somewhat more pronounced. It is possible that this is a

9. It is to be expected that the greatest errors of estimation will appear in the extreme age groups for two reasons. First, these are the groups that have the most options for other than full-time work; young adults are often full-time students, or if they work, work only part time, while elderly adults often retire or reduce their work time before the age of sixty-five. Second, although the equations used to estimate the number of weeks worked included AGE and AGE^2 terms, they were fit to the entire age range, eighteen to sixty-four. It is likely that the second degree polynomial approximation is least accurate at the extremes of the age distribution.

10. The primary problem is one of errors in variables. Of the five variables in Table 4-1, income is most likely to be measured with some error, even if all the data were collected at the same time. That was not the case, and the estimating procedure described above is sure to add "noise." Furthermore, health status is more likely a function of permanent income than measured income. Thus the observed relationship will tend to underestimate the true effects of income (see Friedman, 1957, for a complete presentation of the permanent income hypothesis which can be paralleled here).

11. There are only a total of eighteen cases in the numerators of the six cells for incomes above $6,000 in the two other age groups.

Table 4–1.   Estimated Probability of Disability —U.S., 1967

	Education Level					
	0 Thru 8 Years			9 Thru 12 Years		
Age	18–34	35–54	55–64	18–34	35–54	55–64
White Men						
< $2000	0.0021	0.0393	0.1039	0.0126	0.0123	0.0639
$2–4000	0.0213	0.0337	0.0572	0.0126	0.0260	0.1088
$4–6000	0.0153	0.0266	0.0450	0.0093	0.0137	0.0407
$6–8000	0.0293	0.0209	0.0367	0.0068	0.0126	0.0180
$8–10000	0.0025	0.0190	0.0203	0.0033	0.0071	0.0182
$10000+	0.0329	0.0170	0.0592	0.0033	0.0066	0.0191
Total*	0.0152	0.0212	0.0400	0.0054	0.0077	0.0213
Black Men						
< $2000	0.0359	0.0412	0.1359	0.0308	0.0040	0.0
$2–4000	0.0173	0.0358	0.0988	0.0115	0.0063	0.1645
$4–6000	0.0095	0.0245	0.0325	0.0118	0.0224	0.1235
$6–8000	0.0386	0.0197	0.0071	0.0268	0.0122	0.0031
$8–10000	0.0030	0.0135	0.0021	0.0004	0.0011	0.0
$10000+	0.0064	0.0211	0.0420	0.0003	0.0022	0.0
Total*	0.0156	0.0239	0.0523	0.0099	0.0078	0.0257
White Women						
< $2000	0.0405	0.0608	0.0482	0.0215	0.0191	0.0390
$2–4000	0.0342	0.0291	0.0767	0.0142	0.0241	0.0226
$4–6000	0.0133	0.0294	0.0305	0.0066	0.0134	0.0147
$6–8000	0.0142	0.0170	0.0374	0.0061	0.0097	0.0364
$8–10000	0.0240	0.0244	0.0441	0.0066	0.0070	0.0029
$10000+	0.0260	0.0171	0.0311	0.0090	0.0081	0.0202
Total*	0.0219	0.0253	0.0408	0.0073	0.0085	0.0185
Black Women						
< $2000	0.0270	0.0833	0.0482	0.0223	0.0322	0.0546
$2–4000	0.0382	0.0533	0.2037	0.0130	0.0233	0.0264
$4–6000	0.0224	0.0370	0.0024	0.0087	0.0056	0.0011
$6–8000	0.0025	0.0194	0.0435	0.0064	0.0191	0.0911
$8–10000	0.0	0.0297	0.0143	0.0141	0.0013	0.1602
$10000+	0.3167	0.0469	0.0098	0.0052	0.0089	0.0
Total*	0.0272	0.0466	0.0630	0.0100	0.0129	0.0267
All Persons						
< $2000	0.0274	0.0585	0.0644	0.0199	0.0187	0.0430
$2–4000	0.0268	0.0354	0.0828	0.0133	0.0228	0.0426
$4–6000	0.0145	0.0281	0.0360	0.0081	0.0135	0.0245
$6–8000	0.0209	0.0192	0.0351	0.0072	0.0115	0.0273
$8–10000	0.0099	0.0211	0.0271	0.0054	0.0067	0.0126
$10000+	0.0305	0.0182	0.0475	0.0063	0.0073	0.0193
Total*	0.0190	0.0254	0.0427	0.0069	0.0083	0.0200

*Total includes some cases with unknown levels.
Denominators based on less than sixteen cases are underlined.

Table 4–1. continued

Education Level			All Education Levels*		
13+ Years					
18–34	35–54	55–64	18–34	35–54	55–64
0.0034	0.0096	0.0351	0.0073	0.0247	0.0854
0.0112	0.0167	0.0202	0.0148	0.0313	0.0690
0.0096	0.0137	0.0345	0.0102	0.0192	0.0430
0.0123	0.0134	0.0390	0.0099	0.0147	0.0287
0.0046	0.0108	0.0302	0.0037	0.0104	0.0241
0.0046	0.0085	0.0234	0.0046	0.0085	0.0286
0.0059	0.0073	0.0191	0.0065	0.0105	0.0278
0.0315	0.0	0.0	0.0329	0.0343	0.1550
0.0	0.0618	0.0	0.0120	0.0301	0.1066
0.0009	0.0122	0.0	0.0101	0.0262	0.0419
0.0238	0.0	0.0	0.0278	0.0152	0.0056
0.0	0.0	0.0	0.0006	0.0061	0.0014
0.0	0.0005	0.0	0.0005	0.0057	0.0268
0.0062	0.0027	0.0	0.0105	0.0165	0.0539
0.0097	0.0101	0.0470	0.0232	0.0344	0.0459
0.0021	0.0021	0.0641	0.0153	0.0247	0.0469
0.0042	0.0168	0.0500	0.0069	0.0192	0.0242
0.0064	0.0048	0.0173	0.0069	0.0109	0.0326
0.0076	0.0099	0.0114	0.0076	0.0102	0.0169
0.0082	0.0063	0.0195	0.0091	0.0084	0.0218
0.0067	0.0064	0.0175	0.0083	0.0111	0.0261
0.0	0.0253	0.0	0.0227	0.0654	0.0553
0.0	0.0192	0.0127	0.0163	0.0375	0.1531
0.0	0.0200	0.0131	0.0117	0.0203	0.0028
0.0	0.0376	0.0	0.0051	0.0285	0.0447
0.0	0.0	0.0	0.0104	0.0105	0.0559
0.0090	0.0168	0.0	0.0090	0.0177	0.0026
0.0022	0.0153	0.0023	0.0120	0.0274	0.0500
0.0075	0.0111	0.0409	0.0188	0.0376	0.0591
0.0059	0.0118	0.0396	0.0149	0.0292	0.0627
0.0066	0.0156	0.0405	0.0088	0.0199	0.0321
0.0102	0.0099	0.0249	0.0089	0.0136	0.0300
0.0056	0.0098	0.0211	0.0058	0.0102	0.0212
0.0062	0.0076	0.0216	0.0068	0.0086	0.0255
0.0062	0.0070	0.0179	0.0079	0.0119	0.0288

reflection of the other half of the permanent income hypothesis—positive transitory income temporarily brings lower income people with high disability rates into higher income brackets.[12] Probably more important is the fact that one of the primary ways a family can raise its income is by having two wage earners. A larger proportion of women in families with higher incomes are working and subject to occupationally related disabilities or a greater likelihood of having a condition that interferes with their jobs.[13] The data for black women suffer from the same problem of sparse data as for black men.

With due regard for the problems of small sample size, it is worthwhile to consider the pattern of disability rates by income within an age-education group in the main part of the table. In general, the income gradient is still apparent for each race-sex grouping even when education is held constant. Of course, there are a number of outlying observations, but most of these are based on a small number of cases or are likely to be subject to estimation errors. For instance, there are probably not very many men aged eighteen to thirty-four with less than nine years of school who had family incomes over $10,000 in 1966. Therefore, this category will be more sensitive to errors in the income estimate than some of the larger categories. In general, these results support the hypothesis that income (or factors closely associated with income, other than age, race, sex, or education) has a rather strong effect on the probability of disability.

Conventional data generally indicate much higher prevalence and much higher incidence rates for disability among blacks. Looking only at the overall rates in the right-hand part of the table for all income groups for each age group of blacks and whites, it appears that whites have much lower disability rates—on the order of a half to two-thirds the comparable rates for blacks, for both men and women. Closer examination of income-specific rates indicates a much more complex picture. Except for the lowest income category of the two younger male groups and the lowest two income classes for older men, the rates for black males are comparable to those of white males within each income class; in a number of cases they are even lower. A similar relationship holds between black and white women,

12. The procedure for estimating the income of disabled persons, especially the potential upward bias that was imposed whenever an income source was doubtful, may create substantial amounts of what could be treated as positive transitory income. It is unlikely that true positive transitory income is large enough to produce the changes observed (see note 10, above).

13. It is also possible that women who were not working considered themselves disabled only if their disabilities interfered with their housework, regardless of whether they affected their employment possibilities.

although it is not quite as clear. This strongly suggests that the observed difference in disability rates between blacks and whites is not related to specifically racial differences, but instead is income-related.[14]

These data also allow a test of whether education makes a difference in the probability of disability, holding age, race, sex, and income constant.[15] Education would be expected to have an impact in two major ways: first, through entry to safer or less disability-sensitive jobs, and second, through increased knowledge of proper health practices. Examining the disability rates for white men, there is some evidence of a pattern both for the overall groups and for individual income classes. Those with less than eight years of schooling tend to have substantially higher disability rates than the others, but there is little difference between those with high school and college educations. Basically, the same results are obtained for women. It is difficult to determine whether these education results reflect the influence of different occupations or health practices knowledge, but they suggest that the effects of a minimal amount of education are very important.[16]

The principal findings may be summarized in the following way.

14. The exceptionally high rates for blacks relative to whites in the lowest income categories may be due to a number of factors. First, the black rates may be higher because at the same low income levels blacks are in much worse jobs (with respect to health conditions), have even less access to medical care, or have inferior nutrition, housing, and so forth for the same expenditures (see, for instance, Caplovitz, 1967). Second, the observed black rates may be closer to the true values, while the white rates are reduced because of incorrect income estimates. (It is much more likely that the errors in income estimation account for a larger proportion of low income whites than low income blacks. As blacks generally have lower incomes, the misclassification of some with lower than true incomes will have a smaller effect.) Third, in the few instances where there are enough observations to allow comparison (for instance, men aged thirty-five to fifty-four with zero to eight years of school), the similarity between black and white disability rates holding everything else constant is apparent.

15. It is important to recognize that education and income are not completely independent variables and, in fact, that years of schooling is thought to be a prime determinant of income levels. Thus, controlling for income and education implies that care must be taken when interpreting the results in specific cells. For instance, well-educated white men would be expected to have relatively high incomes, everything being equal. It may be reasonable to surmise that those well-educated white men with very low incomes are somewhat "different" than the average and that such "differences" may underlie some of the unusual results for (1) well-educated people with low incomes and (2) poorly educated people with high incomes.

16. See Leveson (1972: 26) for a discussion of the importance of education, both for having specific knowledge and for the likelihood of obtaining health information in time of need. Lefcowitz (1973: 6) also emphasizes the role of education.

There is a substantial income gradient with respect to the probability of disability when predisability incomes are used. This relationship holds within each age group, each race-sex group, and within sample constraints, even when education is held constant. The much higher observed disability rate for blacks relative to whites is due almost entirely to differences in income. In fact, it appears that the age-income-specific rates for blacks and whites are about equal, especially if allowances are made for potential biases in the data. Finally, education appears to have an influence independent of income; persons with less than nine years of school tend to have substantially higher disability rates, controlling for other factors, than do those with more education.[17]

The Probability of Disability: Adjusted Rates

The five way presentation in Table 4–1 makes it possible to consider the effects of the various factors on the probability of disability and to examine whether variables other than the one of interest were responsible for the observed differences. For instance, the racial differences were found to be primarily attributable to differences in income. Unfortunately, the underlying samples are too small to allow extensive detailed analysis of the data at the most disaggregated level. It also becomes difficult to visually evaluate the effect of a single variable because of the large number of cells in the table. One method of circumventing these problems is to consider the disability rates with respect to just a few variables of interest, adjusted to a given distribution of the suppressed variables. This standardization procedure makes it possible to examine the effects of the variables in question, knowing that the observed differences are not due to differences in

17. A similar table and analysis was carried out using the ratio of family income to the "poverty line income" for the family in an attempt to control for differences in family composition. Although these results are similar to those presented, the "income" gradient is not nearly as clear. There are several potential explanations. First, the poverty line measure may not be an adequate adjustment for family composition given differing expenditure patterns. For instance, the "low income" cutoff may be more appropriate. Second, while the poverty line may be correct, the effect of income on health may be more closely related to the absolute difference (in dollars) from poverty rather than the ratio form. Third, even if a ratio form is correct, the intervals used in the analysis (< 0.5, 0.5 – 0.75, 0.75 – 1.0, 1.0 – 1.5, 1.5 – 2.5, 2.5+) were chosen arbitrarily and may hide the underlying relationship. Fourth, the total income available to the family, rather than a crudely adjusted per capita income level, may be critical for health. Fifth, and most importantly, it is possible that the factor related to disability is not income but something correlated with income, such as occupation. There is no reason to think that poor working conditions and demanding job requirements, while correlated with family income, are also correlated with the poverty ratio measure.

the suppressed variables. For instance, Table 4–2 presents the disability rates by race-, sex-, age-, education-, and income-specific rates of the main part of Table 4–1 with the weights given by the overall distribution of population by education and income.[18]

These results clearly indicate that the difference in disability rates between black and white men is due almost solely to their income and education. When standardized for income and education, the age-specific rates are almost the same; in fact, the black rates are lower for the two older age groups. The differences between white and black women are still evident after standardization, and the "excess probability" of disability for black women increases substantially with age. White women tend to have a greater likelihood of disability than white men in the youngest age group and a substantially lower likelihood in the oldest group. The rates for black men and women are the same in the first age group, but diverge sharply as older black women are much more likely to become disabled.

Table 4–3 presents the age and education standardized rates for each race, sex, and income category. For each race-sex combination there is a fairly clear income gradient. Problems in estimating the predisability income of individuals can partially account for low dis-

Table 4–2. Estimated Probability of Disability by Age, Race, and Sex—U.S., 1967 *(Standardized to the U.S. Education and Income Distribution)*

	Men		Women	
Age	*White*	*Black*	*White*	*Black*
18–34	0.0070	0.0085	0.0097	0.0082
35–54	0.0114	0.0083	0.0117	0.0162
55–64	0.0286	0.0279	0.0217	0.0317

18. Let $d_{r,s,a,e,i}$ be the specific disability rate associated with one race, sex, age, education, and income cell in the main section of Table 4–1. Let $n_{e,i}$ be the number of persons in the U.S. in each education and income category. Then the disability rates in Table 4–2 are

$$d'_{r,s,a} = \frac{\sum_e \sum_i d_{r,s,a,e,i} \cdot n_{e,i}}{\sum_e \sum_i n_{e,i}}$$

Similar adjustments are made for the other tables in this subsection. The problem of small denominators is still present in creating the weighted averages. The tables were computed three times, eliminating cells with less than four, ten, and sixteen cases in the denominators. In general, the results are stable, although in some instances the results with the four case cutoff are somewhat questionable. The values presented are those with the sixteen case cutoff and thus are least subject to the effects of sampling error.

Table 4−3. Estimated Probability of Disability by Income, Race, and Sex—
U.S., 1967 *(Standardized to the U.S. Age and Education Distribution)*

	Men		Women	
Income	White	Black	White	Black
< $20000	0.0244	0.0341	0.0292	0.0359
$2-4000	0.0271	0.0201	0.0230	0.0359
$4-6000	0.0174	0.0220	0.0148	0.0120
$6-8000	0.0153	0.0189	0.0126	0.0188
$8-10,000	0.0092	0.0028	0.0129	0.0105
$10,000+	0.0130	0.0070	0.0130	0.0135

ability estimates of the lower income groups and the higher than
expected probabilities for the upper income groups. The bias at the
low end is probably more important for whites than blacks and for
men than women; at the high end of the distribution, the reverse is
true. In spite of these minor difficulties, it is clear that income (or
factors correlated with income) is important in determining disability
rates. The likelihood of disability for a poor person is at least twice
that of one in the $8,000 and over income class. The differential is
even larger for blacks than whites, possibly reflecting the even lower
availability of medical care in poor black than poor white neighbor-
hoods. There is no clear racial effect in the disability rates for men.
The higher disability rates for black women relative to white women
is largely due to much higher rates in the lowest income categories.
One possibility is that because a greater proportion of black women
are working, they may report more job-related or job-caused disabilities, or may be more likely to report any disability (see footnote 13).

Table 4−4 provides an indication of the differences in disability
by educational attainment while controlling for age and income. For
each of four race-sex groups, there is a clear gradient with respect to
education. For all except black men, however, there is a very large
difference between those who had no high school education and
those with at least nine years of school, while the difference between

Table 4−4. Estimated Probability of Disability by Education, Race, and
Sex—U.S., 1967 *(Standardized to the U.S. Age and Income Distribution)*

	Men		Women	
Years of School	White	Black	White	Black
< 9	0.0212	0.0190	0.0228	0.0288
9-12	0.0100	0.0087	0.0095	0.0104
13+	0.0090	0.0038	0.0083	0.0081

high school and college is relatively small. The very low rate for black men with thirteen or more years of schooling can be explained on two grounds. First, until very recently, only very exceptional black men went to college, and those who did were probably likely to have been exceptionally healthy to have "made it up out of the ghetto." Second, given the small number of black men with any college education, the sampling error for this cell is rather high.

The comparison between black and white men indicates that once age, income, and education differentials are held constant, blacks tend to have a lower probability of disability. A number of factors may lead to this result. Given the general discrimination against blacks, it is unlikely that black and white men with the same age, education, and other characteristics will earn the same income. One way for them to have equal incomes is for there to be something "wrong" with the white man. This may well be a poor medical history leading to a high absentee rate and a higher probability of long-term disability. Alternatively, the black man may have some special qualities that enable him to achieve a higher than would be predicted income level. These conjectures are strengthened by the fact that a given education level tends to be worth less to blacks than whites (Weiss, 1970). Thus, controlling for income and education tends to select blacks from the upper end of the education distribution within a given income level.

The probabilities of disability for white men and women are almost the same for each education group. Black women, on the other hand, have consistently higher disability rates than black men, but, except for the lowest education group, they are comparable to those of white women. Taken together, these three tables indicate that the excess disability rates among black women are concentrated among low income, low education, older women.

A Summary Measure

The previous subsection collapsed the detail of Table 4—1 so that the broad outlines of the findings would be apparent. An even more concise presentation is possible through the use of a regression equation. The body of Table 4—1 contains 216 cells (three age groups, two races, two sexes, three education groups, and six income groups). The disability rate in each may be considered a separate observation and the mean values for age, race, sex, education, and income the independent variables.[19]

19. Approximate mean values were used for each variable, rather than the actual values of the people assigned to each cell. Thus, substantially less than all the potential information was used, and the error in measurement will bias the

The summary equation is:

$$\text{PROB} = .0265 + .0007 \text{ AGE} + .0033 \text{ BLACK} + .0020 \text{ FEMALE}$$
$$(.0001) \qquad (.0031) \qquad\qquad (.0030)$$

$$- .0025 \text{ ED} - .0013 \text{ INCOME}.$$
$$(.0005) \qquad (.0004) \qquad\qquad R^2 = .303$$

Clearly, age, education, and income are highly significant, with coefficients that are three to seven times their respective standard errors. These three variables alone can explain nearly 30 percent of the variance in disability rates. Better measurement is likely to substantially increase that fraction.

A minor respecification of the equation to allow separate coefficients for the different education levels highlights the more detailed findings:

$$\text{PROB} = .0130 + .0007 \text{ AGE} + .0033 \text{ BLACK} + .0022 \text{ FEMALE}$$
$$(.0001) \qquad (.0031) \qquad\qquad (.0030)$$

$$- .0163 \text{ ED9T12} - .0189 \text{ ED13PLS} - .0013 \text{ INCOME}$$
$$(.0036) \qquad\qquad (.0042) \qquad\qquad (.0004)$$

$$R^2 = .310$$

As with any set of dichotomous variables, one must be left out, so people with less than nine years of schooling are included in the constant term. This second equation indicates very large, significant, and approximately equal coefficients for people with nine to twelve and thirteen plus years of schooling, relative to people with less than nine years of school.

The three levels of examining these data concerning the probability of disability all point toward the substantial role of predisability income and minimal levels of education. For instance, these two factors essentially account for the observed differences in disability rates by race. However, it is important to determine whether educa-

---

coefficients toward zero. (Computational costs precluded the more precise approach.) The following values were used: Income—(in thousands of dollars) 1.5, 3.0, 5.0, 7.0, 9.0, 15.0; Age—26.0, 44.5, 59.5; Education—6.0, 11.0, 14.0.

The wide variation in the number of observations available for each cell implies that the error terms will not be homoscedastic. More importantly, cells based on a small number of observations are subject to substantial error. To reduce these problems, the 216 cells were weighted by the square root of the number of observations upon which the denominator of the disability rate was based. Therefore, a cell with the denominator based on 144 observations would be weighted three times as heavily as one based on 16 observations.

tion and income are the true causal factors or are merely factors correlated with the cause of disability. The policy implications of such a determination are enormous. If low education and income were the cause of a substantial fraction of disability, then more education and income transfer payments could substantially improve health status in the United States. If education and income are primarily, or partially, proxy measures for some other factors, then such a policy would be misdirected and other paths should be investigated. A prime potential relationship is through occupation, a variable highly correlated with both income and education.

OCCUPATIONAL FACTORS
AND THE CAUSES OF DISABILITY

The investigation of disability with respect to occupation can be broken down into two major segments. First, there is the likelihood that an individual considers him or herself disabled, and second, the impact of that disability in terms of the person's original occupation. The former segment may be further divided into two factors that determine reported disability. The first factor is the likelihood that the job or working conditions lead to a given medical condition. This factor, the occupational disease or hazard, is the subject of much of the interest in occupational health and safety literature. The second factor is the likelihood that this condition, regardless of its cause, interacts with the requirements of the job to make normal work activity difficult. This issue is often considered a problem of vocational rehabilitation. Finally, if a person is disabled, the requirements of the job, in combination with his or her handicap, skills, and job alternatives will help determine whether he or she keeps that job, moves to another job, or is unable to work at all. This second segment—the role of occupational factors on the impact of a condition—will be examined in the next chapter.

The empirical analysis of this section will rely on the two basic data sources of the previous section, the Survey of Disabled Adults and the Survey of Economic Opportunity, and add data from a third source, the Dictionary of Occupational Titles (DOT). The method of analysis, however, is substantially different. Rather than cross-classifying individuals by the variables in question, such as income and age, the individual observations are aggregated by their occupations. Disability rates for each occupation group are then considered as a function of characteristics of all people within that occupation. Multiple regression techniques are used in this analysis. This approach allows a much richer set of variables, but it also involves fewer observations that are more aggregate and involve more approximations. The next subsection outlines the data and methodology in somewhat more detail. The two subsections that follow examine two aspects of the influence of job characteristics on disability. The first aspect is causal in the usual sense—job characteristics that bear an etiological relationship to specific conditions, especially those considered to be caused on the job. The second aspect is more subtle. It ignores the biomedical causation and focuses on whether a specific limitation, in conjunction with specific job requirements, results in a disability. A final section summarizes the results of the whole chapter.

Data and Methods

The estimation of the probability of disability by occupation requires not only estimates of disability rates, but also characteristics of individuals in the occupations and the working conditions associated with the occupations. These data were obtained from three sources. Data referring to the persons in each occupation are from the 1967 Survey of Economic Opportunity (SEO), the number and characteristics of the disabled are from the 1966 Survey of Disabled Adults (SDA), and the job descriptions are from the Dictionary of Occupational Titles (DOT).

The SEO, which provides the data for the denominator, also makes possible some overall estimates of the coverage provided by this analysis. Approximately eighty-seven million people reporting a recognizable occupation are represented by 38,722 individual cases.[20] Initially, the 296 occupation categories of the 1960 census were used to group the individuals by sex and link the three data sources. Even with this large data base, there were some occupations that had too few cases to provide reliable results. A population base (as estimated in the SEO) of about 24,000 persons of a given sex was used to determine whether an occupation would be aggregated; this cutoff is equal to about ten cases. Those occupations with fewer than the requisite number of persons were grouped into aggregates that were designed to meet two constraints: (1) to be as homogeneous as possible, and (2) to be sufficiently inclusive so that the cutoff requirement would be met.[21] When occupations were grouped, the

20. For both the SEO and SDA, observations were not omitted if data were missing for specific questions. Instead, separate counts were maintained for each question, and the results for each occupation are presented in terms of the number of legitimate responses. In this way, a "no answer" is implicitly given the value of the average response of persons in that occupation.

21. Copies of the aggregate occupations and their associated components are available from the author.

relevant characteristics were combined in an average weighted by the number of persons of that sex in the occupation.

The Survey of Disabled Adults was used to obtain estimates of the number and characteristics of disabled persons in each occupation. The relatively small number of persons in the survey who became disabled in the preceding year precludes the use of just the one year disability sample. Instead, the entire sample of persons with occupations at the time of disability (5,700 cases) was used, and the total number of persons was adjusted to result in an overall disability rate of 1.24 percent, the observed rate for 1965.[22]

The job characteristics are based on the detailed descriptions for 14,000 jobs found in the 1966 Dictionary of Occupational Titles (U.S. Employment Service, 1966). Jobs are evaluated by inspectors from the Bureau of Employment Security (BES) of the U.S. Employment Service and are rated with respect to aptitudes required, working conditions, physical demands, and training time. These data were then aggregated into the 296 census categories.[23] DOT did not specify whether jobs were "male" or "female." To the extent that there are sex differences in the work requirements and conditions within an occupation at the three-digit level, the data will be inappropriate for use in sex-specific regressions.[24] As a partial control for this problem, the "male sample" was restricted to occupations that were at least 40 percent male. This results in 161 "male" occupations.[25]

The relatively small sample involved in creating the numerator for the dependent variables (the SDA) makes it necessary to place some further constraints on the values that are to be used. For instance, it is highly unlikely that, in a given year, no one became disabled. Therefore, only the 144 occupations with a nonzero disability rate are included in analyses concerning overall disability or the five im-

22. The same scheme described above was used to weight the observations. The 1955 cutoff (see footnote 5) was not used because many of the 4,100 people used in the previous section's analysis were women who had had no full-time occupations prior to the onset of their disability.

23. Appendix E in Luft (1972) gives a complete description of these data.

24. The problem arises because the disability rates and socioeconomic variables, such as income, are sex-specific, while the job characteristics are a weighted average of those of all workers in the occupation. If women do the same job for less money, as has often been found, the income coefficient will be biased. If men and women do different things in the same broad occupation, say as waitresses and maitre d's, and get paid different amounts, then the results of the sex-specific equations will be difficult to interpret.

25. The sex ratios across occupation are heavily skewed: of the 161 occupations with at least 40 percent of the workers being men, 51 had no women and 118 had less than 20 percent women. Results for predominantly "female" occupations are reported in Luft (1972).

Table 4–5. Probability of a Condition Happening on the Job—Zero Order Correlations[a]

	INCOME	AGE	BLACK	YRSSCHL	URBAN
ONJOB	−0.300	0.145	0.069	−0.326	−0.555
OJACCID	−0.378	0.091	0.075	−0.355	−0.526
OJDISEAS	−0.113	0.111	0.006	−0.112	−0.055
OJLABOR	−0.083	0.133	0.163	−0.165	−0.252
OJTEMP	−0.335	−0.123	0.321	−0.305	−0.408
OJSTRESS	0.147	−0.010	−0.169	0.079	−0.026
OJDUST	−0.346	0.284	0.087	−0.302	−0.475

[a]Five percent confidence interval for this sample size (104) is ± 0.192.

pact measures. It is possible, however, that there was no on the job disability, so for that group of variables it is only required that there be at least three SDA cases in the occupation. The effective sample in this instance is 104. In all cases the observations are weighted by the number of men in the occupation.

On the Job Disability

Although there is an extensive body of literature concerning occupational hazards and vocational rehabilitation, most of the work has concentrated on specific industries or occupations or, in the rehabilitation case, on individuals and the jobs to which they can move.[26] In spite of the narrow focus of most such studies, many people have a vague impression that some factors, such as race, education, income, physical effort, and age, are related in one way or another to (1) on the job disabilities, (2) the overall disability rate, and (3) the effects of disability. These general impressions can be compared to the simple correlation coefficients between seven measures of on the job disability and a number of independent variables presented in Table 4–5. The dependent variable ONJOB is the likelihood that an individual in the occupation becomes disabled with a condition that was caused by, or happened, on the job. About 29 percent of the disabilities reported in the SDA were classified as job related.[27] These

26. See, for instance, Ashford, 1975, and Conley, 1965.
27. This is the weighted average of the proportion of disability in each occupation that is classified as ONJOB. When these values are adjusted by the overall probability of disability in each occupation, the mean value for ONJOB becomes .0040, indicating that on the average about 0.4 percent of the workforce becomes disabled in a year because of job-related conditions.

Table 4-5. continued

PHYSICAL	VIBES	HAZARDS	FUMES	GED	STRESS	HOT
0.187	0.186	−0.013	0.056	−0.064	0.039	0.001
0.245	0.222	−0.003	0.094	−0.169	0.066	0.012
−0.011	0.060	0.078	0.041	−0.091	0.078	−0.017
0.081	0.125	0.129	0.035	0.053	0.034	0.032
0.270	0.267	0.153	0.198	−0.173	0.012	0.188
−0.101	−0.101	−0.162	−0.148	0.143	−0.045	−0.120
0.242	0.046	0.022	0.111	−0.035	−0.028	0.072

disabilities were further identified as being caused by accidents (OJACCID), occupational disease (OJDISEAS), heavy labor (OJLABOR), extremes of temperature or humidity (OJTEMP), pressures and stress or overwork (OJSTRESS), and dust, fumes, and noxious conditions to breathing (OJDUST). For each occupation, the sum of these components, plus an "other" category, add up to ONJOB.

The zero order correlations between the measures of job-related disability and a number of independent variables tend to approximate one's expectations. Significant coefficients are found for the socioeconomic variables, and in most cases, the results are as expected. The general belief that low-paying jobs are more subject to occupational disability than high-paying jobs is borne out by the simple correlations with total family income. The positive correlation between income and job-stress-related problems stands out. The proportion of blacks is positively related to conditions caused by heavy labor and temperature extremes and is negatively related to those caused by job stress; this is in line with the jobs in which blacks were concentrated. The correlations for number of years of school (YRSSCHL) appear to be very similar to INCOME. This is not surprising, given the high correlation (0.80) between them. The very high negative correlation coefficients for URBAN are partly due to the fact that disability rates are much higher in those occupations that are predominantly rural.

The remaining seven factors are job characteristics derived from the Dictionary of Occupational Titles. The likelihood that the job requires medium or heavy physical labor (PHYSICAL) is positively related to a number of job disabilities, including accidents, but, surprisingly, is not significantly correlated with conditions caused by heavy labor. It is possible that those jobs that are recognized as needing heavy labor (1) tend to hire men capable of doing the work and (2) are more likely to provide the training and assistance necessary to accomplish the job. The worker who is unaccustomed to heavy labor may be more likely to strain himself in an infrequently performed heavy task. Noise and vibrations (VIBES) on the job are positively associated with overall on the job disabilities, accidents, and temperature-related disorders. Surprisingly, hazards on the job are not related to accidents. This may be attributable to the expectation that safety precautions are more likely to be taken when hazards are known to be present. Fumes are positively, but not significantly, related to dust and fumes disorders. General educational development (GED) is a measure used in the DOT to evaluate the amount of formal and informal education required for the job. It tends to be negatively related to accidents and conditions caused by temperature extremes but is positively related to stress problems. On the other hand, the variable indicating jobs evaluated as requiring workers to "perform adequately under stress when confronted with the critical or unexpected or when taking risks" (STRESS) is not related to any of the variables (U.S. Employment Service, 1965: 645). Finally, jobs subject to extreme heat are more likely to be associated with conditions caused by temperature extremes.

In summary, the zero order correlations between the measures of job related disability and a number of independent variables tend to approximate expectations based on common experience. Highly significant coefficients are found for the five socioeconomic variables, and in most cases, the results are as expected. The job characteristics tend to have somewhat lower correlations, possibly because they are more subject to error.[28] In addition, in some cases (such as PHYSICAL and OJLABOR, HAZARDS and OJACCID), it appears that the recognition of a possible danger area leads to safety precautions that eliminate the excess risk that would otherwise be present. In a num-

---

28. Aside from problems in the actual rating of jobs by DOT, there are a number of other factors that make these variables more subject to misspecification. First, the sample used to weight the DOT occupations to form census groups was small relative to the number of occupations. Second, the mere presence of a particular type of working condition may not be a good measure. For instance, it may be necessary to know the likelihood of noise levels above x decibels. In some cases, DOT notes only the presence or absence of a particular condition. In others, although a distribution was generated in the aggregation procedure, a cutoff value was chosen, and thus information was lost. The cutoff procedure was used because the scales were ordinal, not cardinal, and it is thus inappropriate to use the mean or similar measure. Third, the occupation groups in some cases may be too crude to measure the more subtle relationships. For instance, a small group of the workers in an occupation may have hazardous jobs and an extremely high accident rate while other workers have safer jobs.

ber of other cases, the expected relationships are confirmed by the data.

In Table 4−6, the socioeconomic and job characteristics are combined in multiple regressions for each of the on the job conditions. In addition to the characteristics already described, a measure of the amount of eye-hand-foot coordination (EHF); working conditions that require climbing (CLIMB), stooping (STOOP), or outside work (OUTSIDE); tasks that are highly repetitive (REPEAT); and wet work places (WET) are included. These job characteristics are not very important in terms of statistical significance.[29] They are, however, valuable for the understanding of what lies behind the relationships found with the socioeconomic variables.

The overall probability of an on the job disability, even when controlled for a number of job characteristics, is negatively related to years of schooling. The impact of this variable is rather large. Given the estimated coefficients, the average man with a 0.4 percent risk of disability would have twice that risk if he had only 5.5 instead of the mean of 10.5 years of school. As the variable is designed to measure job-caused conditions, it is unlikely that "health education" plays much of a role in lowering the disability rate. It is more likely that the education variable measures job differences more finely than do the job characteristics. Some of the other important findings are that, contrary to expectations, heavy physical labor, climbing, stooping, outside work, and hazards are not significantly related to on the job disability (nor to accidents, which are a major component of ONJOB). This is probably due to the fact that these are visible, much publicized factors, and thus are likely to be the subjects of special safety programs. The relatively large and nearly significant coefficients for repetitive work and stressful working conditions are not surprising in light of the evidence concerning the effects of monotony and work under pressure.[30]

The regression equation predicting the incidence of on the job accidents (OJACCID) is basically similar to the one for all job-related

29. An F test of the null hypothesis that the job characteristic (as distinct from the socioeconomic) variables were not significantly different from zero could not be rejected for any equation. Furthermore, there were few substantial changes in the coefficients of the socioeconomic variables when the job characteristics were added to the regressions. These results should be considered exploratory, especially given the quality of the data. If further research is to be pursued, or if the equations are to be used for detailed analysis, more care should be taken in the choice of variables, both on a priori and on statistical grounds.

30. See, for instance, Ashford, 1975: 124–26; Margolis, Kroes, and Quinn, 1974.

Table 4–6. Probability of a Condition Happening On the Job—Socioeconomic Factors and Job Characteristics[a]

	ONJOB		OJACCID		OJDISEAS		OJLABOR	
	Coefficient	t Ratio	Coefficient	t Ratio	Coefficient	t Ratio	Coefficient	t Ratio
INCOME	$0.268 \cdot 10^{-4}$	0.72	$-0.168 \cdot 10^{-5}$	-0.07	$-0.281 \cdot 10^{-5}$	-0.74	$0.151 \cdot 10^{-4}$	1.42
AGE	$-0.156 \cdot 10^{-2}$	-0.20	$0.122 \cdot 10^{-2}$	0.24	$0.115 \cdot 10^{-2}$	1.44	$0.228 \cdot 10^{-3}$	0.10
BLACK	-0.281	-0.41	-0.896	-2.04*	$-0.264 \cdot 10^{-3}$	-0.38	0.699	3.59**
YRSSCHL	$-0.661 \cdot 10^{-1}$	-1.72	$-0.229 \cdot 10^{-1}$	-0.93	$-0.808 \cdot 10^{-1}$	-0.21	$-0.178 \cdot 10^{-1}$	-1.63
URBAN	-1.321	-4.10**	-0.798	-3.86**	$0.152 \cdot 10^{-1}$	0.47	-0.167	-1.83
GED	0.147	0.65	$-0.493 \cdot 10^{-1}$	-0.34	$-0.125 \cdot 10^{-1}$	-0.55	0.135	2.10*
EHF	$0.393 \cdot 10^{-1}$	0.22	$0.305 \cdot 10^{-1}$	0.26	$0.614 \cdot 10^{-2}$	0.33	$-0.907 \cdot 10^{-1}$	-1.76
PHYSICAL	$-0.429 \cdot 10^{-1}$	-0.27	$0.233 \cdot 10^{-1}$	0.23	$-0.107 \cdot 10^{-1}$	-0.67	$-0.323 \cdot 10^{-1}$	-0.83
CLIMB	0.156	0.50	0.100	0.51	$-0.191 \cdot 10^{-1}$	-0.61	$0.968 \cdot 10^{-1}$	1.10
STOOP	-0.119	-0.63	$0.107 \cdot 10^{-1}$	0.09	$-0.170 \cdot 10^{-1}$	-0.88	$-0.158 \cdot 10^{-1}$	-0.29
OUTSIDE	-0.116	-0.64	-0.121	-1.04	$-0.667 \cdot 10^{-2}$	-0.36	$0.353 \cdot 10^{-1}$	0.68
VIBES	0.201	1.05	$0.928 \cdot 10^{-1}$	0.75	$0.168 \cdot 10^{-1}$	0.09	$0.826 \cdot 10^{-1}$	1.51
HAZARDS	-0.217	-0.84	-0.206	-1.23	$0.344 \cdot 10^{-1}$	1.30	$0.178 \cdot 10^{-1}$	0.24
FUMES	-0.209	-0.70	$-0.989 \cdot 10^{-1}$	-0.52	$0.207 \cdot 10^{-1}$	0.69	$-0.247 \cdot 10^{-1}$	-0.29
REPEAT	0.310	1.69	0.213	1.81	$0.579 \cdot 10^{-2}$	0.31	$0.678 \cdot 10^{-1}$	1.30
STRESS	0.653	1.58	0.423	1.59	$0.948 \cdot 10^{-2}$	0.23	0.209	1.78
HOT	0.490	0.94	0.202	0.61	$-0.710 \cdot 10^{-1}$	-1.34	$0.775 \cdot 10^{-1}$	0.52
WET	-0.488	-1.08	-0.232	-0.80	$0.324 \cdot 10^{-1}$	0.71	-0.225	-1.75
Constant	1.89	2.92**	1.10	2.64**	$-0.438 \cdot 10^{-2}$	-0.07	0.101	0.55
DF	85		85		85		85	
SEE	0.336		0.216		0.034		0.096	
R^2	0.419		0.422		0.121		0.279	
$\bar{R}^2$	0.295		0.299		0.0		0.126	

Table 4–6. continued

	OJTEMP		OJSTRESS		OJDUST	
	Coefficient	t Ratio	Coefficient	t Ratio	Coefficient	t Ratio
INCOME	$-0.378 \cdot 10^{-5}$	-0.60	$0.174 \cdot 10^{-4}$	1.13	$-0.440 \cdot 10^{-5}$	-0.95
AGE	$-0.244 \cdot 10^{-2}$	-1.85	$-0.550 \cdot 10^{-2}$	-1.70	$0.234 \cdot 10^{-2}$	$2.41*$
BLACK	0.325	$2.82**$	-0.196	-0.69	$-0.733 \cdot 10^{-1}$	-0.87
YRSSCHL	$-0.163 \cdot 10^{-2}$	-0.25	$-0.171 \cdot 10^{-1}$	-1.08	$-0.193 \cdot 10^{-2}$	-0.41
URBAN	-0.128	$-2.36*$	$-0.768 \cdot 10^{-2}$	-0.58	$-0.710 \cdot 10^{-1}$	-1.78
GED	$0.689 \cdot 10^{-1}$	1.81	$-0.344 \cdot 10^{-2}$	-0.04	$0.873 \cdot 10^{-2}$	0.31
EHF	$-0.393 \cdot 10^{-1}$	-1.29	$0.824 \cdot 10^{-1}$	1.10	$0.457 \cdot 10^{-1}$	$2.04*$
PHYSICAL	$-0.122 \cdot 10^{-1}$	-0.46	$0.308 \cdot 10^{-1}$	0.47	$-0.303 \cdot 10^{-2}$	-0.16
CLIMB	$0.506 \cdot 10^{-1}$	0.97	$0.438 \cdot 10^{-1}$	0.34	-0.109	$-2.84**$
STOOP	$-0.453 \cdot 10^{-1}$	-1.42	-0.104	-1.33	$0.177 \cdot 10^{-1}$	0.75
OUTSIDE	$0.328 \cdot 10^{-1}$	1.07	$-0.215 \cdot 10^{-1}$	-0.29	$-0.108 \cdot 10^{-1}$	-0.48
VIBES	$0.674 \cdot 10^{-1}$	$2.08*$	$0.274 \cdot 10^{-2}$	0.04	$-0.314 \cdot 10^{-1}$	-1.32
HAZARDS	$-0.204 \cdot 10^{-2}$	-0.05	$-0.866 \cdot 10^{-1}$	-0.81	$0.430 \cdot 10^{-1}$	1.34
FUMES	$-0.325 \cdot 10^{-1}$	-0.64	$-0.807 \cdot 10^{-1}$	-0.66	$-0.420 \cdot 10^{-2}$	-0.11
REPEAT	$0.308 \cdot 10^{-1}$	0.99	$-0.480 \cdot 10^{-1}$	-0.64	$0.912 \cdot 10^{-2}$	0.40
STRESS	$0.270 \cdot 10^{-1}$	0.39	$-0.175 \cdot 10^{-1}$	-0.10	$-0.451 \cdot 10^{-1}$	-0.88
HOT	0.102	1.16	$0.769 \cdot 10^{-1}$	0.35	0.110	1.72
WET	$-0.261 \cdot 10^{-1}$	-0.34	$-0.642 \cdot 10^{-1}$	-0.35	$0.119 \cdot 10^{-1}$	0.21
Constant	0.206	1.88	0.423	1.58	$0.316 \cdot 10^{-1}$	0.39
DF	85		85		85	
SEE	0.057		0.139		0.042	
R^2	0.368		0.149		0.437	
$\overline{R}^2$	0.234		0.0		0.318	

[a]For each equation, the first column provides the estimated coefficients while the second gives the estimated t ratio.

*indicates significance at the 5 percent level.

**indicates significance at the 1 percent level.

disability with one major difference—the highly significant negative coefficient for proportion of blacks. This is the opposite of what would normally be expected (it is the reverse of the simple correlation) and is due to the fact that education, income, and job characteristics have already been held constant. The low explanatory power of the OJDISEAS equation is not surprising considering that most such diseases are related to specific chemicals and compounds not readily identified in these data. The positive and relatively significant coefficient for age with respect to OJDISEAS is probably a measure of the time that most occupational diseases take to become apparent. Conditions caused by heavy labor (OJLABOR) are not particularly related to jobs that require heavy labor, probably because the workers are prepared for and know how to handle the tasks. Such conditions are, however, positively related to jobs requiring a substantial amount for formal and informal training, as measured by GED. Given the level of education required by the job, high attained education is negatively related to conditions caused by heavy labor, while the proportion of blacks is positively related. This suggests that the better educated are more able to avoid such disorders, which may be "forced" upon blacks through activities for which they are not prepared. The negative relationship for EHF and the positive one for STRESS support the conclusion that conditions caused by heavy labor are most common among those occupations that are not labor oriented but may involve occasional spurts of effort.

Temperature-related disorders (OJTEMP) are significantly associated with the proportion of blacks and the presence of vibrations, as well as with high GED and low mean age. The coefficient for hot working conditions is positive but not significant. The results for blacks may be due to the selective placement of blacks in undesirable jobs.[31] Stress and overwork (OJSTRESS) are rather nebulous factors, so it is not surprising that this equation is very poorly estimated.

Dust-related conditions (OJDUST) are fairly well predicted. Age is a critical variable, in line with the evidence that emphysema, for instance, is most common among older workers (Knowles, 1966: 907). The large positive coefficient for EHF may indicate that jobs requiring active, close physical activity, although not of a particularly strenuous nature, may be associated with causes of these conditions. Jobs that require much movement, such as climbing, may result in short, rather than continuous, exposure to dangerous areas so as to reduce risk. Particularly hot jobs may be associated with a lack of

31. See, for instance, Doeringer and Piore, 1971: 141; Lloyd et al., 1970: 157; and Lloyd, 1971: 59.

ventilation and consequent breathing problems. The actual presence of dust and fumes on the job is not associated with the condition.

This subsection has investigated some of the factors related to disabilities caused on the job. In general, the simple correlation coefficients between the on the job disability rate and the rates for its various components are consistent with a priori expectations. The correlations tend to be somewhat higher for socioeconomic variables than for the job characteristics, probably because of greater errors in the measurement of the latter variables. When these variables are combined in an equation predicting the disability rates for on the job conditions, many of the simple relationships are altered. The strong effect of family income is not found when the other variables are included. Education is sometimes important, although it is clear that in the zero order correlations, income and education were largely reflecting job characteristics and urban-rural effects. Aside from this, perhaps the most important conclusion is that the specific, identifiable factors that should logically be related to specific on the job conditions are either not related or have the wrong sign. This is especially true for the more visible factors, such as hazards and accidents, heavy physical labor and labor-related disorders, and dust on the job and dust-related conditions. It appears that when such specific, visible conditions appear, adequate safety precautions are taken to avert health hazards.[32] For some of the less obvious potential hazards, this is not the case. The data indicate that accidents, for instance, are related to monotonous and stressful jobs, while injuries due to heavy labor seem to be related to jobs that do not "officially" require regular heavy labor but instead have many fairly well educated men who may only occasionally be active.

The Overall Probability of Disability

While job characteristics are important variables in determining the likelihood of a specific condition occurring on the job, they are also important in the overall probability of disability, regardless of the cause of the condition. When examining the causes of an impairment, the important characteristics are specific working conditions and labor requirements. These variables are expected to contribute to the likelihood of an accident, injury, or disease occurring on the job. In the second case, whether or not a specific impairment or functional

---

32. Of course, it is possible that the DOT investigators actually based their evaluation of, for instance, whether fumes were present on the job not on a detailed examination of the job situation but on whether safety precautions indicated that fumes were present. There is no detailed information on the procedures used for job evaluation.

limitation will result in disability, the job characteristics of interest are the required activities associated with the job such as reaching, vision, finger dexterity, and basic mobility. Some jobs that have essentially no conditions that lead to disability are nonetheless very "sensitive" to certain functional limitations and will have high disability rates. For example, watchmakers with arthritis of the hands probably have a high disability rate.

The factors likely to be involved in the determination of disability are the characteristics representing the job's work requirements and the corresponding limitations of the individual. DOT provides estimates of *job requirements* in a number of areas: heavy physical labor (PHYSICAL), climbing (CLIMB), stooping (STOOP), reaching (REACH), talking (TALK), finger dexterity (FINGER), and vision (SIGHT). SDA allows the estimation of corresponding *functional limitations* for disabled persons who had been in each occupation. These are lifting or carrying heavy objects (LIFTS), climbing stairs (STAIRS), stooping (STOOPS), reaching (REACHS), speech difficulties (SPEECH), difficulty in handling objects (HANDLES), and vision problems (SIGHTDP).[33]

The interactions between the two sets of variables are approximated by taking the product of each limitation-requirement pair. If the DOT data truly measure the probability that a certain task is necessary in an occupation and the SDA data measure the probability that a person originally in that occupation has that limitation, and if the two probabilities are independent, then the product of the two is the probability that the disabled person was in a job that required a task that he or she is now unable to perform. The assumption of independence is probably not completely justified, but it is impossible to test with the available data.

The variables described above are combined in regressions presented in Table 4-7. In addition to the variables already mentioned, the proportion of men who are household heads (HHEAD) is included as a measure of the demands for income that may affect work choice after disability, the number of years since the onset of disability (YRSAGO), and the number of years on the job before disability (YRSONJOB). When only the five basic socioeconomic variables are

---

33. These variables were constructed in the following manner: in the SDA survey each person was asked whether their condition limited them in any of a list of activities. Possible answers were that there was no limit, some limit, or that they were unable to do the activity at all. The proportion of disabled persons who were limited or unable is used to create the variables used here. The sight limitation was based on those who were blind or had trouble seeing even with glasses.

included (column 1), URBAN is the only significant coefficient, but age and education both have the "right" sign and t ratios greater than one. The coefficient of income is negative but less than its standard error. (The simple correlation between DISRAT and INCOME is − 0.446 and is significant at the 0.05 level.) If the job characteristics are added (column 2), the explanatory power is only marginally improved. All the socioeconomic variables become less significant with the exception of YRSSCHL; it and GED both take on negative coefficients, suggesting that education confers some immunity to disability beyond the effects of jobs identified as requiring substantial education. The results for the socioeconomic variables and functional limitations alone (column 4) are not very different. One surprising feature is that the two nearly significant variables, LIFTS and HANDLES, both have negative signs, perhaps because some occupations tend to have very serious disabilities (as these are) without many less serious ones. This result is carried over when the interaction between job characteristics and limitations is considered in column 3. LIFTS*HVYLABOR is significant and negative, although HANDLES*FINGER is only the size of its standard error.

In this interaction equation, the coefficients for years of school and GED are both negative, and the latter is almost significant at the 0.05 level. This education effect may be due to at least two factors. First, it may indicate greater knowledge about health problems and therefore a greater ability to prevent disability or to treat an illness once it occurs. Second, more education enables an individual to be more flexible in job choice. Flexibility may be used to shift jobs at the onset of a mild disabling condition. This, in turn, can lead to a remission of symptoms or a negative response to the disability question because it no longer interferes with work. The greater significance of GED and the very low value for income (which is important in the purchase of medical care, particularly in this pre-Medicaid era) suggest that the second factor is more important. The role of education in mediating the effects of functional limitations will be considered in more detail in the next chapter.

The number of years since the onset of disability is positively related to the disability rate, supporting the view that minor disabilities may lead to adjustment and a withdrawal from disability status.[34]

---

34. This interpretation stems from the fact that the numerator in the disability rate is derived from the number of people in the SDA survey, all of whom admit to being currently disabled. Suppose that several cohorts of people in two occupations with equal true disability rates were followed from the onset of their disabilities. Over time those in occupation A with relatively minor limitations return to work and no longer consider themselves disabled, while those

Table 4-7. DISTRAT: Overall Probability of Disability

	(1) Socioeconomic Factors		(2) Job Characteristics	
	Coefficient	t Ratio	Coefficient	t Ratio
INCOME	$-0.418 \cdot 10^{-4}$	-0.84	$-0.161 \cdot 10^{-4}$	-0.30
AGE	$0.194 \cdot 10^{-1}$	1.82	$0.162 \cdot 10^{-1}$	0.76
BLACK	0.471	0.51	0.139	0.11
YRSSCHL	$-0.550 \cdot 10^{-1}$	-1.05	$-0.779 \cdot 10^{-1}$	-1.12
URBAN	-2.22	$-5.40**$	-2.17	$-4.29**$
HHEAD			0.173	0.24
YRSAGO			$0.237 \cdot 10^{-1}$	1.35
YRSONJOB			$0.229 \cdot 10^{-1}$	1.74
GED			0.422	-1.53
HEARING				
HYVLABOR[a]			-0.177	-0.64
CLIMB[a]			$-0.103 \cdot 10^{-1}$	-0.03
STOOP[a]			-0.296	-1.02
REACH[a]			0.441	0.85
TALK[a]			-0.151	-0.57
FINGER[a]			-0.589	-1.47
SIGHT[a]			0.357	0.90
Constant	3.11	$4.65**$	2.91	$2.71**$
DF	138		126	
SEE	0.722		0.714	
R^2	0.398		0.462	
$\bar{R}^2$	0.377		0.390	

[a]Variables subject to interactions. In column 2, the variables listed at the left were used; in column 4, those on the right; and in column 3, the product of the two variables, e.g., HVYLABOR * LIFTS.

  *Indicates significance at the 5 percent level.
**Indicates significance at the 1 percent level.

The variable representing job tenure is also positive and significant. If the job characteristics had been shown to be clearly related to disability, then the longer a worker was subject to such conditions, the more likely they would have a deleterious effect. As this does not seem to be a strong relationship, and as the question would most

from occupation B remain disabled. A cross-sectional survey of only those people who considered themselves disabled would find more disabled people from occupation B and a higher average number of years since the onset of disability.

Table 4-7. continued

(3) Interaction		(4) Functional Limitations		
Coefficient	t Ratio	Coefficient	t Ratio	
$-0.208 \cdot 10^{-4}$	-0.41	$-0.422 \cdot 10^{-4}$	-0.83	
$0.180 \cdot 10^{-1}$	0.94	$0.132 \cdot 10^{-1}$	0.70	
0.488	-0.42	0.345	0.33	
$-0.802 \cdot 10^{-1}$	-1.30	$-0.586 \cdot 10^{-1}$	-1.04	
-2.07	$-4.42**$	-1.82	$-3.85**$	
-0.178	-0.28	-0.129	-0.19	
$0.293 \cdot 10^{-1}$	1.77	$0.275 \cdot 10^{-1}$	1.64	
$0.306 \cdot 10^{-1}$	$2.41*$	$0.295 \cdot 10^{-1}$	$2.23*$	
-0.485	-1.93			
0.559	0.76	$0.926 \cdot 10^{-1}$	0.13	
-1.00	$-2.61*$	-0.639	-1.74	LIFTS[a]
-0.445	-0.81	0.206	0.50	STAIRS[a]
$-0.486 \cdot 10^{-1}$	-0.12	0.312	0.71	STOOPS[a]
$-0.261 \cdot 10^{-1}$	-0.07	0.186	0.43	REACHS[a]
0.385	0.41	0.368	0.51	SPEECH[a]
-0.422	-1.02	-0.664	-1.71	HANDLES[a]
0.222	0.66	$0.208 \cdot 10^{-2}$	0.01	SIGHTDP[a]
3.29	$3.01**$	2.69	$3.18**$	
126		127		
0.695		0.714		
0.491		0.459		
0.422		0.391		

likely have been interpreted as the length of time with that employer, it is probably a reflection of the impact of job seniority and pension plans. It is not surprising that workers more likely to receive disability benefits are more likely to list themselves as disabled.

These relatively poor results for the DISRAT variable are not unexpected. The overall disability rate is an extremely broad concept and includes those who are bedridden and those with essentially no activity limitation. Furthermore, the data, although more comprehensive than any other available, are the result of numerous approximations and aggregations, each of which is likely to introduce some random (or nonrandom) error that serves to mask the true relationships. Thus, these results should be considered very exploratory. Hopefully, they will engender further research in this area.

SUMMARY AND CONCLUSIONS

This chapter has presented two approaches to investigating the role of socioeconomic and occupational factors in the causation of disability. Hints of the importance of such factors could be seen in the various sets of data presented in Chapter 3. The difficulty in evaluating the importance of income-education-occupation as a cause of disability from the published data is that currently measured variables are likely to be biased by the effects of poor health. Income is clearly influenced by health status, and very often people will shift occupations after an impairment prevents them from performing their previous work. Education is not subject to this bias, but it is a rather crude measure, and a number of policy actions rest on whether there are separate income, education, and occupation effects. The two analyses of the probability of disability presented in this chapter are, to our knowledge, the first to use predisability data for income and occupation on large-scale national samples. Both are based on multiple sets of data that underwent several stages of aggregation and approximation. Thus, the results in this chapter should be considered tentative. But, the biases that were introduced are likely to minimize the estimated relationships.

The first of the two investigations estimated the probability of disability by age, race, sex, education, and predisability income. The results clearly supported the hypothesis that there are strong and separate income and education effects. There is a negative income gradient evident even within age, race, sex, and education groups. In addition, there appears to be a major difference between a little education (zero to eight years) and at least some high school. The importance of these results are underscored when one realizes that the substantial racial differences in probability of disability for men are entirely due to the different education and income distributions. Income and education account for a large part of the differences between white and black women.

Although the second analysis of the probability of disability was restricted to previously employed men in a wide, but not complete, range of occupations, it provides a very useful complement to the understanding of the results in Chapter 3 and the first half of this chapter. The approach in this case was to use each occupation as the unit of observation and to examine the factors related to the proportion of workers who become disabled for various reasons. When relevant socioeconomic and job characteristics are included in the equations predicting overall disability rates, the income term becomes insignificant and slightly positive. This suggests that at least a major part of the usually observed negative income gradient is a reflection of differing work conditions and activity requirements.[35] There still appears to be some education effect, probably indicating higher levels of medical information and health care and perhaps the ability to fully adjust to the limitations so as not to be considered disabled. The results for on the job conditions are noteworthy and call for further investigation: in a number of specific conditions, such as accidents and heavy labor, the "obvious" working conditions were not important determinants of the likelihood of occurrence. Instead, a number of more subtle factors, such as monotony, were clearly implicated, suggesting that "obvious" hazards are met with safety measures, while sufficient care is not taken for other occupational hazards.

It is helpful to summarize some of these results with a few examples. The probability of a man, aged eighteen to sixty-four, becoming disabled through a condition occurring on the job is 0.397 percent in any one year. This represents a third of all disabilities. Consider the average worker facing these probabilities. If, instead of the average 10.5 years of school, holding other factors constant, he has only a fifth grade education, the likelihood of an on the job condition will almost double. Similarly, if the job is highly repetitive, the probability doubles; if it is subject to stress and action in critical events, the probability triples. The most significant change in likelihood of occupationally related disability is if he is working in a job that is primarily rural. Some other factors are notable for their unimportance. Higher family income is positively, but weakly, related to disabilities occurring on the job. Age and race are similarly unrelated.

The likelihood that a man will become disabled during the year for any reason is 1.26 percent. The man with a fifth grade education has a likelihood of disability that is nearly a third higher, a substantial difference but much less than that for an on the job condition.[36] Life in rural areas is again associated with a greatly increased risk of disability. Longer job tenure will tend to increase the likelihood that a person will report himself as disabled. If, instead of the average of 11.7 years on the job, the worker is a newcomer, he is estimated to have only three-fourths the probability of disablement. Although

35. In fact, economic theory would predict that a risk premium should exist for jobs that are more hazardous, and thus income would be positively related to risk. There is some evidence supporting this hypothesis with respect to risk of death (see Thaler and Rosen, 1973).

36. Given that on the job conditions account for about a third of overall disability, this suggests that education's primary influence is through on the job disability.

statistically significant, this factor, which is probably related to pension coverage for disability, is not of major importance. Income is again negatively, but insignificantly, related to disability.

The major findings of this chapter can be summarized as follows:

1. The overall (unadjusted) disability rates for black men and women tend to be between 50 and 100 percent higher for each age group than the comparables rates for whites.
2. For men, the difference in disability rates by race is due almost entirely to differences in the education and income distributions for each race. For many cell pairs, the black rate is lower than the white rate.
3. For women, a large part of the racial differential is due to differences in income and education, but there appears to be a substantially higher probability of disability among older, less educated, lower income black women.
4. Even within age, race, sex, and education groups, there appears to be a negative income gradient with respect to disability that is quite substantial.
5. Controlling for the other four factors, education has an important influence on disability rates. The most important impact is in the difference between just a little education (zero to eight years of school) and nine or more years. The differential between some high school and some college education, although in the expected direction, is small. This tends to point toward the effects of schooling in attaining a small amount of health information, the ability to obtain more information and to utilize health care facilities, and probably the occupations that can be entered with higher levels of education.
6. The expected impact of biases in the estimation of the income term and of general errors in variables will tend to strengthen these results with respect to the influence of income on disability.
7. In spite of these caveats, mean values for the age, education, and income variables can explain 30 percent of the variation in disability rates.
8. The various socioeconomic factors (age, income, race, education, and urban-rural location) are related to measures of on the job and overall disability in the ways suggested by "common knowledge" only when the simple correlations are considered. The relationships become much more complex when other factors are held constant.

9. In general, income bears no significant relationship to the probability of disability when job characteristics are controlled. If anything, there appears to be a slight positive relationship.
10. Education is marginally related to lower disability, especially for conditions occurring on the job. Some of this effect is probably due to differences in job characteristics not captured by the variables used in the analysis.
11. For a number of specific on the job conditions, such as accidents, heavy labor, and dust-related disabilities, the specific working conditions associated with these disabilities tend not to be related or to be negatively related to the probability of their occurring. This suggests that when specific, observable conditions known to lead to disability are present on the job, safety precautions are taken.
12. On the other hand, conditions more closely integrated in the work process and less obvious to the observer, such as stress and repetitive jobs, seem closely related to accidents and conditions due to heavy labor.
13. The most important measured factor in determining the overall disability rate is residence in rural areas.
14. Job tenure is also related to the probability of disability, although in this case it is likely that the availability of disability benefits results in a greater likelihood of reporting a disability, rather than in the occurrence of a true organic defect.

Chapter 5

Determinants of the Outcomes of Disability: The Influence of Nonmedical Factors

This chapter and the next will focus on the second half of the model presented in Figure 2–1—the factors that interact with functional limitations to result in disabilities of varying severity and the impact of these disabilities. Chapter 5 emphasizes the various outcomes of disability: job changes, altered labor force participation, hours worked per week, and the like. Chapter 6 focuses on the overall effects of disability in terms of earnings, income, and poverty status.

Obviously, a major determinant of the severity or outcome of disability is the person's actual functional limitations. A paraplegic is much more likely to be severely disadvantaged than someone with a minor back problem that keeps him from lifting weights of over thirty pounds. But, to take an extreme example, a paraplegic radio announcer may suffer fewer occupational consequences than the manual laborer with a relatively minor back problem. The effects of a given set of functional limitations are likely to be dependent on the requirements of the person's job. If there is an interaction between functional limitations and the requirements of the job, certain factors such as the person's age, education, and sex, as well as general labor market conditions, may help determine the extent of the adjustment that is necessary. This adjustment may take several forms: the person may drop out of the labor market, reduce the weeks worked per year, or hours per week, or change jobs and earn less per hour.

The motivation for examining the influences of factors other than the specific health problem on the extent of disability should be clear. If things such as education, job skills, and labor market factors are important, then policies can be designed to alter these variables to reduce the economic effects of health problems. As will be seen in the next chapter, these economic effects account for a substantial fraction of poverty in the United States.

A few statistics will highlight the potential role of occupation and other factors in the effects of disability. In 1966, 13.5 percent of all employed men in the U.S. aged eighteen to sixty-four reported some disability. This proportion ranged from 8.6 percent of professional and technical workers to 38.0 percent of farm laborers and foremen (Stanley, 1971: 22). While the incidence of disabling conditions is higher in agricultural jobs, the fourfold difference is at least partially attributable to the greater degree of flexibility in farm jobs.[1]

As always, the available data are not precisely what one would desire. The nature and extent of the health problem are defined by the individual and are not verified by any health professionals. Some of the potential biases with this type of data have been outlined in Chapters 2 and 3. The major difficulties are potential under- and overreporting of disabilities. Minor functional limitations and embarrassing problems, especially mental illness, are likely to be underreported. If the problems are truly minor, then their exclusion will not substantially alter our conclusions. The problems of underreporting mental illness are more serious, and this limitation must be clearly recognized when interpreting the results. Overreporting of health problems may occur because of the social stigma that is attached to unemployment among certain groups, such as middle-aged men. The hypothesis would be that an unemployed man may tell an interviewer that he is unable to find a job because of a health problem even if none exists because there are few socially acceptable alternatives to working. A five year longitudinal study of a cohort of middle-aged men found that this potential problem is of no real importance and that health limitations at the beginning of the period were a major factor in subsequent decisions to retire early and were not post hoc rationalizations (Parnes and Nestel, 1974A: 191).

One other issue is whether it is tautological to use data that define a disability in terms of a health problem that affects the kind or amount of work that a person can do. This would clearly be a difficulty if health problems defined in this way were used to "predict" or "explain" work limitations. Instead, the health problems will be used in one of two ways. In some cases, they will be very specifically defined as functional limitations in reaching, fingering, lifting,

1. See, for instance, Haber, 1970.

hearing, and so forth that are not directly related to the effect on the job. In other cases, the presence of health problems affecting work will be used to segment the population. The magnitude of the labor force changes attributable to those problems that do affect the ability to work can then be measured. Nothing can be said about health problems that don't have an impact on work but almost by definition, they are likely to have relatively minor effects on subsequent socioeconomic status. The question of tautology becomes even less important when one considers the very wide range of health problems included and that most of them lead to changes in jobs rather than to preventing the person from working. For instance, in 1966, among noninstitutionalized men aged eighteen to sixty-four, 73.7 percent of the disabled were in the labor force, in contrast to 94 percent of the nondisabled. Even for the slightly more than a quarter who were in the most severely disabled category, 26.7 percent were in the labor force. For the other two levels of severity, 95.1 percent of the secondarily and 88.9 percent of the occupationally disabled were in the labor force, in contrast to the overall rate for disabled and nondisabled men combined, 90.5 percent (Haber, 1968: 5).

This chapter will use three methods to examine the factors that influence the different impact of disabilities. The first will investigate the importance of the interactions between functional limitations and job requirements in determining whether a worker continues to do the same type of work, different work, or is unable to work at all. This section will use the aggregate occupation data drawn from SDA, SEO, and DOT, as described in the second half of Chapter 4. The second section will focus on the factors that allow disabled persons to maintain a high ratio of current weekly earnings to earnings at the time of disability onset. This analysis will use the SDA and DOT data, but with the individual as the unit of observation. Of course, because this section is restricted to people who are disabled, the findings actually refer to the importance of certain variables in lessening the impact of disability, relative to the average disabled person. The third section measures the magnitudes of the impacts of disability on various components of earnings. It uses comparisons between the disabled and nondisabled, controlling for other factors. The analysis in this section will rely on the SEO data set. Some comparative results from other studies will be included in all three sections. A final section will summarize the major findings of this chapter.

FACTORS INFLUENCING OCCUPATIONAL
CHANGE AFTER A DISABILITY

The "overall disability rate" used in Chapter 4 is a rather loose concept. As used in this chapter, it refers to the probability that an individual in a given occupation will be listed as disabled in an SDA type survey. This measure, of course, includes the whole spectrum of severity and is not sufficiently fine for many purposes. It may be broken down into the likelihood that an individual in the occupation (1) is unable to work at all, (2) can work, but only at a different kind of work, or (3) can continue to do the same kind of work, but for fewer hours than before the disability. Two additional measures may be used to check the respondent's evaluation of his ability to do the same work as before: (4) whether he actually did the same kind of work on his next job and (5) whether he returned to his old employer.

It is hypothesized that the sociodemographic factors, functional limitations, and work requirements of the "old" job will be differentially important for the various outcomes. For instance, the primary factors responsible for leading a person to be unable to work are likely to be functional (physical) limitations. Implicitly, the work requirements of all jobs, not just the previous one, are too demanding. Interactions between requirements and limitations should not add much to the understanding of the severity of disability that can be gleaned from the limitations information alone. On the other hand, interactions between limitations and requirements are likely to be very important in predicting which people continue to do the same work. For those who can work, but only at different occupations, we would expect factors indicative of job flexibility, such as education and youthfulness, to be important. These hypotheses will be tested with the combined SDA–SEO–DOT data grouped by occupation.

The Inability to Work

Given that an individual becomes disabled, what are the factors that determine an inability to work? Table 5–1 presents the regressions for the proportion of men in each occupation who say they are unable to work. The socioeconomic variables alone explain very little of the variation. The job characteristics are almost all positive, although on a priori grounds they should not be very important. Only if the individual feels that all the jobs potentially open to him are similar to the one he was in should these variables be important.

In contrast, the physical limitations are very important. A man who experiences problems in lifting even relatively light objects finds almost no jobs open to him. Similarly, speech difficulties boost the probability of not being able to work by 36 percentage points. Difficulty in handling things also makes work less likely. With the functional limitations held constant, the socioeconomic factors do not make much difference, but more education will ease the impact of the health problem. Although the job characteristics-limitations interactions were not expected to be very important, they do boost the importance of the HVYLABOR−LIFTS variable. This suggests that if their disability makes lifting difficult, men whose jobs usually required heavy physical labor cannot find alternative jobs that do not require that type of work. Other things being equal, if a man is in that situation, the chances of his being unable to work increase by nearly 50 percentage points relative to a mean value of 0.24.

Being Able to Do the Same Work

At the other end of the disability range are those workers who are able to do the same work as before the onset of their conditions (Table 5−2). In this instance, it is hypothesized that the interaction between job characteristics and functional limitations will be critical. If the socioeconomic factors are considered alone, or only with the functional limitations, the number of years of school and race tend to be important. When the job characteristics are added, it is clear that most of the significance of the socioeconomic variables was due to their role as proxies for different types of jobs. The functional limitations alone indicate that difficulty in lifting weights and in climbing stairs makes it much less likely that the individual can continue to do the same work. Although these tend to be rather basic mobility activities, the results of the interaction variables indicate that if they are likely to be important on the job, they further decrease the chances of continuing in the occupation. When these interactions are included, education becomes insignificant, although workers in jobs requiring a high GED still have a slightly better chance of continuing. Being black, however, still markedly decreases the likelihood of being able to do the same work. This is consistent with the view that to get a given job, blacks must be able to indicate that they can do it better than comparably situated whites.

Being Able to Work in a Different Job

The intermediate outcome of disability is being able to work, but only in a job different from the one prior to disability. It is difficult to hypothesize the variables that will be important in predicting

Table 5–1. UNABLE: Proportion of Disabled Men Unable to Work

	(1) Socioeconomic Factors		(2) Job Characteristics	
	Coefficient	t Ratio	Coefficient	t Ratio
INCOME	$0.163 \cdot 10^{-5}$	0.12	$-0.128 \cdot 10^{-4}$	-0.87
AGE	$-0.576 \cdot 10^{-2}$	-1.97	$0.209 \cdot 10^{-2}$	0.36
BLACK	$-0.965 \cdot 10^{-1}$	-0.38	-0.260	-0.76
YRSSCHL	$-0.187 \cdot 10^{-1}$	-1.29	$0.977 \cdot 10^{-2}$	0.51
URBAN	0.223	1.97	0.223	1.60
HHEAD			-0.158	-0.79
YRSAGO			$0.348 \cdot 10^{-2}$	0.71
YRSONJOB			$0.405 \cdot 10^{-2}$	1.12
GED			$-0.395 \cdot 10^{-2}$	-0.05
HEARING				
HVYLABOR[a]			$0.817 \cdot 10^{-1}$	1.07
CLIMB[a]			$0.273 \cdot 10^{-1}$	0.30
STOOP[a]			$0.145 \cdot 10^{-1}$	0.18
REACH[a]			0.216	1.51
TALK[a]			0.165	2.27**
FINGER[a]			$0.124 \cdot 10^{-1}$	0.11
SIGHT[a]			-0.222	$-2.01*$
Constant	0.490	2.65**	$-0.789 \cdot 10^{-1}$	-0.27
DF	138		126	
SEE	0.199		0.197	
R^2	0.085		0.183	
$\bar{R}^2$	0.052		0.073	

[a]Variables subject to interactions. In column 2, the variables listed at the left were used; in column 4, those on the right; and in column 3, the product of the two variables, e.g., HVYLABOR * LIFTS.

* Indicates significance at the 5 percent level.

**Indicates significance at the 1 percent level.

DIFFWORK status because of this intermediate position. For instance, if a condition is severe, the person will be in the UNABLE category, but if it is rather minor, then he will probably be in the SAMEWORK group. Thus a rather subtle scale of disability is needed that cannot be met with the available data.

The regressions for DIFFWORK reflect this problem and explain only 16 percent of the variance, with few significant coefficients.[2] The only consistently important result is that being black substan-

2. For a detailed analysis of the results for DIFFWORK and for SAMEJOB and SAMEKIND, which are discussed below, see Luft, 1972: Ch. iv.

Table 5-1. continued

(3) Interaction		(4) Functional Limitations		
Coefficient	t Ratio	Coefficient	t Ratio	
$-0.301 \cdot 10^{-5}$	-0.24	$0.388 \cdot 10^{-5}$	0.32	
$-0.441 \cdot 10^{-3}$	-0.09	$-0.398 \cdot 10^{-2}$	-0.89	
$-0.693 \cdot 10^{-1}$	-0.24	$-0.714 \cdot 10^{-1}$	-0.29	
$0.624 \cdot 10^{-2}$	0.41	$-0.131 \cdot 10^{-1}$	-0.98	
0.248	$2.16*$	0.168	1.51	
-0.130	-0.82	$-0.192 \cdot 10^{-1}$	-0.12	
$0.184 \cdot 10^{-2}$	0.45	$0.407 \cdot 10^{-2}$	1.02	
$0.147 \cdot 10^{-2}$	0.47	$-0.543 \cdot 10^{-3}$	-0.17	
$-0.246 \cdot 10^{-1}$	-0.40			
$0.739 \cdot 10^{-1}$	0.41	0.102	0.58	
0.484	$5.11**$	0.327	$3.76**$	LIFTS[a]
0.179	1.33	$0.726 \cdot 10^{-1}$	0.74	STAIRS[a]
-0.108	-1.09	$-0.564 \cdot 10^{-1}$	0.54	STOOPS[a]
$0.882 \cdot 10^{-1}$	0.98	$-0.401 \cdot 10^{-1}$	-0.44	REACHES[a]
0.431	1.89	0.359	$2.11*$	SPEECH[a]
$-0.261 \cdot 10^{-1}$	-0.26	0.169	1.84	HANDLES[a]
$0.229 \cdot 10^{-1}$	0.28	$0.217 \cdot 10^{-1}$	0.30	SIGHTDP[a]
$-0.299 \cdot 10^{-1}$	-0.13	0.188	0.94	
126		127		
0.171		0.169		
0.384		0.394		
0.300		0.318		

tially increases the probability of having to find different work. (The coefficient ranges from 0.537 to 0.649 across the five equations with t ratios from 1.59 to 2.26.) As the physical conditions and job requirements have been held constant, this is probably an indication of the previously mentioned job discrimination. This conclusion is supported by the fact that the coefficients for percent black in the SAMEWORK and DIFFWORK equations are of opposite signs and comparable magnitudes. The coefficient in the UNABLE equation is very small, indicating that, *ceteris paribus*, the blacks are shifted into different jobs by disability, although they are still able to work.[3] A

3. Because the three categories (UNABLE, SAMEWORK, and DIFFWORK) are mutually exclusive and collectively exhaustive, the sum of the coefficients for each variable across all three equations must sum to zero, aside from minor rounding errors. What is interesting, of course, is when the effects of a variable such as race are allocated between only two categories.

Table 5-2. SAMEWORK: Proportion of Disabled Men Able to do Same Work as Before

	(1) Socioeconomic Factors		(2) Job Characteristics	
	Coefficient	t Ratio	Coefficient	t Ratio
INCOME	$0.608 \cdot 10^{-5}$	0.42	$0.103 \cdot 10^{-4}$	0.65
AGE	$-0.487 \cdot 10^{-3}$	-0.16	$-0.254 \cdot 10^{-2}$	-0.40
BLACK	-0.480	-1.75	-0.287	-0.77
YRSSCHL	$0.350 \cdot 10^{-1}$	2.25*	$0.154 \cdot 10^{-1}$	0.74
URBAN	-0.176	-1.45	-0.135	-0.89
HHEAD			-0.117	-0.54
YRSAGO			$-0.505 \cdot 10^{-2}$	-0.96
YRSONJOB			$-0.248 \cdot 10^{-2}$	-0.63
GED			$0.975 \cdot 10^{-1}$	1.18
HEARING				
HVYLABOR[a]			$-0.226 \cdot 10^{-2}$	-0.03
CLIMB[a]			-0.187	-1.88
STOOP[a]			$0.641 \cdot 10^{-2}$	0.07
REACH[a]			-0.102	-0.66
TALK[a]			$-0.454 \cdot 10^{-1}$	-0.58
FINGER[a]			$0.629 \cdot 10^{-1}$	0.53
SIGHT[a]			0.171	1.44
Constant	0.131	0.66	0.419	1.13
DF	138		126	
SEE	0.214		0.213	
R^2	0.190		0.269	
$\bar{R}^2$	0.161		0.170	

[a]Variables subject to interactions. In column 2, the variables listed at the left were used; in column 4, those on the right; and in column 3, the product of the two variables, e.g., HVYLABOR * LIFTS.

*Indicates significance at the 5 percent level.
**Indicates significance at the 1 percent level.

similar shift appears to take place from UNABLE to DIFFWORK by household heads, as judged by the coefficients in the three equations. This probably reflects the greater family needs and social pressures for the head to work.

Other Measures of Occupational Change

The above three dependent variables refer to the disabled person's self-classification concerning the type of work that he can do. There

Table 5–2. continued

(3) Interaction		(4) Functional Limitations		
Coefficient	t Ratio	Coefficient	t Ratio	
$0.343 \cdot 10^{-5}$	0.23	$0.922 \cdot 10^{-6}$	0.07	
$-0.536 \cdot 10^{-2}$	-0.96	$0.170 \cdot 10^{-2}$	0.34	
-0.468	-1.38	-0.577	-2.07*	
$0.542 \cdot 10^{-2}$	0.30	$0.301 \cdot 10^{-1}$	2.01*	
-0.127	-0.94	-0.134	-1.07	
$-0.503 \cdot 10^{-1}$	-0.27	-0.252	-1.39	
$-0.477 \cdot 10^{-2}$	-1.00	$-0.982 \cdot 10^{-2}$	-2.19*	
$-0.222 \cdot 10^{-3}$	-0.06	$0.430 \cdot 10^{-2}$	1.22	
$0.774 \cdot 10^{-1}$	1.07			
$-0.199 \cdot 10^{-1}$	-0.09	$-0.349 \cdot 10^{-1}$	-0.18	
-0.299	-2.68**	-0.295	-3.01**	LIFTS[a]
-0.364	-2.29*	-0.195	-1.78	STAIRS[a]
$0.352 \cdot 10^{-2}$	0.03	$-0.586 \cdot 10^{-1}$	-0.50	STOOPS[a]
-0.125	-1.18	$0.831 \cdot 10^{-1}$	0.81	REACHS[a]
-0.137	-0.51	$-0.287 \cdot 10^{-1}$	-0.15	SPEECH[a]
$-0.609 \cdot 10^{-1}$	-0.51	-0.139	-1.35	HANDLES[a]
$0.515 \cdot 10^{-1}$	0.53	$0.588 \cdot 10^{-1}$	0.73	SIGHTDP[a]
0.809	3.01	0.587	2.61**	
126		127		
0.201		0.190		
0.346		0.411		
0.257		0.337		

is the subsidiary question of whether or not he does return to the same job or same kind of work. Unfortunately, the correlation between being able to do the same work as before (SAMEWORK) and returning to the same place is only 0.37, as is the correlation between SAMEWORK and doing the same kind of work as before, although for a different employer. The only significant regresssion coefficients are for the number of years on the job prior to disability and the number of years since disability. These two results suggest that reemployment has to do mostly with seniority, and possibly the flexibility to move to other jobs within the firm, rather than the particular matching of limitations and previous job requirements. Supporting this conclusion is the positive coefficient for years of school in contrast to essentially no relationship for the general educational development (GED) required by the old job. A higher level of schooling may be a good proxy for increased flexibility that enables the worker to be placed at a new job if he cannot perform his old tasks.

Findings from Other Studies

One extremely valuable source for checking our results are the findings from the National Longitudinal Surveys (NLS) of labor market experience. These surveys have been conducted since 1966 by the Center for Human Resource Research of the Ohio State University and the U.S. Bureau of the Census.[4] Their primary strength is that the same panel of people has been reinterviewed almost yearly, and thus it is possible to prospectively measure the effects of certain factors. There are four cohorts, men who, at the inception of the study, were forty-five to fifty-nine years of age; women thirty to forty-four years of age; and young men and women between the ages of fourteen and twenty-four. Each cohort includes about 5,000 people. While the primary focus of the survey is on labor force behavior, there are some health status questions, and some of the analyses have found health to be an important variable. For our purposes, the findings from the cohort of older men are most useful because that age group tends to have a sufficiently high rate of health problems to allow meaningful comparisons.

Parnes and Nestel (1974B) examine factors related to job changes within the same line of work for the middle aged men. Although they hypothesized that health problems would lower the propensity to change jobs because of fear of the unknown and lesser attractiveness to potential employers, men with health problems were more likely to change jobs. While their results are not exactly comparable, because of the focus on people who stay in the same type job, they do support our findings with respect to job tenure and education. Contrary to our findings, however, race does not play any role in the propensity to change jobs.

A study by Smith and Lilienfeld (1971) followed disabled workers who applied for Social Security disability benefits. It offers some support to our findings that the type of job initially held is predictive of return to work. The data in Table 5-3 suggest that the proportion of people not returning to work is strongly related to crude measures of the amount of effort required by the job. Furthermore, former

4. Over fifteen volumes of comprehensive reports and a hundred specific reports have been published analyzing the NLS data (see Center for Human Resource Research, 1977).

Table 5—3. Percentage of Disabled Workers Returning to Work After Disability by Predisability Occupation and Social Security Benefit Status

	Occupation Prior to Onset of Disability						
Benefit Status	*Professional Manager*	*Clerical/Sales*	*Craftsman*	*Operative*	*Service*	*Laborer*	*Total*
Denials							
Not work after onset	39.1	47.4	55.0	56.2	64.1	61.0	53.9
Resume work	42.5	44.7	41.4	39.9	28.4	33.9	39.6
Continuous work	18.4	7.9	3.6	3.9	7.5	5.1	6.5
Return to same work	66.7	67.5	63.0	52.6	75.0	34.8	60.5
Allowances							
Not work after onset	82.0	81.8	88.6	90.6	91.8	93.3	87.9
Resume work	10.8	11.1	8.4	7.2	4.7	6.7	8.3
Continuous work	7.2	7.1	3.0	2.2	3.5	0.0	3.8
Return to same work	71.4	88.9	71.0	66.7	71.4	100.0	74.5

Source: Smith and Lilienfeld, 1971: 157–59.

operatives and laborers who returned to work were least likely to do the same things, again suggesting the influence of job requirements.

A Summary of Occupational Change
After Disability

Of all disabled men who were working at the time of their disability onset, 24 percent feel they are unable to work and 36 percent feel they can continue to do the same work as before their disability. The major factors determining the likelihood of being unable to work are severe physical handicaps. Being unable to lift objects or having a speech difficulty increases the probability by nearly one and a half times the average. Rural residence decreases the likelihood of being unable to work. This suggests that while the factors associated with rural jobs lead to higher disability rates, either they are of a less serious nature or the jobs available to rural residents are more flexible. The job interaction results support the hypothesis that those men who were initially in laboring jobs will be extremely unlikely to find any work if they are unable to perform basic lifting tasks. The likelihood of being able to do the same work as before is dominated by the interaction between functional limitations and job requirements. Difficulty climbing stairs or lifting objects coupled with jobs requiring such activities will eliminate the chances of returning to the same type of work. Being black will also lead to shifting into different work, probably because of labor market conditions.

FACTORS AFFECTING THE IMPACT
OF DISABILITY ON EARNINGS

The primary effect of disability on income is through its impact on the earnings of the disabled individual. Total family income may not fall nearly as much as earned income, because other family members may be able to make up the deficit or income may be received either from disability or public assistance programs. This section will concentrate on the factors related to the ability to maintain previous earnings levels in spite of disability. If certain disabilities or conditions are closely related to wage loss, then they should be emphasized in retraining programs. If certain types of training or backgrounds enable individuals to suffer a smaller loss when and if they become disabled, educational or on the job training programs might concentrate on these aspects.

The emphasis in this section will be on the ratio of current to predisability earnings per week, rather than the absolute level or dollar change in income. This reduces the importance of factors related to the absolute level of earnings. Relative earnings loss also more nearly approximates a measure of welfare loss if one assumes diminishing marginal utility of income. Furthermore, it is possible to examine whether there is a relationship between relative loss and the initial absolute level of predisability earnings.

The results presented in this section will show that for various population subgroups identified by race, sex, and initial earnings level different factors are important in determining the impact of disability on earnings. Although the characteristics of the subgroups are substantially different, most of the differences in retention of earnings are due to different behavioral and labor market responses. For instance, education and job experience tend to be much more important for those who are initially disadvantaged: the blacks and the poor. High initial earnings provide a cushion for some people to accept earnings losses. In addition to these socioeconomic variables, the interactions between job requirements and functional limitations are important.

The remainder of this section is divided into five subsections. The first outlines a general framework. This will include those factors expected to be important in the analysis and a discussion of the causal relationships. The next subsection will briefly discuss the sample used in the analysis, its relationship to the disabled population in general, and the variables describing the interaction between job characteristics and disability. The following two subsections will concentrate on the multiple regression results; first for male, female and racial subgroups, and then for a split of the sample on the basis of initial weekly earnings. A final subsection will summarize the findings.

A Model of the Impact of
Disability on Earnings

Observed earnings are a result of four components. First, a person must actually be in the labor force. Second, he or she must be employed, rather than unemployed. Third, the number of hours worked per week is a decision variable. Finally, the hourly wage rate must be applied to the hours worked to determine total wage income. This section will concentrate on total earnings per week, while the next will examine differences between disabled and nondisabled populations for each of the four components.

Instead of estimating a complete model, several shortcuts can be taken to simplify the analysis. The labor force participation and hours worked per week equations will be rather similar in form. The unemployment equation is composed of two parts, the supply side which is like the labor force participation equation, while the demand side is related to market conditions that generally cannot be precisely measured. The hourly wage equation is somewhat different from the others, with the primary emphasis on education and job experience variables. The basic similarity among the four equations suggests that not too much will be lost if only a reduced form equation is estimated.

A second major source of simplification is made possible by the choice of relative rather than absolute earnings. Thus, many of the variables important in cross-sectional studies to describe differences in preferences or tastes can be ignored because they are likely to be the same for the family before and after disability.

The relative earnings (RELEARN) equation may initially be written in the following form:

$$RELEARN = f[(PERSONS, KIDS6, OTHERDP, YASSETS);$$
$$(AGE, SEX, RACE, YRSSCHL, JOBYRLIM,$$
$$MSPRES, MSABS, URBAN, NORTH, SOUTH,$$
$$NC, HEALTH, YRSAGO);$$
$$(EARNLIM)].$$

The variables are grouped into three categories: the first set represents actual and potential resources of the family, the second set includes measures of job adaptability, and the last is a measure of the predisability earnings.

The number of potential earners in the family is positively related to the total number of persons (PERSONS). This figure will be influenced by the number of very young children who may require the presence of an adult at home (KIDS6). Furthermore, the presence of other disabled adults in the family both increases the need for earnings and reduces the number of potential earners.

High asset levels tend to lead to a reduction in work effort because of alternative means of support, both through income from assets (YASSET) and the use of wealth itself for consumption purposes. There is a high correlation between assets and income from assets, so only one of the two variables will be included. It is likely that asset income is subject to less measurement error.

Four other forms of income available to the family—(1) interfamily gifts; (2) pensions or disability-related income supplements; (3) welfare, public assistance, or other external forms of support; and (4) income earned by other family members—become very troublesome when estimation of the equation is attempted. The appropriate variables are the potential resources available of each type. The observed levels of these income sources are more likely to reflect the influence of disability; people receive such income because their earnings are low. Thus, these income sources are omitted from the equation.

The adaptability factors measure the likelihood that a disabled person can remain at the same or similar job or reduce the impact of disability on earnings. As individuals get older (AGE), it is generally more difficult for them to shift jobs, let alone occupations. Older workers are also more likely to have acquired substantial pension benefits. Furthermore, among men, early retirement in the late fifties is generally socially acceptable, while it is less so for younger men.

Sex is an obviously important factor. Not only do women have fewer alternative job opportunities, but there are several factors contributing to the likelihood that they will drop out of the labor force after disability. The social norms are such that while women are often expected to stay at home, it is extremely unusual for a man to completely drop out of the labor force (generally he must be severely and visibly disabled to obtain social acceptance of his dependent role).[5] The much lower wages for women also have an important role; even a minor reduction due to job change or reduced hours may drive the take-home pay below the equivalent value of home production that is foregone by working. The situation is especially critical if day care or domestic services are purchased because the woman is working.

Race can be expected to operate in a way similar to sex. Blacks generally have lower incomes, even with the same education as whites. Thus, a given reduction in wage income is more likely to force a black below that point at which welfare is more desirable than a job. More importantly, the range of jobs open to blacks, either through outright discrimination, credential requirements, or jobs not being available in the ghettos, is much narrower than that available to whites. This constricted job choice will tend to make it more difficult for a disabled black to maintain his or her wage level in another occupation.[6] It is expected that the relevant labor markets

5. I am indebted to Dr. Robert Weiss for pointing out the importance of visible disability in relation to social acceptance of the sickness behavior (see Weiss and Bergen, 1968: 107–15). Remember that these data refer to the mid-1960s, when sex role stereotypes were more firmly held.

6. There is one important exception to the problem of a narrow range of job alternatives. If they all pay about the minimum wage and the worker is able to get any of the jobs, earnings will remain about constant. The one "advantage" of being at the bottom of the heap is that it is difficult to fall any lower.

and behavior patterns for men and women of each race are suffi-ciently different so that separate equations will be estimated for each to allow for interaction effects.

Education, as measured by number of years of school (YRSSCHL), is expected to influence the impact of disability in two ways. First, more education is generally associated with jobs that are less physi-cally demanding. The education term may therefore serve as a proxy for job characteristics not sufficiently represented by the other variables. A related aspect is that jobs requiring more education are generally more tolerant of disabilities by allowing more flexible working hours or conditions (Haber, 1970: 9). A second, and more important, role of education is in widening the range of jobs open to an individual.

The number of years experience on the job at the time of disabil-ity (JOBYRLIM) may also be an important factor favoring the maintenance of earnings. It is a measure of general on-the-job experi-ence, and since it is related to the particular job, it is a much better measure of the likelihood that an individual will keep his original job after disability.

Bowen and Finegan (1969: 40–49) generally find marital status to be a highly significant variable in determining labor force partici-pation. They feel that it primarily represents a certain set of attitudes and work habits. This is especially true for the distinction between those who have been married at some point and the never-marrieds. In particular, the man who is married with spouse present (MSPRES) is likely to have greater responsibilities and social pressure to work than the single man. The woman in a similar situation who is disabled has both a more secure source of income and more social support for leaving her job. To identify the supposed attitude differences, per-sons who have been married but currently are without their spouse (MSABS) should be distinguished from the never-marrieds. (The last is an omitted dummy variable.)

Two area variables—URBAN, and a set of regional dummies for the major census regions, NORTH, SOUTH, NC (North Central), and WEST (omitted)—can be added to represent differences in the job mix available and in unemployment rates. For instance, Haber (1970: 9) argues that farm work is more flexible than most other kinds of labor and thus attracts disabled workers.

The simple term for HEALTH can be considerably expanded and refined. There are basically two groups of variables that represent the health status of the individual: specific interactions between impairments and job requirements, and general disease types. The interaction variables should be of the form: this person cannot lift weights over fifteen pounds *and* this persons's job at time of disability required lifting weights over fifteen pounds. Such a formulation enables one to distinguish an impairment, that is, not being able to lift heavy weights, that does not interfere with a person's job from one that does imply a job limitation. Thus the lifting impairment would be a disability for a construction laborer but not for a clerk. Some health conditions may affect jobs but not appear as specific impairments; examples are mental illness, heart trouble, and similar disorders that may be sensitive to interactions with people or stress or that may reduce a person's life expectancy. The latter may encourage the individual to cut back on hours or to retire early.

One additional measure of adaptability is the number of years that have elapsed since the onset of the health problem, YRSAGO. It is expected that the more time that has elapsed, the greater the adaptation to the health problem.

The final variable is the level of weekly earnings before limitation (EARNLIM). This serves as a summary measure of the predisability earnings level, standard of living, and preferences for money income. The term is especially important as a proxy for preferences and alternatives available to the family. Thus, if a person had a high level of initial earnings, the family is more likely to be able to "get by" with a greater proportionate reduction in income than is a similar family with lower initial earnings.

This subsection has briefly sketched a model of the impact of disability on earnings. By considering only the ratio of earnings after to earnings before disability, a relatively simple model can be used. There are three groups of variables in the equation: (1) actual and potential resources available to the family, (2) measures of functional limitations and job adaptability, and (3) a term that represents the predisability earnings level. The model is based on fairly standard labor force equations, but the ratio form permits the elimination of a large number of unobtainable variables concerning family preferences and employment opportunities of other family members.

Description of the Data

The basic data concerning the socioeconomic characteristics and functional limitations of the disabled persons are drawn from the Survey of Disabled Adults. For this analysis the sample is limited to those persons with a job at or before the onset of the disability and who were aged eighteen to sixty-four in 1966. The sample is further restricted by excluding cases with missing data and people who were only in part-time jobs at the time of their disability.[7] The final sample is composed of 3,944 cases representing 10.6 million people.

Although the SDA contains a series of questions concerning the extent of impairments, only one question was asked about the requirements of the job: whether heavy physical labor was regularly or occasionally required. To supplement this, the three digit occupation code describing the person's occupation at the time of disability onset was used to link the SDA observations with the job characteristics data from the Dictionary of Occupational Titles. The job characteristics information is represented by the probability that the job requires the activity in question. The interaction variables are defined in the following way: first, it is determined whether the individual has a given impairment, say a speech difficulty. If there is no impairment, a zero is entered for that variable. If the person is impaired, the probability from DOT that talking is required on the job is used. Thus, both the person with no speech problem and the one with a speech defect who did not need to talk on the job would be considered to have no occupational interaction.[8] The seventeen interactions between impairments and job requirements are listed in Table 5−4. The disability information is from SDA and refers to the person's current status, while all but the last job characteristic are estimated from DOT for the job described at the time of initial limitation. The one exception is for PHYSICLS and PHYSICLN, where the respondent specified whether heavy physical labor was required on the job she or he had when disabled. Most of the variables have an S or N suffix; this is to distinguish between impairments that enable the person to do some (S) rather than none (N) of the activity.

To supplement the disability-job interaction variables, a set of five variables describing the individual's condition are included. If the person's condition has gotten better (BETTER), rather than get-

7. Given the reasonably large number of cases and the similarity between cases with and without complete information, it was decided to include only those cases with complete information. This reduces the sample by about 16 percent. People who had extremely low levels of initial earnings, the denominator in the dependent variable, were excluded to avoid absurdly high values of RELEARN. The cutoffs were set at $50 per week for men and $30 per week for women. An analysis of the occupations of these people supports this decision; most were farm laborers, laborers, janitors, private household workers, cooks, and waitresses. These are jobs that are likely to be part-time or involve nonmonetary compensation (see Luft, 1972: Appendix F, for a more detailed discussion).

8. It is, of course, possible that an individual with a given impairment actually needed that activity for his job even though relatively few of the workers in the occupation perform that activity. In this case, the interaction term is misleading. Omitting the interactions, however, is equivalent to assuming that all activities are equally necessary for all jobs.

Table 5-4.   Definition of Impairment—Job Requirement Interaction Variables

Variable Name	Impairment	Job Requirement
LIFTS LIFTN	Lifting: trouble, but can do some[a] Lifting: cannot do at all	Medium or heavy physical labor (basically lifting)
STOOPS STOOPN	Stooping: trouble, but can do some[a] Stooping: cannot do at all	Stooping, kneeling, crouching, and/or crawling
CLIMBS CLIMBN	Climbing stairs: trouble, but can do some[a] Climbing stairs: cannot do at all	Climbing and/or balancing
REACHS REACHN	Reaching: left or right: trouble, but can do some[a] Reaching: left or right: cannot do at all	Reaching, handling, fingering, and/or feeling
HANDLES HANDLEN	Handling: left or right: trouble, but can do some[a] Handling: left or right: cannot do at all	Maximum (finger dexterity, manual dexterity)[b]
WRITES WRITTEN	Writing: trouble, but can do some[a] Writing: cannot do at all	Maximum (clerical perception, job's relation to data)[b]
SIGHT	Trouble seeing even with glasses or blind	Maximum (spatial perception, form perception, color discrimination, seeing)[b]
HEARING	Trouble hearing or deaf	No interaction
SPEECH	Speech difficulty	Talking required
PHYSICLS PHYSICLN	Lifting: trouble, but can do some[a] Lifting: cannot do at all	Heavy physical labor occasionally or regularly on job[c]

[a]Includes cases in which the respondent said she or he is limited in the activity but did not respond to the second question concerning whether she or he could do some of the activity or none at all.

[b]The probabilities for the various job requirements are compared and the largest is chosen for the interaction value.

[c]As indicated by the respondent specifically in reference to his or her job at the time of disability; this is not a probability drawn from the matched DOT data.

ting worse or remaining the same, relative earnings are likely to be higher.[9] Four specific diagnostic groups are included to account for limitations not already captured. These are conditions associated with the lungs or breathing (LUNGS); heart and circulatory conditions (HEART); digestive-genitourinary conditions (DIGGU); and musculoskeletal conditions (MOBILITY).[10]

In summary, the data to be used are drawn primarily from SDA, which provides detailed information on predisability work status as well as current work and health status of disabled persons. These data are supplemented by the estimated set of job characteristics from DOT related to the predisability occupation. To eliminate cases with extremely low wages primarily due to nonmonetary compensation, a minimum weekly wage screen is imposed. Even with this limitation, the sample represents a substantial portion of the adult U.S. population and 60 percent of the disabled population.

Impact of Disability on Earnings:
Sex and Race Differentials

The differences in job opportunities and social roles of men and women and blacks and whites suggest that there will be different functional relationships for each group so that separate equations will be estimated for each. First the racial differences for men will be compared, then the results for men and women, and finally the differences between black and white women.

Table 5−5 presents the mean values for the samples of white and black men. It is clear that black men are more severely affected by disability. The average ratio of current to predisability earnings

---

9. This need not be the case. Given that current physical condition is represented by other variables, the fact that a person indicates that she or he has gotten better implies that his or her health status had been worse before. This previously poorer health might lead to lower earnings.

10. The specific conditions included in each of the four groups are: LUNGS/ BREATHING: asthma, tuberculosis, chronic bronchitis, emphysema, other lung diseases, other respiratory problems, and respiratory problems in addition to disorders other than circulatory; HEART/CIRCULATORY: rheumatic fever, arteriosclerosis, high blood pressure, heart trouble, other circulatory diseases, circulatory diseases plus some other disorder, other diseases of the blood and blood forming organs, and stroke; DIGESTIVE/GENITOURINARY: gallbladder, liver trouble, stomach ulcer, other stomach trouble, kidney stones, prostate trouble, hernia or rupture, other digestive, other genitourinary, and digestive system disorders in combination with other conditions; MOBILITY: missing legs, feet, arms, hands or fingers; palsy; paralysis of any kind; repeated trouble with back or spine; permanent stiffness or any deformity of the foot, leg, arm, or back; other diseases of the bones and organs of movement; varicose veins; and diseases of the bones or organs of movement in combination with other disorders. These four groups account for about 70 percent of the conditions reported by people in the sample.   .

Table 5–5. Mean Values for Disabled Men with Initial Weekly Earnings of $50 or More

Variable Name	White	Black
RELEARN	0.644	0.499
YRSSCHL	10.13	7.21
AGELIM	42.53	42.02
NORTH	0.211	0.186
NC	0.244	0.185
SOUTH	0.316	0.499
URBAN	0.799	0.895
MSPRES	0.861	0.722
MSABS	0.081	0.225
PERSONS	3.45	3.73
KIDS6	0.180	0.286
OTHERDP	0.361	0.318
JOBYRLIM	12.02	8.75
EARNLIM	139.13	95.61
AGEDP	49.26	48.53
YRSAGO	6.73	6.50
YASSET	344.93	63.90
LIFTS	0.255	0.411
LIFTN	0.054	0.162
STOOPS	0.180	0.255
STOOPN	0.040	0.098
CLIMBS	0.075	0.083
CLIMBN	0.008	0.009
REACHS	0.191	0.265
REACHN	0.036	0.061
HANDLES	0.120	0.184
HANDLEN	0.024	0.029
WRITES	0.055	0.032
WRITEN	0.007	0.013
SIGHT	0.120	0.089
HEARING	0.077	0.050
SPEECH	0.006	0.002
PHYSICLS	0.181	0.151
PHYSICLN	0.064	0.132
BETTER	0.245	0.284
LUNGS	0.093	0.104
HEART	0.273	0.256
DIGGU	0.098	0.162
MOBILITY	0.262	0.214
Number of cases	1980	319
Approximate number of persons represented (000s)	3947	636

(RELEARN) for blacks is less than half, while for whites it is almost two-thirds.[11] Disabled black men have much less education, are much more likely to live in the South and urban areas, are as likely to have been married but are much more likely to be currently without spouse, and have much lower earnings initially. The black men are in larger families, with more young children, but with a smaller probability of having another disabled person in the family. Blacks had been working for shorter periods on their job at the time of disability, although they were disabled at about the same time and at the same average age as the white men. The black men, in general, are more likely to have a disability that interacts with their job, although they are less likely to have hearing, seeing, and speech problems as their disabilities.

These differences in underlying characteristics of the two subgroups are quite obvious. It is less clear, however, what lies behind the different effects on relative earnings levels. One approach is to estimate multiple regression equations for each group and compare the findings, as in Table 5−6. A Chow test of the coefficients indicates that the estimated relationships are indeed different at the 1 percent level of significance. Thirty to fifty percent of the variance in RELEARN is explained by the included variables; a substantial proportion for cross-sectional microdata. Even more important is the high statistical significance of the coefficients: almost half of the variables are significant at conventional levels. Most of the socioeconomic variables are of the expected sign; those that are not are not significantly different from zero. One convenient technique for comparing the relative importance of the different variables in the regressions is the use of beta coefficients. These are comparable to regression coefficients based on data normalized to a mean of zero and standard deviation of 1.0 within each sample. One can then interpret a standard deviation in years of schooling as about 2.5 times as powerful for black as for white men in maintaining relative earnings.

The effects of marital status are fairly similar for the two races. The strong positive coefficient for married men with wife present (MSPRES) probably reflects their increased responsibilities and greater attachment to the labor force. This is consistent with Bowen and Finegan (1969). However, their findings of different patterns

---

11. These are the weighted averages of the ratios for each person in the sample. The weights are derived from the sampling scheme and when summed add up to the number of people represented by each subsample.

for previously married and never married men are contradicted by the insignificant coefficients for MSABS.[12]

The effects of the family composition variables are substantially different for black and white men. The number of persons (PERSONS) in the family indicates the potential for other people to substitute for the disabled person's earnings. The negative impact is almost three times as large for black men as for white men. The presence of other disabled persons (OTHERDP) in a black family is not significant, perhaps because there tends to be a somewhat lower prevalence of reported multiple family disability. For white men, it tends to raise RELEARN both because of greater need and fewer alternative earners, controlling for PERSONS. The presence of young children has little effect on the postdisability earnings of either black or white men.

The regional variables tend to affect black and white men differently. For both groups, living in the West (the omitted region) is more advantageous than living elsewhere, and being in the South is a decided disadvantage. This may be a reflection of the relative job opportunities in the two regions.[13] Unlike whites, black men have a substantially more difficult time maintaining their earnings in the North, perhaps because of a relatively tighter job market.

Both black and white men exhibit about the same patterns for the effects of age, earnings when limited, and job tenure, although the last tends to be substantially more important for blacks. In general, similar patterns are also evident for the functional limitation–job requirement interaction variables. The coefficients for these terms are usually of the correct sign and often significant. Men who cannot do anything in a certain activity (N suffix) usually have lower RELEARN than those who can do something (S suffix).[14]

12. As in all instances of dummy (0, 1) variables, one category is omitted, in this case the never-married category. Its influence is implicitly captured in the constant term, while the other coefficients measure the differential effects of the corresponding variables. Thus the coefficient of 0.327 for MSPRES indicates that, everything else held constant, married men with spouse present have a RELEARN value 0.327 higher than men who were never married.

13. There is another possible answer for the strong negative influence of the South in this and other regressions. Some disabled persons may migrate to the South for health reasons. The relatively lower level of wages in the South would then produce a RELEARN less than 1.0 even if there was no reduction in wages corrected for price and cost of living differences. The South had more than its share of disabled persons (31 percent of the population aged eighteen to sixty-four lived in the South versus 38 percent of the disabled sample (U.S. Bureau of the Census, 1967B: 25). It is possible that part of this excess may be due to selective migration.

14. At first glance, one would expect each of the variables to have a negative sign, as each designates a physical disability of the person combined with the

Table 5–6.   1966 Earnings Relative to Earnings at Time of Disability: Men

Variable Name	White Men			Black Men		
	Coefficient	Standard Error	Beta Coefficient	Coefficient	Standard Error	Beta Coefficient
YRSSCHL	0.017	0.003**	0.113	0.040	0.007**	0.289
NORTH	−0.023	0.033	−0.017	−0.216	0.092*	−0.165
NC	−0.038	0.032	−0.029	−0.092	0.092	−0.070
SOUTH	−0.148	0.031**	−0.122	−0.129	0.077	−0.127
URBAN	0.008	0.028	0.006	0.072	0.087	0.043
MSPRES	0.327	0.049**	0.202	0.206	0.106	0.181
MSABS	−0.013	0.060	−0.006	0.097	0.110	0.079
PERSONS	−0.021	0.008**	−0.066	−0.040	0.013**	−0.187
KIDS6	0.031	0.037	0.021	−0.071	0.065	−0.063
OTHERDP	0.077	0.023**	0.066	0.023	0.051	0.021
JOBYRLIM	0.0032	0.0012**	0.062	0.016	0.003**	0.274
EARNLIM	−0.0010	0.0001**	−0.177	−0.0014	0.0006*	−0.102
YASSET	−0.0000	0.0001	−0.003	0.00018	0.00010	0.087
AGEDP	−0.0135	0.0014**	−0.257	−0.021	0.003**	−0.451
YRSAGO	0.0010	0.0015	0.015	−0.0025	0.0031	−0.046
STOOPS	0.004	0.040	0.002	−0.002	0.070	−0.001
STOOPN	−0.365	0.074**	−0.108	−0.194	0.123	−0.100
CLIMBS	0.051	0.063	0.018	−0.141	0.150	−0.045
CLIMBN	−0.272	0.200	−0.028	−0.188	0.433	−0.019
HANDLES	−0.029	0.043	−0.015	−0.022	0.083	−0.016
HANDLEN	−0.247	0.083**	−0.063	0.192	0.197	0.056
WRITES	−0.135	0.054*	−0.051	−0.306	0.187	−0.086
WRITEN	0.134	0.157	0.017	−0.442	0.267	−0.093
SIGHT	−0.091	0.038*	−0.047	−0.207	0.097*	−0.094
HEARING	−0.057	0.041	−0.027	−0.142	0.101	−0.061
SPEECH	−0.221	0.178	−0.024	−0.567	0.666	−0.036
PHYSICLS	−0.219	0.029**	−0.150	−0.246	0.066**	−0.173
PHYSICLN	−0.324	0.050**	−0.141	−0.405	0.070**	−0.269

BETTER	0.127	0.026**	0.098	−0.096	0.052	−0.085
LUNGS	0.016	0.041	0.008	−0.363	0.096**	−0.217
HEART	0.020	0.031	0.016	−0.267	0.072**	−0.228
DIGGU	0.120	0.041**	0.063	−0.112	0.074	−0.081
MOBILITY	0.129	0.030**	0.101	−0.076	0.072	−0.061
Constant	1.066			1.625		
R^2	0.301			0.553		
$\bar{R}^2$	0.287			0.501		
DF	1940			285		

*Significant at 5 percent level.
**Significant at 1 percent level.

The five conditions variables are very different for the two samples; for whites, the coefficients are all positive, and those for BETTER, DIGGU and MOBILITY are significant; for blacks, they are all negative, and those for LUNGS and HEART are significant. There are no a priori reasons for such differences, and it is difficult to work through the effects of such variables when "everything else is held constant."

It is quite obvious that there is a "racial effect" in the impact of disability on earnings.[15] For a number of the most important characteristics, both the coefficients and the observed values in the population are different in the two samples to the detriment of black men. In some cases, this is immediately clear from a comparison of the signs and magnitudes of the coefficients and values, but usually the net effect must be computed. The overall difference in average RELEARN between the two samples $(0.644 - 0.499 = 0.145)$ can be decomposed into a part due to different value of characteristics for the blacks and a part due to a different estimated relationship. If black men had the same estimated equation as whites (in other words, applying the white coefficients to the mean black values for each variable), the estimated average RELEARN is 0.602.[16] This implies that only 0.042 of the differential is due to different attributes while 0.103, or 72 percent, is due to the different impact of disability. An alternative view is to estimate RELEARN for whites using the coefficients of black males. This value is 0.721, indicating that the estimated relationship for blacks gives much more weight

---

likelihood that it affects his job. Consider, however, a person who has none of the listed limitations (or limitations that do not interact with his job) and has none of the listed conditions. If this were a sample of the population in general, it would be likely that the person is perfectly well. But, because in this case the whole sample is of disabled persons, it is known that the individual has some disability not included in the list, for example, mental illness. Therefore, the implicit value of RELEARN is very low for a disabled person with none of the explicitly included disabilities. This may result in positive coefficients for some of the disabilities. The following statement might then explain the coefficient: "If one is disabled, but the only thing wrong is X, then one is relatively (to all disabled persons) well off."

15. If there was no racial effect, one would expect the coefficients in the two equations to be the same. The differences in the observed values of RELEARN in the two samples would be explained by differences in the attributes of the two groups.

16. If the mean values in Table 5-5 for white and black men are designated X_i^w and X_i^b, respectively, and the coefficients in Table 5-6 are C_i^w and C_i^b, then

$$\sum_i C_i^w X_i^b = 0.602.$$

than the white relationship to those variables in which the blacks are most deficient.[17]

A few examples of the differential importance of specific variables may help interpret these results. For blacks, education is more than twice as important as for whites, but they have less education. The number of years on the job is nearly five times as important for blacks, but they average 3.27 fewer years of experience. These differences may be explainable in terms of labor market theories such as discrimination based on cost of information and other factors, as well as different behavior by the two groups. But the important result is that the impact of disability is substantially more severe for black men.

Job opportunities, alternative sources of income, and different social roles, among other factors, lead to the expectation that the behavioral relationships in maintaining earnings levels for men and women will be different. Not only are these a priori beliefs confirmed in an examination of the estimated relationships, but a number of surprising results are apparent.[18] Education is not at all significant in maintaining earnings for women, whereas it is very important for men. This difference probably reflects the different range of job opportunities open to women. In general, they tend to be concentrated in occupations that probably require less education.

The coefficient for MSPRES is highly significant and is opposite in sign to the value for men. This is expected, as married men have a socially determined role that encourages them to work to support their families. Married women, on the other hand, are often encouraged not to work, and if disabled, the presence of a husband to provide family income will strengthen that pressure.

The level of earnings at the time of disability, while highly significant and negatively related to RELEARN for men, is essentially of no importance for women. For men, it can be argued that those who had initially high earnings could afford to reduce their earnings

17. Continuing the notation of the previous footnote, $\sum_{i} C_i^b X_i^w = 0.721$.

There is no theoretically correct set of weights. However, comparing the four values does offer some insight into the overall importance of behavioral parameters and underlying characteristics.

18. Mean values and regression results for white and blacks combined are given in Luft, 1972: Ch. vi. Because of the much larger number of whites, e.g., 1,372 white women versus 273 black women, the estimated relationships for the combined samples are very close to those of the white subgroup. When the combined equations were estimated, a dummy variable for race was included. This was statistically insignificant, indicating the importance of considering the interaction effects for a variable whose importance is as pervasive as race.

if that would result in an easier job with respect to their disability. Those with initially low earnings could not drop much further while remaining in the labor market. In part, this is the result of minimum wage laws that preclude a disabled worker from accepting a job at very low pay even if it reflects his or her low marginal productivity. Unless a man is sufficiently disabled to be accepted in a disability benefit program, there are few alternatives to working that are socially acceptable and financially viable, given the general exclusion of men from other welfare programs. The same explanation would hold for women, except that they are more likely to have the option of dropping out of the labor market, supported either by their husbands or welfare. Thus there is no discontinuity for women with low earnings. In fact, lower initial earnings will result in the break-even point (below which the earnings are not worth the effort and costs in transport, child care, and so forth) being reached sooner.

Urban location is negatively related to earnings retention for women, while it is unimportant for men. If this dummy actually represents a group of rural jobs that is more flexible in terms of time as well as effort requirements, then it is understandable that women, with their traditionally greater home responsibilities, will be more sensitive to such flexibility.

The coefficients for the age of the disabled person are very similar for the two sexes, but the number of years since disability is highly significant for women but not for men. Again, this is explainable in terms of the differences in attachment to the labor force for men and women.

It should be quite clear that the relationships predicting RE-LEARN for men and women are quite different, but it is also obvious that the characteristics of the two groups are also different.[19] For instance, the women are somewhat better educated (the initial sample included only women with work experience and earnings over $30 per week), less likely to have their spouses present, have somewhat smaller families, and are younger. In addition, they had much less job experience, earned less, and were disabled much longer ago than the men.

The net effects of the differences in the relationships and the average values can be seen by applying the men's coefficients to the women's values and vice versa, as in Table 5-7. The observed averages of RELEARN, 0.627 and 0.261 for men and women, respectively, indicate substantial overall differences. If, however, women

19. The characteristics of all women can be derived from Table 5-8 by weighting the two columns. In practice, the column for white women gives a reasonable approximation.

Table 5–7. Estimates of the Effects of Behavioral Relationships and Population Attributes on RELEARN for Men and Women

	Attributes		*Difference*
	Men	*Women*	*Women—Men*
Coefficients			
Men	0.627	0.680	+0.053
Women	0.390	0.261	−0.129
Difference			
Women—Men	−0.237	−0.419	

responded in the same way and faced the same external conditions as men, their average RELEARN would be 0.680. The difference attributable to using the men's coefficients (0.419) with the women's characteristics is even greater than the actual observed differences of 0.366 = 0.627 − 0.261. Under the alternative weighting, if men faced the same conditions and reacted in the same way as women, their RELEARNs would average 0.390, substantially below the observed value, but also well above the value for women. This is an example of the index number problem: women do better than men with the men's coefficients, and men do better than women with the women's coefficients. Essentially nothing can be said about which group is better off.

The results for black and white women are examined next. The mean values for two subsamples are given in Table 5–8 and the regressions in Table 5–9. It is immediately clear that the situation is somewhat different from that of white and black men. Whereas black men have a substantially lower average RELEARN than white men, the situation is reversed for black and white women, with values of 0.319 and 0.250 respectively.

Characteristics across races within each sex are somewhat similar. Like black men, black women have less education, are more likely to live in the South or urban areas, are about the same age, are as likely to have been married but are much less likely to have other disabled persons in the family, and earn less per week than their white counterparts. While black men had substantially less work experience than whites, there is no racial difference for women. There is, however, a large difference for women in the number of years since disability (a shorter span for black women), while there is no such difference for men.

The estimated regression equations suggest that there are also differences in the behavioral relationships for black and white

Table 5–8.   Mean Values for Disabled Women with Initial Weekly Earnings of $30 or More

Variable Name	White	Black
RELEARN	0.250	0.319
YRSSCHL	10.55	8.47
AGELIM	35.33	35.44
NORTH	0.273	0.303
NC	0.267	0.191
SOUTH	0.280	0.435
URBAN	0.833	0.935
MSPRES	0.715	0.511
MSABS	0.230	0.418
PERSONS	3.23	3.59
KIDS6	0.166	0.295
OTHERDP	0.342	0.292
JOBYRLIM	6.47	6.48
EARNLIM	91.02	63.30
AGEDP	48.00	45.24
YRSAGO	12.67	9.80
YASSET	304.15	59.45
LIFTS	0.122	0.219
LIFTN	0.046	0.049
STOOPS	0.070	0.268
STOOPN	0.014	0.078
CLIMBS	0.028	0.052
CLIMBN	0.003	0.011
REACHS	0.220	0.284
REACHN	0.044	0.034
HANDLES	0.123	0.182
HANDLEN	0.017	0.028
WRITES	0.062	0.027
WRITEN	0.007	0.008
SIGHT	0.103	0.186
HEARING	0.038	0.028
SPEECH	0.008	0.001
PHYSICLS	0.104	0.155
PHYSICLN	0.048	0.087
BETTER	0.256	0.295
LUNGS	0.055	0.028
HEART	0.212	0.302
DIGGU	0.108	0.122
MOBILITY	0.239	0.158
Number of Cases	1372	273
Approximate Number of Persons Represented (000s)	3893.0	774.0

women. This is most apparent in the effects of the family structure variables. Although the coefficient for PERSONS for white women is positive but only slightly larger than its standard error, the coefficient is negative and significant for black women. Furthermore, KIDS6 is highly significant for both groups, but negative for whites and positive for blacks. OTHERDP, although positive for both, is more than three times as large for black women. These differences probably relate to the much larger fraction of previously married black women without husbands, and the relative difficulty each subgroup has in finding employment.

Income from assets, although generally not significant in most of the samples, is significant and positive for black women. As asset income is usually very low, this may serve as a proxy for the few blacks with high family income.

Again, the relative impact of differences in the characteristics of the two groups can be compared to differences in the behavioral relationships. The average RELEARN for blacks using the estimated coefficients from the white sample is 0.266, not very different from the actual average for black women of 0.250. When the characteristics of white women are matched with the black coefficients, the estimate of 0.320 is essentially the same as the observed value of 0.319. These results suggest that the different relative earnings for black and white women are not due to differences in either socioeconomic or health characteristics but in the job opportunities faced by, and the behavioral responses of, each group.

The Impact of Disability
for the "Rich" and "Poor"

Among the findings of the previous subsection were significant negative coefficients for the influence of initial earnings levels on the ratio of postdisability to predisability earnings per week. It was hypothesized that the impact of disability may be very different for high and low income workers. Higher income workers may have more alternative jobs open to them, supplemental resources, and the possibility of reducing their standard of living without suffering absolute hardship. This subsection will provide a partial test of the ways the impact of disability varies by income level. This is done by splitting the sample on the basis of the initial weekly earnings level and comparing the behavioral relationships for each subgroup. This allows for an interaction effect between initial earnings and all the other variables, just as was the case with the split by race in the preceding subsection.

Table 5–9.   1966 Earnings Relative to Earnings at Time of Disability—Women

Variable Name	White Women			Black Women		
	Coefficient	Standard Error	Beta Coefficient	Coefficient	Standard Error	Beta Coefficient
YRSSCHL	−0.0003	0.0039	−0.002	0.0056	0.0073	0.052
NORTH	−0.056	0.032	0.059	0.385	0.090**	0.407
NC	0.020	0.032	0.021	0.003	0.096	0.003
SOUTH	0.0054	0.032	0.006	0.028	0.090	0.031
URBAN	−0.061	0.029*	−0.053	−0.111	0.097	−0.063
MSPRES	−0.236	0.048**	−0.251	−0.217	0.104*	−0.249
MSABS	−0.038	0.051	−0.038	−0.199	0.110	−0.226
PERSONS	0.0095	0.0079	0.037	−0.047	0.016**	−0.196
KIDS6	−0.160	0.035**	−0.140	0.192	0.064**	0.202
OTHERDP	0.061	0.022**	0.068	0.201	0.058**	0.210
JOBYRLIM	0.0069	0.0017**	0.115	0.011	0.003**	0.202
EARNLIM	−0.00009	0.0002	−0.013	−0.0007	0.0008	−0.046
YASSET	0.00001	0.00001	0.025	0.0003	0.0001**	0.225
AGEDP	−0.0089	0.0012**	−0.237	−0.0061	0.0027*	−0.155
YRSAGO	−0.011	0.0016**	−0.288	−0.0090	0.0032**	−0.165
STOOPS	−0.156	0.057**	−0.072	−0.075	0.070	−0.066
STOOPN	−0.216	0.138	−0.044	−0.196	0.123	−0.104
CLIMBS	−0.059	0.090	−0.016	0.009	0.149	0.003
CLIMBN	−0.091	0.278	−0.009	−0.868	0.554	−0.149
HANDLES	0.082	0.040*	0.059	0.132	0.073	0.110
HANDLEN	−0.166	0.089	−0.048	−0.593	0.166**	−0.208
WRITES	−0.239	0.054**	−0.124	−0.630	0.227**	−0.181
WRITEN	0.014	0.140	0.003	1.105	0.582	0.182
SIGHT	−0.064	0.041	−0.039	0.049	0.075	0.038
HEARING	0.018	0.054	0.008	−0.334	0.142*	−0.127
SPEECH	−0.132	0.128	−0.026	−0.422	0.642	−0.031
PHYSICLS	−0.004	0.035	−0.003	−0.045	0.064	−0.037
PHYSICLN	−0.096	0.051	−0.048	−0.154	0.095	−0.100

BETTER	-0.057	0.024	-0.058	0.057	0.054	0.059
LUNGS	0.020	0.047	0.011	-0.049	0.131	-0.019
HEART	0.031	0.029	0.030	0.130	0.061*	0.137
DIGGU	0.047	0.036	0.034	-0.197	0.077*	-0.148
MOBILITY	0.029	0.027	0.029	-0.020	0.068	-0.017
Constant	1.015		0.845			
R^2	0.250		0.499			
$\bar{R}^2$	0.232		0.430			
DF	1338		239			

*Significant at 5 percent level.
**Significant at 1 percent level.

The large differences in usual weekly earnings for men and women make it necessary to choose different cutoffs for each sex. For men, weekly earnings of $130 and for women earnings of $80 were chosen to define the boundaries of the two groups that will be loosely termed "rich" and "poor."[20] The differences in the impact of disability on the two groups is shown in Table 5–10. For both men and women the relative earnings after disability are substantially lower for the "rich" than for the "poor." Essentially the same proportion in each group is in the labor force; thus almost all of this difference is either due to lower hourly earnings or shorter work weeks.

Table 5–11 provides the results of regressions of RELEARN for "rich" and "poor" men.[21] It is clear that not only are the mean values for RELEARN rather different, but the behavioral relationships are unlike each other in a number of ways. Most striking are the results for years of schooling—a highly significant positive variable in the overall sample; it is apparent that it is really important only for the "poor" men. This suggests that the functional limitations–job requirements interaction variables capture only part of the labor market effect and that individuals in higher paying jobs can move fairly easily to other jobs without any great importance attached to their "credentials." "Poor" men, however, find that education is very important in trying to maintain their previous level of earnings.

A second important difference is in the estimated coefficients for the two variables concerning marital status. MSPRES is not significant for the "rich" men but is highly significant and positive for "poor" men. Being married with the spouse present will boost the estimated postdisability earnings of a man in the latter group to a

Table 5–10. Measures of the Impact of Disability for "Rich" and "Poor"

	RELEARN		Proportion in Labor Force	
	Men	Women	Men	Women
"Rich"	0.5475	0.2412	0.6758	0.3281
"Poor"	0.6718	0.2759	0.6782	0.3306

20. On a yearly basis, these levels are close to the median levels of wage and salary income for full-time, year-round workers, $6,375 for men and $3,823 for women (U.S. Bureau of the Census, 1967A: 45).

21. In these regressions, EARNLIM and YASSET are expressed in hundreds of dollars, thus shifting their coefficients by two places. These changes cause no alteration in the overall results, except for the constant term.

level even higher than predisability, everything else held constant. The "low income" man probably sees his responsibilities and the likely lack of job opportunities for his wife as an extremely strong incentive to keep working in spite of his disabilities. The behavior of the "high income" man is probably the net effect of his family status, coupled with the greater income earning possibilities of his wife (Benham, 1974). Rich men who have been married but currently are not living with their spouses suffer (or are willing to accept) a substantial loss of earnings relative to other married and single men. Previously married poor men, however, manage to reduce their earnings loss substantially in comparison with poor never-married men. The effects of other family structure variables are comparable for each group, although the presence of another disabled person in the family of a poor man will lead to increased work effort to try to maintain the previous level of income.

The importance of differences in labor market behavior between the two groups is again demonstrated by the variable measuring number of years on the job before disability, JOBYRLIM. As with education, for rich men job tenure is unimportant; they are apparently willing and able to move to somewhat lower paying (and less demanding) jobs with little difficulty. Poor men, even though they tend to have fewer years on the job, find such seniority as they have very important. The average poor man with somewhat more than ten years seniority will add close to ten percentage points to his postdisability wages relative to one with no seniority.

The EARNLIM variable, which was used to split the sample, is no longer significant in the RICH MEN equation, indicating that it is not the ratio form of the dependent variable, but different behavioral relationships that are responsible for the observed results. For poor men, the variable is still highly significant, but its coefficient is less than half the size of the one in the combined regression. This suggests that the $130 limit was too high an estimate of the point separating the two groups, in that many of those earning, say, $120 per week are willing to forego a substantial fraction of their earnings in order to "purchase" an easier job. Those with much lower earnings are unable to make that tradeoff and still have enough money.

Theory predicts that the availability of an alternative source of income, such as interest, rent, or dividends, will reduce the amount of labor supplied. This should be especially true if the person is disabled. Rich men respond as expected with a significant negative coefficient for YASSET, but poor men do not, having a significant positive response. Men who were initially receiving low wages and yet

Table 5-11. 1966 Earnings Relative to Earnings at the Time of Disability—"Rich" and "Poor" Men

Variable Name	"Rich" Men			"Poor" Men		
	Coefficient	Standard Error	Beta Coefficient	Coefficient	Standard Error	Beta Coefficient
YRSSCHL	0.00105	0.00398	0.00892	0.03311	0.00418**	0.19733
NORTH	-0.02626	0.04004	-0.02266	-0.07647	0.04145	-0.05216
NC	0.00785	0.03837	0.00715	-0.09274	0.04088*	-0.06592
SOUTH	-0.14645	0.03828**	-0.13910	-0.15110	0.03885**	-0.12254
URBAN	0.02306	0.03689	0.01873	0.04599	0.03422	0.03068
MSPRES	0.03573	0.07492	0.02452	0.45932	0.05412**	0.29326
MSABS	-0.26417	0.08578**	-0.15259	0.16713	0.06450**	0.08662
BLACK	-0.14526	0.07274*	-0.06040	-0.03535	0.03829	-0.02166
PERSONS	-0.01577	0.01111	-0.05479	-0.03331	0.00886**	-0.10909
KIDS6	0.07958	0.05040	0.05964	0.01800	0.04111	0.01248
OTHERDP	0.00376	0.03026	0.00377	0.09819	0.02731**	0.07947
JOBYRLIM	0.00079	0.00150	0.01938	0.00947	0.00147**	0.16091
EARNLIM	-0.01458	0.01269	-0.03752	-0.45225	0.05934**	-0.17808
YASSET	-0.00252	0.00073**	-0.10885	0.00241	0.00094*	0.05518
AGEDP	-0.01250	0.00187***	-0.26319	-0.01457	0.00160**	-0.26900
YRSAGO	-0.01109	0.00177**	-0.22435	0.00664	0.00177**	0.08658
STOOPS	-0.04441	0.05850	-0.02707	0.02681	0.04297	0.01487
STOOPN	-0.23418	0.10179*	-0.07819	-0.41427	0.07695**	-0.13371
CLIMBS	-0.07676	0.07858	-0.03357	0.05888	0.07771	0.01764
CLIMBN	-0.03219	0.23852	-0.00410	-0.41242	0.24537	-0.03821
HANDLES	0.02006	0.05744	0.01175	-0.02101	0.04779	-0.01144
HANDLEN	-0.18130	0.12216	-0.04650	-0.26351	0.09332**	-0.06838
WRITES	-0.09253	0.06144	-0.04845	-0.15951	0.07621*	-0.04824
WRITEN	-0.30385	0.23065	-0.03884	0.26900	0.16302	0.03833
SIGHT	-0.05921	0.04988	-0.03706	-0.15363	0.04700**	-0.07189
HEARING	-0.07555	0.04726	-0.04757	-0.03527	0.05407	-0.01408
SPEECH	0.06647	0.17905	0.01079	-0.99324	0.28425**	-0.07652
PHYSICLS	-0.13605	0.03906***	-0.11070	-0.27329	0.03554***	-0.17499
PHYSICLN	-0.39982	0.06510**	-0.19022	-0.36255	0.05230**	-0.16698

BETTER	0.05957	0.03340	0.05431	0.10825	0.03050**	0.07900
LUNGS	0.04774	0.05760	0.02726	0.00370	0.04672	0.00189
HEART	0.00436	0.03924	0.00425	0.01307	0.03638	0.00955
DIGGU	0.09402	0.05297	0.05843	0.03840	0.04581	0.02027
MOBILITY	0.02638	0.03878	0.02429	0.13875	0.03607**	0.10221
Constant	1.40960			1.15443		
R^2	0.387			0.359		
$\bar{R}^2$	0.360			0.344		
DF	767			1462		

*Significant at 5 percent level.
**Significant at 1 percent level.

had asset income are probably somewhat different from the average. It is possible that they were more "aggressive"—trying to invest while still earning relatively little, and thus more likely to continue working after a disability.

The two groups of men exhibit similar responses with respect to age but different relationships for the number of years since the onset of disability. The longer a rich man has been disabled, the less likely he is to have relatively high earnings, while the poor man seems to marginally increase his earnings year by year after disability.

Table 5-12 presents the results for women with initial weekly wages above and below $80. Again, there are striking differences in the two subsamples. As with the men, schooling is not important (and is actually negative) for those with initially high earnings, while it has a substantial positive impact for those below the cutoff.

Marital status is among the most important variables, and here too, the results are different in the two subgroups. In both cases, being married with spouse present sharply reduces the expected earnings after disability relative to the predisability level, but for rich women, the coefficient is one third larger. The presence of young children in the families of rich women leads to a much greater relative reduction in earnings (about five times) even though they are less likely to have children under six. Again, it seems as though the rich woman's income is seen as secondary, and if she is married, or if young children are present, she is more likely not to work as much. The earnings of poor women are much more likely to be crucial to the household. If another person in the family is disabled, the poor woman is more likely to attempt to maintain her previous earnings.

The importance of job seniority for poor men is repeated for poor women. Whereas for rich women, seniority is not significantly related to relative earnings, for poor women it is among the most important variables, with each year adding over one percentage point to RELEARN.

The results for the effects of initial earnings (EARNLIM) are partly like and partly unlike those found for the men. In both cases, the estimated coefficient is negative and insignificant for the rich sample. Poor men had a significant negative coefficient, indicating that the cutoff was too high, so that some men in the poor group were willing to accept large income losses for "easier" jobs. For poor women, however, the variable is positive and significant. This further confirms that the importance of this variable is not due to the ratio form of the dependent variable.[22] In the case of poor women, the

---

22. The ratio form of the dependent variable requires that it be bounded by zero. Thus, the distribution of the dependent variable can have a very large tail

EARNLIM variable probably serves to separate full-time and part-time workers. Given a disability, it is much more likely that part-time workers are able to either marginally reduce their work effort or quit completely. Full-time workers, on the other hand, are more likely to have been working because of family income needs and thus are likely to continue working after disability, given the same degree of handicap.

This analysis was extended by further splitting each sample into black and white subsamples, but the lower income of blacks resulted in very small samples of "rich" blacks. In general, the results of the racial subsamples are similar to those already described, but there are a few notable exceptions. The education coefficient, which is significant only for the "poor," is the same for blacks and whites, suggesting that the racial differences observed in the full sample are due to differing distributions by income, not a pure racial effect. The job tenure variable, also significant only among the poor, is more than twice as important for blacks. Finally, asset income has different effects for blacks and whites. Among rich men, it is positive for blacks and negative for whites; among poor men, it is positive for both groups, but nearly thirty times as large for blacks as for whites.[23] There are no consistent differences in the splits for white and black women.

The previous subsection suggested that predisability income levels were an important factor in explaining the ability to maintain earnings; this subsection strongly confirms that view with an investigation of separate regressions for the rich and poor. The results indicate that the rich accept a somewhat greater relative loss in earnings after disability by shifting to alternate jobs. Education, job tenure, and previous earnings level are not particularly important in this shift for the rich, while they are critical factors for the poor. This suggests that the jobs faced by the rich are substantially more flexible and do not place as much emphasis on credentials and experience as those faced by the poor.

Findings from Other Studies

There are relatively few published studies that provide a direct comparison with these results. Substantially more evidence is avail-

---

to the right, but is constrained on the left. The use of a minimum wage cutoff substantially reduces this problem. To the extent that this problem is still present, it would cause the EARNLIM coefficient to be strongly negative.

23. These results suggest that asset income among low income persons is indicative of a high rate of savings and an attempt to raise incomes in the future. Within each income sample, blacks are more likely to be at the lower end of the income distribution where this type of behavior, which will lead to an attempt to maintain incomes after disability, is more common and, hence, will exhibit a stronger effect.

Table 5–12.   1966 Earnings Relative to Earnings at the Time of Disability—"Rich" and "Poor" Women

Variable Name	"Rich" Women			"Poor" Women		
	Coefficient	Standard Error	Beta Coefficient	Coefficient	Standard Error	Beta Coefficient
YRSSCHL	−0.00751	0.00531	−0.05851	0.00836	0.00470	0.06032
NORTH	−0.02707	0.04189	−0.03126	0.00279	0.04561	0.00273
NC	0.06348	0.04313	0.06941	−0.05936	0.04545	−0.05777
SOUTH	0.07255	0.04436	0.07518	−0.04317	0.04356	−0.04661
URBAN	−0.00849	0.04548	−0.00690	−0.08069	0.03590*	−0.06842
MSPRES	−0.26127	0.06283**	−0.28739	−0.20133	0.05981**	−0.21627
MSABS	−0.12055	0.06758	−0.11985	−0.04349	0.06381	−0.04496
BLACK	0.07853	0.05352	0.05659	0.04208	0.03847	0.03514
PERSONS	−0.02476	0.01220*	−0.09693	0.01310	0.00884	0.05156
KIDS6	−0.18928	0.05156**	−0.17017	−0.03568	0.03843	−0.03271
OTHERDP	0.04772	0.03142	0.05656	0.08761	0.02855**	0.09213
JOBYRLIM	0.00293	0.00230	0.05847	0.01030	0.00216***	0.15061
EARNLIM	−0.05047	0.02675	−0.07568	0.20058	0.10137*	0.05947
YASSET	0.00172	0.00137	0.04728	−0.00160	0.00279	−0.01704
AGEDP	−0.01058	0.00185**	−0.27342	−0.00675	0.00145**	−0.18282
YRSAGO	−0.00900	0.00149**	−0.27490	−0.01246	0.00143**	−0.26708
STOOPS	−0.19787	0.08857*	−0.09450	−0.07510	0.05228	−0.04685
STOOPN	0.08823	0.26745	0.01236	−0.28981	0.09587**	−0.10103
CLIMBS	−0.34155	0.14597*	−0.08789	0.08916	0.09350	0.02743
CLIMBN	−1.81674	1.59565	−0.04051	−0.07408	0.23424	−0.01072
HANDLES	0.04511	0.05611	0.03635	0.09262	0.04540*	0.06429
HANDLEN	−0.07428	0.14728	−0.01839	−0.24772	0.09416***	−0.08043
WRITES	−0.15672	0.06981*	−0.10053	−0.27275	0.08189***	−0.09783
WRITEN	−0.34763	0.18918	−0.06785	0.37640	0.19486	0.06287
SIGHT	−0.16040	0.06514*	−0.09047	−0.06819	0.04477	−0.04693
HEARING	−0.09647	0.07727	−0.04532	0.03316	0.06991	0.01374
SPEECH	−0.11451	0.17968	−0.02324	−0.17484	0.17282	−0.02928
PHYSICLS	0.07964	0.05646	0.05236	−0.06637	0.03782	−0.05159
PHYSICLN	−0.01973	0.08721	−0.00861	−0.15516	0.05291**	−0.08910

BETTER	-0.05199	0.03256	-0.05809	-0.05361	0.03035	-0.05214
LUNGS	-0.03466	0.06587	-0.01950	-0.00039	0.06228	-0.00019
HEART	0.03603	0.04013	0.03691	0.08321	0.03417*	0.07912
DIGGU	-0.05202	0.05314	-0.03692	0.04896	0.04167	0.03646
MOBILITY	0.07276	0.03838	0.07754	0.01096	0.03473	0.01013
Constant	1.32947			0.67769		
R^2	0.322			0.246		
$\bar{R}^2$	0.282			0.220		
DF	569			1006		

*Significant at 5 percent level.
**Significant at 1 percent level.

able for the various components of earnings; these will be discussed at the end of the next section.

A study of people who had received temporary disability benefits in California provides support for the strong negative influence of age on maintaining earnings levels. The proportion returning to work fell steadily from 61 percent in the under twenty-five age group to 43.8 percent in the fifty-five to sixty-four age group (Sinai, 1967: 33). Furthermore, even among those who return to work, there is a strong influence of age on the ratio of post- to predisability weekly wages. For those under twenty-five years of age, the ratio was 0.99, and it fell consistently to 0.78 for the fifty-five to sixty-four age group (Ibid, pp. 109, 111).

Nagi and Hadley (1972) provide some analysis of the effects of disability on income and the adjustments that are made by the family. They split a sample of Social Security disability applicants into high and low income groups with a $500 per month cutoff. For the low income families, income maintenance depends on the spouse's working, while many of the higher income families initially had two earners and there was little change in the proportion with spouse working in each group. Income from property, especially renting out the family's original house while moving to rental quarters, was an important source of income for the latter group. Among those with higher incomes, the proportion with at least high school education is greatest in the group maintaining its income level and smallest among those with severe declines; for the low income group, there is no clear relationship. Higher education would be expected to lead to a maintenance of income levels. Nagi and Hadley use this explanation for the high income group and point out that the initially very low incomes of the poorly educated made it easier for welfare and workmen's compensation to make up the lost earnings. It is difficult to reconcile their findings with respect to education with our very clear results. But the differences in sample, approach, and number of other factors held constant suggest that a direct comparison is impossible.

A COMPARISON OF ACTUAL AND PREDICTED LABOR MARKET BEHAVIOR OF DISABLED ADULTS[24]

The preceding two sections have dealt with factors that influence the types of adjustments disabled persons must make in their labor

24. Parts of this section were previously published in Luft, 1975, and are reprinted with the permission of North-Holland Publishing Company.

market behavior. In both cases, attempts were made to control for the interactions between the person's functional limitations and the requirements of his or her job prior to the onset of the disability. Controlling for such factors, it was found that age, race, sex, education, and initial earnings levels all had profound influences on the type of work a person did and his or her current earnings relative to earnings at the onset of disability.

The major limitation in both of those sections is that they present comparisons *within* the group of disabled adults. For instance, the preceding section concentrated on what enables people with a disability to maintain a high level of post- to predisability earnings relative to the other disabled people in the sample.[25] This section will use the nondisabled population as the "norm," to provide more easily understood measures of the effects of health problems. The approach will be to separate the observations in the 1967 Survey of Economic Opportunity into two groups: (1) people who report some health problem that limits the kind or amount of work they can do, and (2) people who are not limited. The latter sample will be used to estimate a series of regression equations for various components of labor market behavior, such as participation, weeks worked per year, earnings per hour, etc. The estimated coefficients from these equations will then be applied to a group of disabled persons to "predict" their labor market behavior had they been well. The differences between actual and predicted behavior of the disabled will be compared to the observed differences between the disabled and nondisabled groups. In all of these comparisons, the samples will be further split by race and sex to evaluate the ways in which these variables interact with disability to influence behavior.

The next subsection will outline in somewhat more detail the labor market equations to be estimated and data to be used. This will be followed by a discussion of the differences between observed and predicated behavior. A final subsection will summarize these findings and compare them with previous studies of the impact of health problems on labor market behavior.

Estimating the Impact of Health Problems on Labor Market Behavior

The primary interest in this chapter is in estimating the importance of the health problems, not in breaking new ground in the

---

25. This problem was clearly demonstrated in the preceding discussion about the effects of certain functional limitations and conditions that had a positive effect on RELEARN. Such health problems are not "good," but they are less serious than those of the rest of the group.

specification of labor force models. Therefore, the equation that is used is similar to that of the preceding section and is drawn from the usual labor force participation literature. The independent variables rather closely follow those of Bowen and Finegan (1969). Both age and the square of age are included to allow for the traditionally demonstrated inverted U-shaped curve with respect to labor force participation and earnings. A dummy variable is used for whether the person was in school during the survey week. The effect of schooling is represented by the maximum number of grades completed. Five variables define the type of family and the person's role in the family. The first is marital status, coded as married with spouse present and married at some time but with spouse currently absent. The individual's responsibility for other persons is approximated by whether or not he or she is the family head. In addition, three indicators of the size of the family and alternative sources of potential labor and responsibility are included: the number of other adults (aged fourteen and over), the total number of other persons in the family, and the number of children under the age of six years. Three regional dummies, Northeast, Northcentral, and South are included, as is a dummy for residence in urban areas. Income from assets is included to control for an income effect on labor market behavior.[26] For women, a measure of other family income is included that is the total of wage, salary, and self-employment income of other family members but does not include welfare payments or other sources of income that are based upon "need."[27]

There are five health status variables that indicate whether a person is prevented from working, limited in the kind and amount of work, limited in the kind of work, limited in the amount of work that he or she can do, or is limited in the amount or kind of housework that she can do.[28] The health (or disability) variables are only used to split the population into well and disabled subgroups. As

26. This variable is computed as a residual and includes a few sources of non-employment income received on a regular basis that are not strictly returns from assets, such as alimony payments. Explicitly excluded are social security, pension, workmen's compensation, unemployment insurance, and public welfare payments.

27. The sexism implicit in this formulation is recognized; it assumes that other family members make their earnings decision and then the woman responds (Poirier, 1977). Two reasons underly the choice of this model. First, it follows a long line of similar economic models, and our intent was to provide comparable results highlighting the effects of disability (Rosett, 1958; Mincer, 1962; Bowen and Finegan, 1969). Second, given data drawn from the mid-1960s, the "secondary female worker" model may well be more appropriate.

28. The first four variables are mutually exclusive. The housework question was asked only of women.

before, the focus is on the noninstitutionalized population aged eighteen to sixty-four. Using the above five disability questions, the SEO identified 14.6 percent of the population as having a health limitation affecting their work. The SDA, using the same questions as a screening device, identified 17.2 percent of the population as being disabled. Given the differences in sampling design in the two surveys, and the efforts taken in the SDA not to miss any disabled people, the two estimates are rather comparable. It is likely that those people not identified as disabled in the SEO tend to have relatively minor limitations.[29]

There are nine dependent variables. The first, LFPYEAR, is a dummy variable equal to one if the individual was in the labor force for any period in the previous year (1966).[30] The second, WRKLSTWK, is equal to one if the person worked at all in the week prior to the survey.[31] A measure of the unemployment rate for persons in the labor force in 1966, UNEMPRAT, can be constructed by dividing the number of weeks they were looking for work by the number of weeks they were in the labor force.[32] The number of weeks worked, WKSWORK, is a straightforward conversion from the six classes given in the SEO to the means for each class. Total earnings per year, EARNYEAR, is the sum of all wage and salary income plus net income from business and farm self-employment for 1966. The estimated weekly earnings throughout the work year, EARNWKYR, is computed by dividing EARNYEAR by WKSWORK. The errors introduced by the conversion from brackets to means, of course, also enter this variable. For those working in wage and salary positions in the previous week, three additional variables can be tested:

29. See pp. 25–27 for a more complete discussion of the two surveys.

30. The (0, 1) nature of this dependent variable suggests that Probit analysis would be a more appropriate estimating technique than the OLS methods that were used. An independent study of labor market behavior by Scheffler and Iden (1974) used a similar set of variables with the SEO data and tried both OLS and Probit with essentially the same results using either technique. Given the cost of Probit analysis and the focus here on the effects of disability, rather than the labor market equations per se, OLS estimates are quite adequate.

31. The SEO did not ask a specific labor force question for the preceding week, so those who were looking for work were not included, nor were data collected concerning the self-employed. Those persons with farm or business income in the preceding year were assumed to be working in the week prior to the survey.

32. Unfortunately, SEO only provides coded values for the numbers of weeks worked and weeks in the labor force. The mean values for each category (1-13, 14-26, 27-39, 40-47, 48-49, 50-52) were used. This may introduce measurement errors when estimates are used in both the numerator and denominator, especially for people who only worked a small number of weeks.

the hourly wage (HOURWAGE), a number of hours worked (HRS-WRKED), and a direct measure of total weekly earnings (WEEK-EARN). All are provided by SEO as continuous variables, although the wage rate is computed from the other two.

The 1967 Survey of Economic Opportunity has been described in some detail in previous chapters. For the analyses in this section, observations missing the necessary data were omitted from the sample.[33] All computations (regressions, means, etc.) are performed using the inverse of the sampling times response rate. The sum of the weights for all observations is equal to the total number of persons represented by the appropriate subsample; for the whole group, this is the 105 million adults aged eighteen to sixty-four in the U.S. in 1967. Three somewhat different samples are used for the nine questions. The equations for LFPYEAR and WRKLSTWK are based on the entire sample of well (nondisabled) adults, 30,864 observations. The equations for UNEMPRAT, WKSWORK, EARNYEAR, and EARNWKYR are based on the 24,130 well persons with some labor force experience in the preceding year. The equations for HOURWAGE, HRSWRKED, and WEEKEARN are based on the 18,609 well persons in wage and salary positions in the preceding week. For each regression the samples were split by race and sex.

The Impact of Health Problems
on the Components of Earnings

Total earnings may be broken into its various components to examine the different effects that disability has for each race and sex group. These results are summarized in Table 5–13, which provides three figures for each component and race-sex group. The first entry in each triplet is the mean value of the variable for those people without disabilities—0.9533 is the labor force participation rate of well white men. The second entry is the gross difference between the first and the observed mean for people with a disability. In this instance, 0.1679 = 0.9533 − 0.7854, with the last value being the observed participation rate for white men with a disability (not shown). The third entry (0.1775) is the difference between the value for the nondisabled group (0.9533) and the estimated value for the disabled group (also not shown). This estimated value is necessary because the underlying characteristics of the two groups differ; the disabled are generally older, less well educated, more likely to live in the South and rural areas, and so forth. In fact, the whole thrust

33. This reduces the total of 45,844 observations to 36,732. While there may be some biases in who chooses not to respond to certain questions, the group providing all the necessary information seems representative of the total.

of Chapters 3 and 4 is that the probability of disability is not equal for all. Thus, to adjust for the sociodemographic differences, a set of regressions was computed for each dependent variable using the sample of well adults.[34] The coefficients of these equations were then applied to the characteristics of the disabled population to estimate the values for the disabled, adjusted for the differences in the two groups—that is, what the earnings variables would have been given the behavior of the "well" group and the characteristics of the disabled.

The importance of the adjustment may be dramatically seen in the results for labor force participation. It is clear that the lower observed rates for the ill are in fact due to their health status and not to other characteristics. Three of the four race-sex groups have adjusted rates that are even higher than the rates found in the well population.[35] This strongly suggests that, at least on the basis of the factors used to predict labor force participation, those people who report poor health are not using it as an excuse to hide other reasons for not working. More precisely, there is no evidence that had disabled persons been well, they would have had a participation rate any different from that of the rest of the population.

These data also allow comparisons of the impact of a disability for various groups that are known to have different labor force behavior patterns, such as whites and blacks and men and women, and thus continue the investigation of the previous section. For both sexes, the net (adjusted) effect of disability on participation rates is larger for blacks than for whites. This is probably indicative of the facts that (1) blacks are less likely to receive medical care either at all, or as early, and thus receive less assistance in adjusting to or curing a given condition, and (2) blacks are more likely to be in occupations that are sensitive to disability so that they drop out of the labor force.

A comparison can also be made between sexes. Overall, the impact

34. The actual equations are not of primary interest for this discussion. The variables and samples in the equations are discussed in the preceding section. The coefficients may be found in Luft, 1975: 43–57.

35. This may be seen by examining the four pairs of gross and adjusted differences in the first column of Table 5-13. For all but white women, the adjusted difference is greater than the gross difference. Thus, for three of the four cases, there was a greater spread between the observed participation rates of the disabled and their estimated participation rates than there was between their observed rates and those of the well population. This implies that the estimated rates were even higher than those observed among the well. Simple subtraction of the two differences shows how much higher—for white men, those who were disabled, had they been well, would have had a participation rate 0.0096 (= 0.1775 − 0.1679) higher than those who actually were well.

Table 5-13. Mean Values of Components of Earnings for "Well" Persons and the Gross and Adjusted Differences Between "Well" and "Disabled" Persons

	LFPYEAR	*WRKLSTWK*	*UNEMPRAT*	*WKSWORK*
White Men				
Well	0.9533	0.8503	0.0236	46.31
Gross Difference[c]	0.1679	0.2178	−0.0217	3.98
Adjusted Difference[d]	0.1775	0.2123	−0.0165	4.39
Black Men				
Well	0.9342	0.8015	0.0640	44.69
Gross Difference[c]	0.2545	0.3411	−0.0320	6.45
Adjusted Difference[d]	0.2692	0.3485	−0.0321	7.15
White Women				
Well	0.5960	0.4500	0.0303	37.78
Gross Difference[c]	0.1897	0.2178	−0.0106	5.57
Adjusted Difference[d]	0.1797	0.2239	−0.0096	8.16
Black Women				
Well	0.7062	0.5149	0.0644	36.77
Gross Difference[c]	0.1974	0.2479	−0.0214	6.37
Adjusted Difference[d]	0.2171	0.2860	−0.0221	7.73

[a] Estimated values for HOURWAGE are used in the computation of the adjusted figures for HRSWRKED in place of the actual wage rate.

[b] Estimated values for WKSWORK are used in the computation of the adjusted figures for EARNYEAR in place of the actual number of weeks worked.

[c] Gross difference is equal to the value for the "well" population minus the observed value for the "disabled" population.

[d] Adjusted difference is equal to the value for the "well" population minus the estimated behavior for the "disabled" population as computed from the regressions on the "well" population and the economic characteristics of the "disabled" population.

of disability is greater for women, especially when considered relative to their initially lower "normal" levels of participation. This is probably due to, among other things, (1) the greater probability of the woman's role as a secondary earner who need not stay in the labor market, and (2) the limited range of occupations open to women, so that it is more difficult to find jobs in which their disabilities do not interfere with the job requirements. Most of the differential between sexes arises from the comparison between white men and women; the impact of disability among blacks is about the same across sexes, especially when considered relative to the "normal" or "well" rates. This lends support to the secondary worker hypoth-

Table 5-13. continued

HOURWAGE	HRSWRKED[a]	WEEKEARN	EARNWKYR	EARNYEAR[b]
$3.29	43.30	$139.79	$140.34	$6633.
0.59	1.69	25.75	29.87	1875.
0.38	1.58	18.26	19.74	1416.
2.32	40.35	93.64	90.66	4148.
0.41	4.62	19.89	19.35	1305.
0.24	4.45	12.89	11.35	1010.
2.14	35.93	76.43	67.16	2654.
0.32	2.89	16.70	16.37	951.
0.21	3.52	13.51	12.07	951.
1.59	35.19	59.12	51.28	1917.
0.23	7.01	18.75	18.15	877.
−0.06	5.46	15.96	6.38	481.

esis, as it is unlikely that black women have a wider range of job opportunities than white women. Black women, however, do tend to provide a greater share of the "necessary" family income.

The proportion of people working in the preceding week (WRK-LSTWK) is a more sensitive measure of disability. Not only is this rate consistently lower than the participation rate for the year (which is usual with these variables), but the absolute impact of disability is greater (implying that the relative impact is even more significant). This difference can be considered in terms of the long- and short-run effects of health problems. As the health questions are related to current health status and not health over the past year, it is not surprising that they are more important for the more recent measure of participation. The sample of people currently listed as disabled include some who became so within the past year and thus were probably working. Similarly, people get better, or at least overcome their disability, and move in the other direction, from the disabled to well category, over a period of a year.

Considering only those persons in the labor force at some time in the last year, it is possible to examine the impact of disability on two other measures—the implicit unemployment rate and the number of weeks worked per year. The unemployment rate for disabled persons is substantially higher than for the well population; for white men it is nearly twice as high. The net differences, however, indicate that for white men and women, part of the health differential is due to the other characteristics of the disabled—that is, they would be expected to have a somewhat higher than normal unemployment rate. In contrast to this, the net differences for blacks are even larger than the gross differences and are about twice those for white men and women, respectively. But the black differentials relative to their higher well unemployment rates are comparable to the similar ratios for whites. Thus, while in absolute terms the impact of illness through unemployment is greater for blacks than for whites, no special interaction with disability is apparent. In other words, the disabled black will face an unemployment rate that is higher than the nondisabled black, but the differential seems to be due to general problems in the black labor market, not in the submarket faced by disabled blacks.

Had the disabled population been well, their socioeconomic characteristics suggest that they would have worked more weeks in the year than was actually worked by the well population. This finding supports the discussion of participation rates concerning the relative attachment of the two groups to the work force. White women who are disabled lose nearly twice as many weeks from their work year relative to their "expected well behavior" as do white men. On the other hand, black men and women who are disabled lose a comparable number of weeks.

These first four variables are all measures of the amount of time that a person is willing or able to work, and thus it is not surprising that disability status is an important factor. The remaining variables, HOURWAGE, HRSWRKED, WEEKEARN, EARNWKYR, and EARNYEAR, all directly or indirectly involve the hourly wage rate, as well as the number of hours worked. Parnes et al. (1970B: 49) indicate that even when occupation was controlled (albeit at a rather crude level), hourly wages for older men differ with health status. By limiting the sample to wage and salary workers who were employed in the week preceding the survey, it is possible to check these results. The data for HOURWAGE indicate a substantial gross difference; even when the data are adjusted for the different characteristics of the two samples, the impact of disability is equal to about 13 percent of the expected rate for men and 9 percent for women. Thus, even when age, education, race, family structure, and other variables are accounted for, health still matters.

A number of comparisons within this set of data are revealing. For the "participation type" or "work effort" measures, the impact of disability was greater for blacks than whites. But the reverse is true for hourly wages, although among men the impacts relative to earnings of well persons are comparable for both races. One explanation of this result may be that many blacks, even when well, earn close to the legal minimum. (Even among well persons, the average black's hourly wage is less than three-quarters that of whites.) Therefore, if they become disabled, they cannot shift to still lower paying jobs: the only alternative may be to drop out of the labor force. Second, as was discussed in previous sections, relative to disabled whites, disabled blacks are more likely to say they are limited in the amount of work or prevented from working. This may be a reflection of the interaction of their skills, discrimination, and market opportunities. Alternatively, blacks may actually suffer from a different mix of illnesses and disabling conditions.

The impact of disability on wage rates is greater for men than for women in both races, even when the differential is considered in relation to the base wage rate. These results tend to lend support to the suggestion that the smaller impact for blacks relative to whites is due to the "bottom of the wage range effect" because women, too, are generally found in low wage jobs.

A final comparison supports our previous findings concerning which persons are most likely to become disabled. If the probability of disability was independent of income, the expected income levels of the disabled would be the same as those of the well population. It has already been shown that the disabled population would be expected to have labor force participation rates and weeks of work per year comparable to the well population. In addition, as will be seen below, they would be expected to work about the same number of hours per week. The differences in expected hourly wage of the disabled and actual wage of the well are, therefore, particularly revealing. These differentials are fairly large: 6 percent for all men and 9 percent for all women.[36] (Note that the major sociodemographic variables have already been taken into consideration.) These results strongly suggest that those people who have lower than aver-

---

36. These estimates can be derived from Table 5-13 with a little effort. The adjusted hourly wage rate for disabled white men is $3.08 = $3.29 − 0.59 + 0.38, and the comparable rate for disabled black men is $2.15. Weighting these two figures by the proportion of white and black men in each group and comparing them to the weighted average wage rate for all well men yields a ratio of 0.94, or a 6 percent lower wage rate. The predominance of whites in the population allows a reasonable approximation of the total to be derived from just the white subsample.

age wages (on the basis of sociodemographic characteristics) are also more likely to become disabled.

The findings with respect to hours worked per week (HRS-WRKED) are similar to those obtained for the other measures of participation and amount of time worked: the impact of health is much greater for blacks than whites, and for women than for men. One change is that the sex differential is maintained across races, although white women suffer a greater loss relative to white men than black women relative to black men. This is probably indicative of the greater proportion of black men who are in the secondary labor market and may thus only obtain part-time jobs. Women, on the other hand, are much more likely to be in part-time jobs regardless of race.

Two measures of weekly earnings are available from slightly different populations: WEEKEARN is the reported weekly earnings of wage and salary workers for the week prior to the survey; EARN-WKYR is a computed variable based on the number of weeks worked and total earnings (including self-employment) for all persons working in the past year. The results for both variables tend to be similar so they will be considered together.[37] By comparing the gross and net differentials for WEEKEARN, it may be estimated that no more than a third of the gross difference in weekly earnings is attributable to different population characteristics; the remainder seems to be due to health differences. Analysis of the relative impact of disability by race and sex is confounded by the combination of work effort and hourly earnings effects. Instead of the "usual" case of the black differentials being larger than the white differentials, the results are reversed for men, as they are for hourly wages. This is the case in absolute terms; if the differentials are examined relative to the overall weekly wage level, the situation changes. In that case, the relative impact of disability is comparable for men of both races, while among women, blacks tend to be more severely affected.

Finally, the impact of disability for those persons who were in the labor force may be summarized by the differentials in total earnings per year. The evaluation of these results is dependent on the measures used in making the comparisons. In absolute terms, the

37. The mean values tend to be rather close, although the results for women tend to be more divergent than for men. Because the WKSWORK variable was only available as an interval, some errors were introduced in the estimation of EARNWKYR. It is reasonable that these errors would be greater among women, who are more likely than men to be in the labor force for less than a year. Not only are the percentage errors created by the conversion from categories to means greater for smaller numbers of weeks, but the intervals used in the SEO are larger at the low end of the range (see note 31).

effects of disability on annual earnings are greater for men than for women and for whites than for blacks. In this instance, the pattern found in the examination of the hourly wage dominates the pattern of the number of weeks worked. The importance of the base earnings level for each group is clear if the earnings loss is evaluated relative to the estimated earnings level. Women suffer a greater relative decline than men due to disability, and black men have a greater relative loss than white men. But even this measure masks part of the impact of disability on earnings: the adjusted earnings levels for black men and women in general is so low that the individual may respond to a health problem by dropping out of the labor force, as was seen in the participation equations.

These results strongly indicate that the impact of disability is felt in all the components of the earnings function, although the relative effects vary. In some cases, the different characteristics of the well and disabled populations account for a substantial fraction of the observed differentials between the two groups. These characteristics have the greatest effect on the hourly wage and variables that include the wage rate. This, of course, is a reflection of the fact that the poor are more likely to become disabled than the rich. At the other extreme are the measures of labor force participation and weeks worked per year for which the adjustment for characteristics makes almost no change or implies that the disabled population would have worked even more than the well.

It may be inferred from the hourly wage results and the comparisons between men and women and between blacks and whites that when a health problem strikes, its impact varies with the initial status of the person. Thus, these findings build upon and expand those of the preceding sections. If the person is male, well-educated, white, and has other attributes that lead to high-paying jobs, much of the accommodation is through a change in jobs to one that either pays less for less demanding work or is part-time.[38] The person is still

---

38. The role of education also became apparent as a by-product of this investigation when the basic equations were estimated for well adults. It was found that the coefficient of years of schooling was negative (-0.0019) in the labor force participation equations for men, a result contrary to that predicted by theory and generally reported in the empirical literature. Further investigation using the complete sample of well and disabled men showed the usual positive and highly significant coefficient for schooling, 0.0043, with a standard error of 0.0006. If dummy variables were included identifying the people with a disability, this coefficient changed to an insignificant negative value, -0.0008. This
(0.0006)
suggested that the education variable in conventional equations was serving largely to identify people without health problems and those people with disabilities who were best able to stay in the labor force. This hypothesis gained

likely to be employed, but will be earning a smaller, although still substantial, amount. An individual starting near the bottom of the earnings ladder has a much more constricted range of alternative jobs, so the hourly wage, if he or she is working at all, experiences a smaller decline. Likewise, a person already working part-time or irregularly can make relatively smaller adjustments in his or her total earnings. The initially disadvantaged person is more likely to respond to disability by dropping out of the labor force entirely. Of course, these actions are a combination of constraints imposed by the labor market, abilities of the individual in terms of job skills and potential, and possible differences in disabling conditions.

Findings from Other Studies

There are a great many studies that indicate the importance of long-term health problems or disabilities on various measures of labor market behavior.[39] Most of these, however, do not control for the different characteristics of those who become disabled or otherwise make it possible to clearly attribute the differentials in behavior to health problems. There are two major exceptions: the cross-sectional study by Morgan et al. (1962) and the longitudinal studies derived from the National Longitudinal Surveys of labor market experience.[40] The Morgan et al. study examines each of the components of earnings by spending units in a national cross-sectional survey. Variables such as age, education, marital status, children, unemployment rate in the state, race, plans for future expenditures, and measures of attitude and need-achievement are included, in addition to self-reported disability status. The measure of health problems was found to be highly significant in the equation for labor force participation of spending unit heads. Their results indicate net and gross effects of about the same size, whereas my findings indicate net (or adjusted) effects that exceed the gross effects (Morgan et al., 1962: 42). This relatively minor difference is

---

support from a final regression that added an interaction term between years of schooling and the presence of a disability. This term was highly significant, positive, +0.0084, and about twice the size of the "conventional" value. Fur-
       (0.0014)
thermore, the "regular" years of schooling coefficient remained negative and significant, −0.0022. All of this suggests that the primary effect of schooling
       (0.0006)
with respect to labor force participation is to increase the likelihood of participation if one has a disability and to decrease the likelihood of participation if one is well. For details, see Luft, 1974.

39. See, for instance, Haber (1968), Flaim (1969: 3–14), Berkowitz and Johnson (1971), and Bowen and Finegan (1969: 64–65).

40. See footnote 4.

largely attributable to their use of spending unit heads as the unit of observation with no age constraint. Thus, many of the people in question are beyond retirement age, so that the age of disability effects are confounded. Similar results were found in their investigation of the behavior of wives of spending unit heads, but with evidence of relative effects of disability that were even larger than for the heads, as was the case in our results (Morgan et al., 1962: 117).

One of the most important findings of our analysis is that those people who are disabled appear to have had at least as strong an attachment to the labor force as those who are well. This is based on a retrospective comparison of various characteristics of each group and thus is not as strong as one would like. But, after a detailed analysis of the prospective, longitudinal data of men aged forty-five to fifty-nine who dropped out of the labor force, Parnes and Meyer (1971: 22–23) reach a similar conclusion.

[T]he longitudinal nature of the present data permit us to be more confident than we otherwise could be that poor health is actually a cause of, rather than a mere rationalization for, withdrawal from the labor force. We know, for example, that even at the time they were in the labor force in 1966 about three-tenths of those who later dropped out reported their health as "poor," in contrast to fewer than one in 20 of all of the labor force members at that time. Six-tenths of the dropout group reported a health problem that limited the amount or kind of work they could do, a proportion three times as high as that which prevailed among all labor force members.

It is also worthy of note that the men who were to drop out of the labor force between 1966 and 1967 registered no weaker commitment to work in the former year than all men in the labor force at that time. Two-thirds of the black men and three-fourths of the white said that they would wish to continue to work even if they were to get enough money to live comfortably without working—proportions that differed very little from those prevailing among all of the labor force members in 1966. Indeed, the proportion of the dropouts who expected in 1966 to retire prior to age 62 was only about one-tenth in the case of the blacks and two-tenths in the case of the whites, proportions smaller than those that prevailed among all labor force members.

Another analysis of the same group considered the likelihood of becoming "retired from a regular job" within the period 1966 to 1971, based on 1966 characteristics, for men who were not retired in 1966. Estimates were derived controlling for the effects of age, race, marital status, number of dependents, net assets, duration of pension coverage, class of worker, average hourly earnings, attitude toward job, and commitment to work. Adjusting for all these factors, among those whose health affected their work in 1966, 15.6 percent retired by 1971, while only 7.7 percent of those without a health problem retired. In terms of the F ratio, health was the most significant variable after age. Furthermore, these figures are not very different from the unadjusted values—16.5 percent and 7.5 percent, respectively—indicating that it is, in fact, a health effect and not a proxy for other variables when health problems are found to be highly predictive of dropping out of the labor force (Parnes and Nestel, 1974A: 172–76). Very comparable results are reported by Parnes and Nestel for the proportion of men who reduced their hours worked per year from 3,000 or more in 1965–1966 to less than 1,000 in 1969–1971. This supports both the participation rate finding and the findings with respect to weeks worked per year and hours worked per week.

Cruder, unadjusted results for 1965 show substantial impacts of health problems on both the unemployment rate and the number of weeks unemployed for this population of older men. Furthermore, these data show that the impact of health problems tends to be substantially greater for men in blue collar and service occupations than in white collar occupations, thus supporting the findings concerning RELEARN in the previous section (Parnes et al., 1970A: 99).

The results in Table 5–13 indicate that adjusting for sociodemographic characteristics increases the estimated negative effect of health problems on the number of weeks worked and tends to reduce the estimated effect on the number of hours worked per week. Morgan et al. only present adjusted data for the combination of these two effects, the number of weeks worked per year. They, of course, indicate a rather substantial reduction in hours worked per disabled spending unit head, 256 fewer hours per year relative to a mean of 2,092. More importantly, even when adjustments are made for a broad range of characteristics, health problems account for a reduction of 199 hours, or 78 percent of the gross figure.[41] These findings are rather consistent with those that can be derived from our analysis. Combining the separate effects of health problems on WKSWORK and HRSWRKED for black and white men, there is a 266 hour gross reduction and a 289 hour adjusted reduction. Given the differences in the two studies, these figures are rather comparable. Basically similar patterns were found for wives of spending unit (Morgan et al., 1962: 131, 136).

41. The variables considered in the adjustment are (1) adult unit composition, (2) education and age, (3) occupation, (4) hourly earnings, (5) plans to help parents or children, (6) attitude toward work, (7) religious preference, (8) race, (9) state unemployment rate, (10) education difference between husband and wife, and (11) immigration status of the head and his or her father (see Morgan et al., 1962: 78).

Perhaps one of the most surprising findings of our study is that people who are disabled have lower hourly earnings than would be expected had they been well; for men, there is a 12 percent average reduction.[42] These results strongly support the interpretation of the previous section that disability leads to a shift to lower paying jobs for those persons able to remain in the labor force. These results are supported by both the Parnes and Morgan studies. Parnes et al. report for their group of older men average pay per hour classified by health limitation and occupation. In both 1966 and 1969, those men with a health problem had lower earnings in almost every occupational group (Parnes et al., 1970A: 49; Parnes, Nestel, and Andrisani, 1972: 69–72). The major exceptions were white managers and proprietors in each year. Regressions for average hourly earnings in 1966, holding other things constant, exhibit significant negative disability coefficients and reductions in hourly wages of $0.36 for white men and $0.14 for black men, very close to our findings.[43] The results from the Morgan et al. study are also consistent with ours. Gross reductions in hourly earnings of $0.46 and $0.36 are found for spending unit heads and their wives, respectively, who have health problems. Controlling for the relevent sociodemographic factors reduces these to $0.21 and $0.29, relative changes comparable to the ones that we found and adjusted differences that still imply a substantial effect of disability on hourly earnings (Morgan et al., 1962: 58, 127).

Taken as a whole, these results from very differently designed cross-sectional and longitudinal studies offer strong support for the sets of findings presented in this chapter. Not only do they show substantial effects of disability on the various components of earnings, but they exhibit the same patterns and imply that the observed effects are truly due to disability and are not merely capturing the effects of other factors.

SUMMARY AND CONCLUSIONS

This chapter has drawn together various measures of the factors that influence the effects of health problems on labor market behavior. Three rather different empirical approaches were used. In the first, the unit of observation was the detailed occupation group, and the

---

42. It is not surprising that adjusting for their sociodemographic characteristics substantially reduces the gross effect of disability on hourly wage. The previous chapters showed that people with initially lower income-education-occupation status had a greater risk of becoming disabled.

43. These regressions include years of school, age, region, occupation, job tenure, and training prior to 1966. See Parnes et al., 1974 :285–90.

dependent variables were the proportion of disabled men unable to work, able to work at the same job, and able to work only at different jobs. In the second, a broad sample of disabled men and women was used to estimate the relative influence of various sociodemographic factors on the ratio of current weekly earnings to earnings at the time of the disability onset. The richness of this data set of individual observations allowed the splitting of the sample into subgroups based on race, sex, and initial earnings level. The third approach also used individuals as the unit of observation, but in this case behavioral relations for various types of labor market activity were estimated for well adults. These relationships were then combined with the sociodemographic characteristics of the disabled to approximate how they would have behaved had they been well. In addition to these three new approaches, the literature was combed to find applicable studies bearing on our results.

Overall, the various approaches provide a remarkably consistent picture of the factors that influence the effects of health problems on economic behavior. Severe functional limitations appear to be the primary factor in rendering someone unable to work. Such limitations are probably best handled on a one-by-one basis with expert medical and rehabilitation consultation. However, only a small fraction (less than a quarter) of the disabled population is so seriously limited. For the rest of the people with functional limitations, various socioeconomic factors, many of which are policy variables, influence the ultimate changes attributable to disability. Some of these major findings are outlined below:

1. While people who live in rural areas have higher disability rates, they seem to be better able to obtain some type of work after their disability. This supports the hypothesis that nonindustrial work can be more flexible and thus is better able to meet the limitations of the disabled worker.
2. Men who used to perform heavy labor jobs before their disability find it very difficult to get a job if they can't perform basic lifting tasks—for example, disabled longshoremen don't get desk jobs.
3. As expected, the interactions (or more precisely, the lack thereof) between functional limitations and previous job requirements are crucial to being able to do the same type of work.
4. On the other hand, actually staying with the same employer is primarily the result of job tenure.
5. In terms of maintaining a high ratio of current to past earnings, job tenure appears to be very important only for people in initially low-paying jobs. This suggests that when the poor be-

come disabled, they face a much more competitive labor market and their tenure is very important to maintaining their relative position.

6. Race plays a very important role in determining the effects of disability. Blacks are not only less well-educated, skilled, and so forth, but they appear to face a segmented labor market that leads them to exhibit very different behavioral relationships.

7. Controlling for functional limitations, and other variables, blacks will be more likely to shift into different types of jobs than whites.

8. The average ratio of earnings among black men (0.499) is substantially lower than that of white men (0.644), but only 28 percent of this differential is due to differences in the attributes of the two races. Most of the effect is caused by different behavioral relationships. Among women, although blacks have higher average ratios than whites, again almost the whole difference can be attributed to different job opportunities and behavioral responses.

9. The various components of labor market behavior indicate the different ways in which health problems affect different racial groups. Black men are much more likely to drop out of the labor force or work fewer weeks than white men. The latter take larger cuts in hourly wages and earnings if the comparison is among working men of each race. Among women the impacts are similar—black women are more likely to drop out and reduce their hours per week, while white women have a larger loss in wage rate and overall earnings.

10. Education, hypothesized to be an important variable in determining the ability of an individual to shift jobs without substantial income losses, proved to be critical for some groups. It is very important for black men and for poor men and women, while it is insignificant for the rich, and not very important for white men in general. Apparently, relatively high-paying jobs are also those that enable the individual, if disabled, to move to similarly high-paying jobs. Although educational credentials may be important in getting the initial job, they thereafter have little effect unless one becomes disabled.

11. These findings are supported by the surprising result that education appears to have no positive influence on the labor force participation of men if they are well. For disabled men, however, it has a strong positive role.

12. The predisability earnings level is very important for men but not for women, and this difference holds for both races. For the samples split by initial earnings level, the variable is no longer

significant for the rich, further suggesting that the job alternatives available to those with initially high earnings are available in a wide range of wage levels. These people then tend to shift downward in income but with no particularly large relative losses within the group. Among poor men, the ratio of post- to predisability earnings bears a significant negative relationship to previous earnings level, while for poor women it is positive. In both cases, the results seem to be a reflection of alternative job opportunities. Poor men find that, for a given educational level, they have difficulty finding jobs paying comparable wages. The minimum wage laws set a floor to the hourly rate, and social pressures and the unavailability of welfare make it more difficult for them to drop out of the market. The negative relationship is merely a reflection of the fact that if one is near the bottom of the distribution, it is hard to fall any further. Among women, earnings are often seen as secondary, so that when initially low so constricted and the importance of home activities are so great that they drop out of the labor force.

13. Given the different educational backgrounds and jobs open to blacks and whites, the following summary description of the impact of disability may be suggested. Whites, with their higher education and earnings, are able to shift to alternative jobs that do not interfere with their disabilities. This job shift is sometimes accompanied by a substantial reduction in hourly wage and thus yearly earnings, but the initial earnings are usually high enough so that this change can be absorbed without impoverishment. (For instance, the average yearly earnings of *disabled* white men is $610 greater than the earnings of *well* black men.) The blacks are not in nearly so flexible a position. The effects of lower education and job discrimination make alternative jobs difficult to find. Their hourly wage rate cannot drop much because it tends to be close to the legal minimum even without a disability. By being at the bottom of the scale, they have little more to lose and they cannot trade off income for less painful work. The blacks are therefore much more likely to be forced out of the labor force if they become disabled.

14. Health problems can be seen to affect almost every aspect of labor market behavior. Furthermore, the various approaches taken in this chapter and the supporting findings of other studies leave little doubt that it is a "real" health effect and not something else.

❋   *Chapter 6*

Disability and Social Welfare

The preceding chapters have outlined the importance of various socioeconomic factors in determining the likelihood of a disability and the severity of its effects. The focus was primarily on the relative importance of such factors and the findings that disability and its effects are not purely random or chance events. Instead, they seem to be causally related to a number of variables such as income, education, labor market factors, and other variables, many of which may be subject to policy intervention. This chapter will explore the magnitudes of the economic effects of disability and show that they are very substantial. This will serve as a backdrop for policies to lessen the impact of disability, which will be presented in Chapter 7.

The first question that must be addressed is the appropriate unit of observation. Should the effects of disability, and health problems more generally, be evaluated with respect to the individual, the family, or some larger unit? The first section of this chapter will briefly explore this question. The second section will focus on the magnitude of earnings losses from two extreme viewpoints—the individual and society as a whole. The former measures the implicit loss imposed upon the person who is disabled, while the latter provides an estimate of the gross social loss attributable to disabilities. Of course, earnings losses are not necessarily the variables of interest; policymakers may well be more interested in the income and poverty status of the disabled person's family, thus allowing for the effects of both other potential workers and transfer payments. The third section provides an analysis of earnings, transfers, income, and poverty status and concludes that, while earnings losses are somewhat offset by transfer payments and other sources of income, disability is nevertheless responsible for a substantial fraction of poverty in the United States. The fourth section offers a brief discussion of the importance of macroeconomic variables such as the unemployment rate in the overall analysis of the causes and consequences of health problems. A final section provides a brief summary.

WHO IS AFFECTED BY DISABILITY?

The clearest and most direct effects of disability are felt by the disabled person. But examining merely these direct effects can provide misleading estimates of the overall impact. For instance, if we are concerned with personal income and the disabled person has insurance coverage to replace lost earnings, then he or she suffers no financial loss. Of course, this rather trivial example explicitly excludes everything but financial losses. Disability almost always involves a disruption of the normal daily activities and a change in social role. While it is difficult, if not impossible, to attach values or costs to each disruption, most people would prefer not to be disabled even if they had full insurance coverage.[1]

The Effects of Disability on Family Roles

It is rare that the effects of a disability stop with the affected person and do not affect his or her family. The reduction in the earnings potential of the disabled person raise the pressures for other family members to increase their earnings. If the disabled person had been primarily a household worker, then family chores will be reallocated. Table 6–1 gives some indication of the extent of such reallocation. The changes involve people who perform the activities now but do not do as much as before their condition began and those who do not perform the activities at all but had done so before. (Data are not available on people who perform certain tasks now but did not do them before.[2]) These shifts range from 14.5 percent of

1. This is not to say that insurance coverage has no effect on the behavior of the disabled person or even that providing coverage might not lead a few people to be more careless. It does imply that most people would probably prefer to be "well" and live a "normal" working life than have a disability that caused them to reduce their earnings by x percent and then to receive insurance payments to cover that loss. The question of the incentive effects of disability insurance will be discussed in more detail below.

2. The questionnaire does not precisely capture role changes. For instance, it is difficult to predict the responses to the survey of a disabled man who now stays home and does light housework and shopping while his wife has become the full time earner in the family.

Table 6–1. Percent Changes in Performance of Specific Activities Since the Onset of Disability [a]

| | Does Activity Now | | Does Not Do Activity Now | |
| | Do As Much As Before? | | Did This Activity Before Onset? | |
	Yes	No	Yes	No
Shopping for family needs	51.1	25.0	8.0	15.9
Heavy household chores	22.5	16.9	39.3	21.3
Light household chores	54.5	26.1	4.6	14.8
Taking care of money and bills	66.6	7.8	6.7	18.9
Parties at home, friends for dinner	37.5	17.0	17.1	28.4
Family outings, visits, clubs	47.2	27.0	13.5	12.3

[a]Based on the noninstitutionalized population aged 18–64 in the United States, 1966, with a disability onset after childhood. This is 89 percent of the total Survey of Disabled Adults. Special tabulation from the 1966 SDA.

disabled adults changing who takes care of money and bills to 56.2 percent who have reduced their heavy household chores. (Changes are indicated by the sum of columns 2 and 3.) Changes of these magnitudes imply that the usual family roles may become altered, or at least become subject to substantial strain. While the women's movement is currently challenging the standard roles in the family, role changes can impose substantial psychic costs upon the family when such changes are externally imposed.[3]

The Effects of Disability on Family Composition

A disability may even lead to a change in family composition so that a discussion of the effects on the family becomes even more complicated. For example, the nuclear family, having suffered the loss of primary income earner or home worker may invite relatives to live with them or may go to live with relatives. Furthermore, children who otherwise may have moved out may stay with their disabled parents.

It is extremely difficult to measure such changes in family composition because the census definition of a family includes all persons in the household who are related by blood, marriage, or adoption. The Survey of Disabled Adults, however, defines a "disability unit" as the disabled person, his or her spouse, and their unmarried children under age eighteen. Using this definition, 31 percent of disabled married persons and 61 percent of disabled unmarried persons have other relatives living with them (Swisher, 1970: 3). In contrast, estimates obtained from the U.S. Survey of Economic Opportunity suggest that only 15 percent of the "census definition families" include more than a single unit.

While these data suggest that the family composition of the disabled is substantially different than the average, Morgan et al. (1962: 237-38) came to the opposite conclusion:

> [C]ontrary to what might be expected, less combining of households occurs among the disabled than in the national population at large. Seventeen percent of all adult units in the national sample live in a relative's household, while 12 percent of all adult units with disabled members live in a relative's household. . . . The number of disabled who themselves house relatives is about the same as the national sample.

These conflicting results are probably attributable to (1) the differences between the rather narrowly defined "disability unit" and the broader "family-spending unit" and (2) the inclusion of the whole

3. See, for instance, Safilios-Rothschild, 1970: 271-78.

age range in the Morgan study. Very old and very young families are more likely to live with relatives regardless of disability status.

A second set of evidence concerning changes in composition can be drawn from SDA. About 11 percent of the disabled population whose onset of disability was in the previous five years reported a change in living arrangement. Health was given as the reason for this change in a quarter of these instances. The dominant reasons for family changes among the disabled, as with the nondisabled, are death of spouse or relative, divorce or separation of spouse, children left home, or marriage. Of course, disability may have been a factor in the reasons for divorce or marriage. It is also not known how many children did not leave home because of a disabled parent.[4]

Initial data from a followup survey of about a third of the people in the 1966 SDA are particularly revealing. The three year followup sample was limited to people who were disabled less than ten years in 1966 and who were not disabled in childhood.[5] Table 6—2 presents the distribution of these people according to their living arrangements in 1966 and 1969. A quick glance at the table suggests substantial stability in living arrangements but a more careful consideration raises a number of questions. (Unfortunately, there are no comparable followup data for a cohort of well adults.) For instance, it is not surprising that a very large fraction of disabled men and women aged eighteen to forty-four who were initially living with a spouse but not children in 1966 either remained in the same situation or added children in the three year period. It is surprising that even 3 percent of disabled males aged fifty-five to sixty-four added children to their households. These were probably grown children rather than infants. Among young childless couples, 8.7 percent of the disabled women and 18.4 percent of the disabled men were living alone three years later. This high separation rate may be a reflection of the strain on a relationship imposed by disability. Another situation in which disability affects family composition may be seen when the disabled person, spouse, and children lived together in 1966. The rather high proportions of older disabled men in this category (23 percent of those aged fifty-five to sixty-one and 10 percent of those aged sixty-two to sixty-four) suggest that the children are still in the household to replace the lost earnings of the father. This interpretation is supported by the very low proportion of disabled women in the same arrangement (5 and 0 percent, respectively).

4. These data are drawn directly from SDA.
5. Of course, not all of these people were still disabled in the followup survey—10.5 percent of those with a clear health status were listed as recovered. See Burdette, 1975: 34-35.

Table 6–2. Changes in Living Arrangements for Noninstitutionalized Disabled Adults, 1966 to 1969, Percentage Distribution by Age and Sex[a]

	Men					Women				
		Age in 1966					Age in 1966			
	Total	18–44	45–54	55–61	62–64	Total	18–44	45–54	55–61	62–64
Number (in thousands)	2,749	781	842	747	379	3,516	1,174	1,088	801	452
Living Arrangements of Disabled Persons										
Total percent	100.0	100.0	100.0	100.0	100.0	100.0	100.0	100.0	100.0	100.0
Alone in 1966	7.0	2.2	7.5	9.5	11.1	6.3	3.1	5.6	6.7	16.1
In 1969: Total percent	100.0	100.0	100.0	100.0	100.0	100.0	100.0	100.0	100.0	100.0
Alone	74.3	9.1	72.0	76.8	96.4	73.0	100.0	58.9	76.1	70.2
With spouse	7.1	45.5	—	7.4	—	7.9	—	7.2	3.0	16.8
With others	18.6	45.4	28.0	15.8	3.6	19.1	—	33.9	20.9	13.0
With spouse, no children in 1966	40.4	11.3	37.8	58.6	69.9	39.1	10.2	42.7	63.7	61.8
In 1969: Total percent	100.0	100.0	100.0	100.0	100.0	100.0	100.0	100.0	100.0	100.0
Same	91.3	60.5	94.7	94.2	91.0	85.2	74.8	87.6	86.6	82.2
With spouse, children	4.2	21.1	2.1	3.4	3.1	3.5	15.5	2.1	3.3	1.6
Alone	3.7	18.4	1.6	1.4	5.6	5.9	8.7	1.9	4.4	14.7
With others	0.8	—	1.6	1.0	0.3	5.4	1.0	8.4	5.7	1.5
With spouse, children in 1966	42.1	68.1	48.7	23.3	10.4	34.2	68.8	32.2	5.3	0.1
In 1969: Total percent	100.0	100.0	100.0	100.0	100.0	100.0	100.0	100.0	100.0	100.0
Same	73.8	83.5	72.3	49.4	65.4	75.4	84.0	59.3	43.4	—
Alone	1.0	1.8	0.2	—	—	—	—	—	—	—
Spouse, no children	23.5	11.5	27.1	50.2	32.7	17.9	7.7	37.0	54.7	100.0
With others	1.7	3.2	0.4	0.4	1.9	6.7	8.3	3.7	1.9	—

With others, or relatives in 1966										
In 1969: Total percent	10.5	18.4	6.0	8.6	8.6	20.4	17.8	19.5	24.3	22.0
	100.0	100.0	100.0	100.0	100.0	100.0	100.0	100.0	100.0	100.0
Same	52.8	55.1	59.0	39.5	58.1	58.3	64.8	51.3	66.4	43.3
Alone	20.8	20.0	26.2	23.3	15.1	14.7	10.6	14.9	13.9	27.7
With spouse	13.2	21.6	9.8	1.2	1.2	7.4	6.7	11.3	5.3	4.6
All others	13.2	3.3	5.0	36.0	25.6	19.6	17.9	22.5	14.4	24.4

[a] All persons included in this table were aged eighteen to sixty-four, did not have a childhood disability, and were disabled less than ten years in 1966.

Source: Derived from Burdette, 1975: 34–35.

While these interpretations must be considered tentative because there is no adequate control group, it does seem reasonable that disability affects family structure, thus making it particularly difficult to develop unambiguous measures of welfare based on the family unit. For example, how does one evaluate the effects on a family in which the children continue to live with their disabled parents and the resulting extended family is well above the poverty line? Some of the estimates to be presented below try to approximate "what would have been," but it should be recognized that this is basically an area about which little is known.

Societal Measures of Disability

It is also possible to develop measures of the effects of disability at a relatively global level, say for the nation as a whole. In that case, the variable of concern is the total productivity loss attributable to disability, or an estimate of how much larger gross national product would be if disability were to be eliminated. If one assumes that earnings reflect the marginal product of labor, then forgone earnings approximates the national cost of disability. Of course, what is true at the margin may not hold for large changes. The data presented here indicate that about 17 percent of the population aged eighteen to sixty-four has some disability. If they were to be cured overnight, it would take a while for the economy to adjust to that large an increment in the labor force. However, the aggregate measure is a useful one to consider when evaluating alternative programs.[6] As an example, a 10 percent reduction in the disabled population would probably reduce the aggregate loss by close to 10 percent and the adjustment problems would be minimal. This would not be true for a 50 percent reduction in disability.

EARNINGS LOSSES ATTRIBUTABLE TO DISABILITY[7]

The estimates derived in Chapter 5 for the effects of disabilities on the various aspects of labor market behavior may be used to calculate both individual and aggregate earnings losses attributable to disability, as shown in Table 6-3. (Note that these estimates only refer to the noninstitutionalized population and thus omit many of the most seriously disabled.) As was discussed before, health problems affect every aspect of labor market behavior, so the calculations must take

6. See, for instance, Rice, 1966.
7. Parts of this section were previously published in Luft, 1975 and are reprinted with the permission of the North-Holland Publishing Company.

into account not just the change in earnings per year for those who still work, but also the change in the overall participation rate. The losses attributable to the latter are straightforwardly estimated as the product of the adjusted difference in the participation rate and the estimated earnings per year for the disabled group. The losses for those who continued working is either obtained directly from the adjusted difference in EARNYEAR (Method A) or from its components, which are reduced weeks per year and reduced earnings per week (Method B). The two sets of estimates are within a few percent of each other.

The last four lines of the table provide summary measures of the average effects of disability on earnings. The average loss due to health per disabled adult is $1,445; this ranges from $575 per disabled black woman to $2,208 per disabled white man. The magnitudes of these losses may be seen by comparing them to the expected yearly earnings of these people (line 22). The average disabled black woman suffers an earnings loss equal to 37.8 percent of her yearly earnings. For a white man the figure is 35.8 percent. The greatest relative loss is suffered by a black man, who, with an average level of impairment, education, and job opportunities, can expect to lose nearly 45 percent of his already meager earnings because of his health problem.

Two measures of the sources of these losses are given in lines 23 and 24. Overall, a little more than half of the earnings loss is attributable to those people who drop out of the labor force because of their health problems. This proportion is much larger for black men than it is for white men, mirroring the discussion of the components of earnings in the previous chapter. The same relationship between races holds for women. These figures gain increased importance when it is remembered that this loss of more than half the earnings is borne by the 19 percent of the disabled who drop out entirely. In contrast to the average earnings losses of $1,445, their losses are $4,026 (line 5/line 3).

About a quarter of the total loss is atrributable to lower earnings per week, a combination of fewer hours and, more importantly, lower hourly wages. Nearly 30 percent of the earnings loss for white males comes from lower weekly earnings while the proportion for blacks is only about 17 percent. These figures reflect the greater ability of the white male, with an initially high earnings level, to adjust to a disability by continuing work at a lower paying job. Blacks and women, on the other hand, start out earning much less and are much more likely to drop out of the labor force because substitute jobs paying less are not as available.

Table 6–3. Earnings Losses Attributable to Disability—U.S. Noninstitutionalized Population Aged Eighteen to Sixty-Four, 1966

	Men		Women		Total
	White	Black	White	Black	
1. Population of Disabled Adults (000s)	6,396	855	6,847	1,290	15,388
Losses Due to Those Who Drop Out of Labor Force					
2. Adjusted Difference—LFPYEAR[a]	0.1775	0.2692	0.1797	0.2171	—
3. Person Years Lost (000s) (line 1 × 2)	1,135	230	1,230	280	2,875
4. Estimated Earnings per Year for the Disabled[a]	$ 6,174	$ 3,823	$ 2,264	$1,521	—
5. $ Loss, Millions (line 3 × 4)	$ 7,007	$ 879	$ 3,264	$ 426	$ 11,576
Losses Due to Those Who Remain in the Labor Force					
6. Method A: Labor Force (000s)	5,024	582	2,781	657	9,044
7. Adjusted Difference—EARNYEAR[a]	$ 1,416	$ 1,010	$ 951	$ 481	—
8. $ Loss, Millions (line 6 × 7)	$ 7,114	$ 588	$ 2,645	$ 316	$ 10,663
9. Method B: Labor Force (000s)	5,024	582	2,781	657	9,044
10. Adjusted Difference—WKSWORK[a]	4.39	7.15	8.16	7.73	—
11. Weeks Lost (000s) (line 9 × 10)	22,055	4,161	22,692	5,079	53,987
12. Expected EARNWKYR for the Disabled[a]	$130.21	$ 82.66	$ 62.86	$39.51	—
13. $ Loss for Lost Weeks, Millions (line 11 × 12)	$ 2,872	$ 344	$ 1,426	$ 201	$ 4,843
14. Actual WKSWORK[a]	42.33	38.24	32.21	30.40	—
15. Adjusted Difference EARNWKYR[a]	$ 19.74	$ 11.35	$ 12.07	$ 6.38	—
16. $ Loss for Weekly Wage, Millions (line 14 × 15)	$ 4,198	$ 253	$ 1,081	$ 127	$ 5,659
17. $ Loss Total, Millions (lines 13 + 16)	$ 7,070	$ 597	$ 2,507	$ 328	$ 10,502
18. Total Losses Due to Disability, $ millions (lines 5 + 8)	$14,121	$ 1,467	$ 5,909	$ 742	$ 22,239
19. Total Earnings in 1966, $ Millions—All Adults	$259,417	$19,109	$70,733	$7,489	$356,748

20. Earnings Loss Relative to Total Earnings (line 18/line 19)	0.054	0.077	0.084	0.099	0.062
21. Earnings Loss per Disabled Adult (line 18/line 1)	$ 2,208	$ 1,716	$ 868	$ 575	$ 1,445
22. Earnings Loss Relative to Annual Earnings per Disabled Adult (line 21/line 4)	0.358	0.449	0.325	0.378	—
23. Proportion of Loss Attributable to "Dropping Out" of the Labor Force (line 5/line 18)	0.496	0.599	0.552	0.574	0.521
24. Proportion of Loss Attributable to Lower Earnings Per Week (line 16/line 18)	0.297	0.172	0.183	0.171	0.254

aThese figures are derived from Table 5-13.

Comparisons with Other Studies

The rest of Table 6—3 provides aggregate measures of earnings losses for the noninstitutionalized population that give an estimate of the magnitude of the problem and allow a comparison with previous studies. The aggregate loss was $22.2 billion in 1966, or somewhat over 6 percent of the total earned income received by adults aged eighteen to sixty-four.[8] The total figures may be compared to the estimated loss of $14 billion for all spending unit heads in 1959 (Morgan et al., 1962: 248). Aside from the impact of inflation, that number should be smaller than ours because it refers only to spending unit heads; but on the other hand, it is inflated because there are no age limits. Two additional comparison figures are provided by Rice (1966) and by Cooper and Rice (1976). For 1963, Rice (1966: 41) estimated $15.1 billion as the earnings losses attributable to illness among the noninstitutionalized population. Aside from inflation and population growth adjustments, there are difficulties in comparing the two figures because Rice only uses age-sex-adjusted participation rates and does not consider the earnings losses attributable to lower earnings per hour, nor does she adjust for socioeconomic factors. Cooper and Rice (1976) have recently estimated the cost of illness in 1972 and find a total of 4.3 million person years or $36.1 billion in lost productivity among the noninstitutionalized population. Of this, $15.2 billion, or about half, was attributable to people "unable to work," a description similar to those who drop out of the labor force. Cooper and Rice include in their estimates an imputed value of the time lost by housewives due to illness, $4.4 billion for those still able to do some work. Our estimates do not include such a valuation, and if they are used to estimate the overall costs of disability, they should be revised to include such estimates (Brody, 1975).

If crude adjustments are made to control for differences in population coverage and inflation, all of these estimates are reasonably consistent. Thus, it appears that earnings losses attributable to health problems accounted for about 6 percent of total earnings, or $1,445 per disabled adult, over a third of their estimated earnings had they been well. The next section will translate these earnings losses into family income changes to estimate the influence of disability on the income distribution.

8. The overall earnings estimates are derived directly from the SEO sample of people aged eighteen to sixty-four. There is some evidence that the SEO estimate of total earned income is about 8 percent below the national income estimates (U.S. Office of Economic Opportunity, 1970: 10).

FROM EARNINGS TO INCOME:
THE EFFECTS OF DISABILITY
ON POVERTY

Most studies of poverty in the U.S. have concentrated on the money income of the family as the criterion for the evaluation of well-being. Although this measure has many shortcomings, it is useful to consider the family income of the disabled to obtain some overall estimates of the effects of health problems. The first part of this section will provide some overall, unadjusted estimates of the proportion of people who are poor and disabled. These figures will both set the stage for the estimates of the fraction of poverty caused by disability and provide some insight into who becomes impoverished and how some of the disabled escape poverty. The second part of the section offers our adjusted estimates concerning the effects of disability and the degree to which various transfer payments alleviate such poverty.

Estimates for Disability Units:
The Nuclear Family

Table 6—4 shows the median disability unit income by the life cycle status of the disabled person, as well as the proportion with unit incomes below the poverty level. Disability unit income refers to income from all sources received by the disabled person, his or her spouse, and their minor children. The life cycle status describes the overall family structure of the household, some of whose members may not be in the disability unit but who may contribute substantial income to the family. The income levels may be compared to approximate absolute levels or to the incomes of those with secondary disabilities whose incomes tend to approximate those of well adults. These data indicate the extremely low incomes of the nonmarried disabled household heads and severely disabled married men. Married women who are disabled have lower family incomes but do not suffer extensive losses even if they are severely disabled. The lower incomes for married men and women without children in the household are probably due to the fact that most of these couples are substantially older than the others, and it is in this group that both husband and wife are more likely to be disabled.

The effects of disability can also be evaluated by considering the proportion of families with unit income at or below the Social Security Administration poverty line adjusted for family composition.[9]

9. This poverty line is adjusted for family size and composition, urban-rural residence, and other factors to provide a measure of equivalent levels of living for families of different size. See Orshansky, 1965: 3–29, for a more extensive discussion.

Table 6—4. Median Unit Income and Percentage At or Below Poverty Line by Life Cycle, Disability Status, and Sex of Disabled Persons Aged Eighteen to Sixty-Four, U.S., 1965

Disability Status	Young Dependent Adults < 45	Married Head or Spouse			Non-married Heads	Older Dependent Adults
		With Minor Children	Adult Children Only	No Children		
Median Unit Income						
Men: Severe disability	$ 397	$2,939	$3,890	$3,251	$1,204	$ 911
Occupational disability	1,007	6,547	5,874	5,528	3,128	1,515
Secondary disability	2,081	6,742	7,123	6,103	3,045	840
Women: Severe disability	550	5,348	5,907	3,979	1,266	553
Occupational disability	406	5,556	5,693	4,659	1,716	474
Secondary disability	782	7,545	7,179	6,245	2,681	1,571
Percent At or Below Poverty Line						
Men: Severe disability	91.2	60.0	20.4	30.0	66.9	72.8
Occupational disability	66.5	20.0	10.4	13.5	46.7	49.7
Secondary disability	43.9	11.0	6.2	13.9	31.9	61.3
Women: Severe disability	86.2	28.8	13.1	20.6	70.1	82.4
Occupational disability	75.7	27.9	18.9	18.2	55.5	79.1
Secondary disability	60.3	10.1	13.0	21.2	33.8	46.3

Source: Swisher, 1971: 62, 66.

Except for those who are married, almost any degree of disability will result in incomes such that there is nearly a 50 percent chance of being poor. More importantly, even among the category of husband-wife families with either the head or spouse disabled, there were 2.45 million such families below the poverty line. This was about 77 percent of all poor, nonaged husband-wife families in 1966.[10]

Estimates for the Extended Family

Table 6−4 presented data concerning the situation of the disability unit, namely, the disabled person, spouse, and minor children. The first section of this chapter pointed out that one way in which people may adjust to the earnings losses caused by disability is by expanding the family unit. Table 6−5 provides the median family income of all related persons in the household, by the life cycle status of the disabled person.[11] These data show that the median incomes of married couples with no children or only minor children are only slightly higher if all family income is considered, indicating that few other income recipients are in such families. The presence of adult children in the family does boost the pooled resources substantially. But such families comprise only 13 percent of the "married head/or spouse" families. Similar increases are found for dependent adults, although substantial numbers of them are still poor, especially the more seriously disabled older men. The disparity between median unit and family incomes for "dependent" adults and husband-wife families with adult children strongly suggest that these unusual family structures were created to pool incomes and cushion the effects of disability.

Although the proportion of families with *family* income under the poverty line is not available, it is possible to consider the number of families with incomes below $3,000. In 1965 there were 5,022,000 families and 3,448,000 unrelated individuals with the head of household between the ages of fourteen and sixty-four who had incomes under $3,000 (U.S. Bureau of the Census, 1966: 2). Of this group, 4.86 million, or 57 percent, included at least one disabled person. Furthermore, between 56 and 76 percent of the 5.02 million families with incomes under $3,000 included a disabled adult.[12] Considering

10. This estimate is derived from Swisher, 1971: 62; and Orshansky, 1967: 188, 192; with a few adjustments described in Luft, 1972: 200.

11. In a few cases the median income of the family is shown to be below that of the unit. This may be due to business losses of other family members, but it is more likely due to somewhat different samples. This results from nonresponses about family income although unit income was available.

12. These proportions are derived from data presented in Swisher (1970) and the data discussed in the preceding census reference. Luft (1972: 202-203), dis-

Table 6—5. Median Family Income by Life Cycle, Disability Status, and Sex of Disabled Persons Aged Eighteen to Sixty-Four, U.S., 1965

Disability Status	Young Dependent Adults < 45	Married Head or Spouse			Non-married Heads	Older Dependent Adults
		With Minor Children	Adult Children Only	No Children		
Men: Severe	$4,384	$3,188	$5,848	$3,201	$1,315	$1,927
Occupational	6,682	6,820	8,238	5,514	4,331	1,657
Secondary	9,434	7,106	10,699	6,232	3,090	4,263
Women: Severe	3,936	5,631	8,610	3,791	1,355	3,981
Occupational	3,827	5,862	7,947	4,762	2,427	4,812
Secondary	6,684	8,099	11,331	6,250	3,284	10,886

Source: Swisher, 1970: 26.

only families with at least a husband and wife and the man under age sixty-five, about 64 percent of such families with incomes under $3,000 include a disabled adult. An alternative way of examining the relationship between disability and income is by noting that, although 11 percent of nondisabled families and individuals aged fourteen to sixty-four had incomes under $3,000 in 1965, the comparable proportion for the disabled is 32 percent.

Three Estimates of Family Income of the Disabled

The above estimates clearly indicate that disabled persons comprise a very large fraction of people who are poor. But results in Chapters 3 and 4 have shown that the poor are more likely to become disabled. Furthermore, once a person becomes disabled, he or she may alter living arrangements and/or receive transfer payments to reduce the effects of his or her own earnings loss. Using the SEO sample and some of the equations discussed in Chapter 5, it is possible to obtain three estimates of family income for disabled persons in 1967. These values are (1) expected family earnings had the individual been well, (2) actual family earnings, and (3) actual family income including all transfer payments.[13] Several measures of the effects of disability based on these data are given in Table 6–6.

The relative losses of earnings and income are substantial and in the expected pattern. Overall, health problems reduce expected family earnings by nearly 16 percent (line 4), but this varies from 28 percent among black men to 11 percent among white women. The effects are relatively greater for men than for women and for blacks than for whites. If the loss in income (line 5) is considered, the relative pattern is the same for men, but the high poverty levels among black women, even if they were well, produces unclear results. The

cusses the estimation of the upper and lower bounds on the proportion with incomes under $3,000.

13. These figures are derived in the following manner. "Expected yearly earnings" is the sum of the actual earnings of all adult family members living with the disabled person and the "expected" earnings of the disabled person. (This imparts an upward bias to the estimates of family income if the family is larger or if some members are working who would not have been had there not been a disability in the family.) The "expected" earnings figure is derived from the predicted level of labor force participation and of yearly earnings if in the labor force. These values, in turn, were derived by using the appropriate race-sex equation from the sample of well adults and the specific characteristics of the disabled person, as in Chapter 5. "Actual family earnings" includes all reported income (including that of the disabled person) minus transfers (social security, government pensions, veterans' pensions, private pensions, workmen's compensation, public welfare payments, and unemployment insurance payments). "Actual family income" does not exclude these transfers.

Table 6—6. Measures of Earnings and Income Losses Among the Families of Disabled Persons Aged Eighteen
to Sixty-Four, U.S., 1967

	White Male	Black Male	White Female	Black Female	Total
Estimated earnings and incomes					
(1) Expected earnings	$8,468	$4,923	$6,621	$3,760	$7,043
(2) Actual earnings	6,789	3,524	5,929	3,279	5,922
(3) Actual income (including transfers)	7,404	4,111	6,509	3,911	6,522
(4) Relative earnings loss ((1) − (2))/(1)	0.198	0.284	0.105	0.128	0.159
(5) Relative income loss ((1) − (3))/(1)	0.126	0.165	0.017	−0.040	0.074

Source: See footnote 13.

difficulty is that the expected earnings levels for disabled black women is even below their actual incomes, seemingly suggesting that it pays to become disabled. It is unlikely that such is really the case. The reason for the anomalous results rests with the exclusion of all transfer payments from the "expected" income measure and attributing all such payments to disability. This was done because it is impossible to determine the true reason for transfer payments. However, it is clear that many black women would have been poor even if well, and thus probably would have received some transfers anyway.

Disability and Income Distribution

The availability of individual observations in the SEO makes it possible to examine the effects of disability in changing the shape of the income distribution curve. As the basic interest is in the effects of disability on family well-being, a poverty ratio measure is used. This is simply the relevant family income divided by the Social Security Administration income cutoffs for the poverty line. These figures are provided by SEO and are based on farm, nonfarm status, age and sex of family head, and number of related children under the age of eighteen. These cutoffs are the ones used to officially define the extent of poverty and are based on estimates of living costs. To provide a benchmark, the cutoff for a nonfarm, male-headed family with spouse and two children is $3,473. Table 6–7 provides estimates of the proportion of families with poverty ratios below specific levels.[14]

These figures make possible a number of comparisons and interpretations. First, a rough comparison may be made between the distributions of well families and disabled families based on expected earnings. Because transfer payments and some other minor income sources are omitted in the latter measure, it would be expected that the income distributions in column 2 are biased downward.[15] Even with this bias, the distributions in columns 1 and 2 are roughly similar for white and black men. In fact, the proportion of disabled white

---

14. These figures help explain the anomalous results for black women in the preceding table. For instance, column 1 indicates that almost 36 percent of black women without a disability were in families below the poverty line. Furthermore, this figure includes transfer payments, many of which are dependent on the extent to which a family is impoverished. Thus, it is very likely that at least some of the transfers received by disabled black women would have been given them even if they had been well. The same is true, but to a much lesser degree, for white women.

15. In conventional terms, the graph of families plotted against the income measure would be shifted to the left, or the proportion apparently in poverty is greater than is truly the case.

Table 6–7. Proportions of Families with and without a Disabled Adult, Aged Eighteen to Sixty-Four, with Family Incomes Below Various Poverty Ratios—1967

Race-Sex Group and Income Category	(1) Well Families — Total Income Including Transfers	(2) Expected Earnings	(3) Actual Earnings	(4) Total Income Including Transfers	(5) (Col. 3) – (Col. 2)	(6) (Col. 4) – (Col. 2)	(7) (Col. 3)/(Col. 2)	(8) (Col. 4)/(Col. 2)
		Families With A Disabled Adult						
All Persons								
Poverty Ratio < 0.50	0.043	0.067	0.239	0.081	0.172	0.014	3.57	1.21
< 0.75	0.072	0.115	0.298	0.164	0.183	0.049	2.59	1.43
< 1.00	0.110	0.168	0.351	0.241	0.183	0.073	2.09	1.43
< 1.50	0.210	0.285	0.462	0.389	0.177	0.104	1.62	1.36
< 2.50	0.488	0.546	0.669	0.635	0.123	0.089	1.23	1.16
White Men								
Poverty Ratio < 0.50	0.023	0.016	0.185	0.050	0.169	0.034	11.56	3.13
< 0.75	0.041	0.030	0.239	0.120	0.209	0.090	7.97	4.00
< 1.00	0.069	0.047	0.291	0.186	0.244	0.139	6.19	3.96
< 1.50	0.155	0.123	0.398	0.325	0.275	0.202	3.24	2.64
< 2.50	0.435	0.389	0.615	0.568	0.226	0.179	1.58	1.46
Black Men								
Poverty Ratio < 0.50	0.084	0.054	0.402	0.192	0.348	0.138	7.44	3.56
< 0.75	0.149	0.161	0.492	0.358	0.331	0.197	3.06	2.22
< 1.00	0.232	0.274	0.566	0.493	0.282	0.219	2.07	1.80
< 1.50	0.417	0.469	0.726	0.684	0.257	0.215	1.55	1.46
< 2.50	0.703	0.782	0.868	0.857	0.086	0.075	1.11	1.10

White Women

Poverty Ratio								
< 0.50	0.044	0.070	0.228	0.064	0.158	−0.006	3.25	0.91
< 0.75	0.072	0.127	0.285	0.137	0.158	0.010	2.24	1.08
< 1.00	0.106	0.195	0.332	0.212	0.137	0.017	1.70	1.09
< 1.50	0.200	0.329	0.434	0.351	0.105	0.022	1.32	1.07
< 2.50	0.478	0.599	0.648	0.618	0.049	0.019	1.08	1.03

Black Women

Poverty Ratio								
< 0.50	0.150	0.310	0.457	0.243	0.147	−0.067	1.47	0.78
< 0.75	0.246	0.432	0.529	0.391	0.097	−0.041	1.22	0.91
< 1.00	0.355	0.538	0.604	0.499	0.066	−0.039	1.12	0.93
< 1.50	0.531	0.710	0.750	0.709	0.040	−0.001	1.06	1.00
< 2.50	0.778	0.870	0.916	0.900	0.046	0.030	1.05	1.03

Note: The "identified person" in the table, e.g., white man, was identified as being between eighteen and sixty-four and either well or disabled. Then the data from the rest of the family was included to derive the family poverty ratio. Thus, many disabled families include well persons and some well families include a disabled adult; that is, families are included as many times as there are adults aged eighteen to sixty-four. This should not cause any difficulty in interpreting the results.

men with low expected family earnings is even smaller than the actual proportions for well white men. This is consistent with the findings of the latter part of Chapter 5 that showed higher participation rates and weeks worked for disabled white men, had they been well. Furthermore, the data in Table 6–7 are not adjusted for the different age distributions in the two groups; the disabled are older, and older workers tend to earn more. Among women, the expected earnings levels indicate greater degrees of impoverishment. In part, this may be due to the exclusion of transfer payments.

The evaluation of the impoverishing effects of disability depends, in large part, on the choice of measures. One can examine the absolute proportion of people with incomes under various poverty ratios, as in columns 2 to 4; the fraction of people who shift below a given ratio, relative to their expected position, as in columns 5 and 6; or the relative shifts, as in columns 7 and 8. For instance, from column 3 it is apparent that 29 percent of disabled white men would have family earnings below the poverty line, rather close to the 33 percent for disabled white women. However, less than 5 percent of the men would have been poor if not disabled (column 2) versus nearly 20 percent of the white women. Thus, disability may be seen as the cause of shifting 24 percent (column 5) of all white men from above to below the poverty line, while "only" 14 percent of white women suffer a similar movement. Another way of looking at the effects of disability is to say that, based on actual versus expected earnings, 6.2 times as many white men are poor because of their disability (column 7). In contrast, "only" 1.7 times as many white women are poor as would be otherwise expected. The primary focus here is on the consequences of health problems, not the overall inequity of income distribution. It must be remembered, however, that the relative effects of disability-caused impoverishment are likely to be very different if some major income redistribution scheme is adopted. (In particular, the "relatively small" effects of disability for women are due to their greater general levels of impoverishment.) On the other hand, the more modest changes necessary to correct some of the purely health effects may be more politically feasible.

The various measures in Table 6–7 point to a number of important results. First considering all persons, the basic effect of disability is to reduce family earnings such that 18 percent of the families are moved from above to below a poverty ratio (PR) of 1.50. More importantly, column 5 indicates that all of this shift appears in the very lowest category, PR $<$ 0.50, while the fraction of families in each of the other categories remains about constant.[16] This shift would more than triple the number of families in the very lowest category and double the number below the poverty line (column 7). Transfer payments considerably improve the picture. Only 8.1 percent of all "disabled families" are actually in the lowest bracket, in contrast to an expected fraction of 6.7 percent had they been well, an increase of about 20 percent (column 8). However, while it appears that transfers are primarily helpful in removing families from the very lowest levels, there are still 43 percent more families below the poverty line (0.241 of the total) than would be expected based on predicted earnings levels (0.168 of the total).

The impoverishing effects of disability are very different for each race-sex group. Among white men, there is generally very little poverty, less than 5 percent of the families would be expected to be below the poverty line. Based on actual earnings, almost a quarter of the families shift below the poverty line, yielding a total of 29 percent poor, a sixfold increase. By far the greatest shift is into the very lowest poverty ratio bracket, but there are net increases for all four of the bottom categories. Transfers make the largest absolute and relative difference for the very lowest levels, but even so, 14 percent of disabled white men are in families below the poverty line that would normally be expected to be above the line.

Black men are much more likely to be in poverty even if well, so the relative effects of disability are smaller for them than for white men. The absolute effects, however, are even greater. Among white men, while a quarter were shifted below the poverty line based on earnings, only 17 percent fell as far as 50 percent below the poverty line. For black men, only a somewhat larger fraction, 28 percent went from above to below the poverty line, but there was substantially more shifting to the very lowest levels; fully 35 percent moved

---

16. This is implied by the nearly constant difference in the first four categories between the cumulative distributions for expected and actual earnings. This can be seen rather vividly if the proportion of families in each category, rather than the cumulative proportion, is computed from columns 2 and 3. These figures are given below:

Proportion of Families in Each Poverty Ratio Category

	≥ 0.50 < 0.50	≥ 0.75 < 0.75	≥ 1.00 < 1.00	≥ 1.50 < 1.50	< 2.50	≥ 2.50
Expected Earnings	0.067	0.048	0.053	0.117	0.261	0.454
Actual Earnings	0.239	0.059	0.053	0.111	0.207	0.331

It is clear that the proportion of families in categories 2 to 4 is essentially constant while the large net shift into the lowest category is balanced primarily by families shifted out of the PR ≥ 2.50 category.

below the 0.50 PR level. (These findings confirm those of Chapter 5 concerning relative earnings before and after disability.) Furthermore, transfer payments are not nearly as effective in removing disabled black males from poverty; 22 percent more than would be expected are still below the poverty line.

The effects of women's health problems on their family income is substantially different. For both white and black women, disability leads to a net shifting of families from all categories but the bottom into the lowest bracket, if transfer payments are not considered. This pattern is similar to that shown by black men. Transfers help bring the income distributions for families of disabled women about back to what would be expected based on predicted earnings levels. This is a reflection not so much of the effectiveness of transfer payments as the very large fractions of disabled women who are poor by any standard—about 20 percent of white women and 50 percent of black women. The results for women are clouded by the fact that there are two distinct subgroups: (1) unmarried women who are very likely to be poor and also to be eligible for some transfers regardless of their health, and (2) married women whose earnings are likely to be small relative to their husbands' and who, therefore, are unlikely to receive transfer payments.

Disability, Transfer Payments, and Income

The various measures of impoverishment and the ameliorating effects of transfers are summarized in Table 6−8. This can be seen by examining lines 1 to 3: less than 5 percent of white men but almost 54 percent of black women who became disabled would have had less than poverty level earnings even if they were well. Thus, the results for black women and some of the other groups must be treated with caution. Line 5 provides an estimate of the proportion of families that are currently measured as being poor but who would not have been poor had they been well. Nearly three-quarters of disabled white men who were poor would not have been so had they been well. The impact is less among the other groups but, in part, this is due to the omission of all transfer payments from "expected income" where the effect of this bias is greater. As was discussed above, the low estimates for the effects of disability on women are a result of the much larger fraction of women who are "usually" in poverty, the availability of other earnings if they are married, and data limitations. The results of the preceding chapter indicate that the economic effects of disability are comparable for men and women. Given the steadily increasing role of women in the labor force and the increase in single parent families, it is reasonable to expect

Table 6—8. Proportion of Families of Disabled Persons Aged Eighteen to Sixty-Four in Poverty, Based on Several Measures of Income—U.S., 1967

	White Male	Black Male	White Female	Black[a] Female	Total
Proportion in poverty based on:					
(1) Expected earnings	0.047	0.274	0.195	0.538	0.168
(2) Actual earnings	0.291	0.566	0.332	0.604	0.351
(3) Actual income (including transfers)	0.186	0.493	0.212	0.499	0.241
(4) Proportion shifted below the poverty line, based on family earnings (line 2 − line 1)	0.244	0.282	0.137	0.066	0.183
(5) Proportion currently poor because of disability (line 3 − line 1)/line 3	0.747	0.444	0.080	−0.078	0.303
(6) Proportion impoverished by disability who are lifted out of poverty by transfers (line 3 − line 1)/line 4	0.570	0.777	0.124	−0.591	0.399

Source: See Table 6–7.
[a]See text and footnote 14.

196 Poverty and Health

that the relative effects of disability on women in 1977 are even greater than they were in 1967.

The last line in Table 6−8 provides a crude measure of the effectiveness of transfer payments in raising disabled families who otherwise would be poor back above the poverty line. Overall, only about 40 percent of those families impoverished by disability were lifted out of poverty. It must be remembered that all forms of transfer payments are included in this estimate, not just those related to disability.[17]

These data also allow a rough computation of the effects of disability on the overall distribution of income.[18] As indicated in Table 6−7, 11 percent of well families are below the poverty line. If the actual population weights are used to combine the well and disabled groups using the actual income, including transfers, of the disabled, then 13 percent of the total are in poverty, an 18 percent increase. It must be remembered that the disabled are somewhat more likely to have been poor even if well. Based on their expected earnings, 16.8 percent of the disabled would have been poor (this is an upper estimate because it excludes all transfers), implying that for the total distribution, 11.9 percent of the families would have been poor. Thus, disability accounts for between 9.2 and 18.2 percent of the poverty population. For white men, who are much less likely to be impoverished if well, the figures are substantially more dramatic. Between 23.2 and 30.8 percent of all poverty among white men is attributable to disabilities. These figures may even underestimate the role of disability in poverty because they do not take account of families with more than one disabled person. Data from the Survey of Disabled Adults indicates that about 40 percent of disabled persons had a disabled spouse.[19]

17. The reasoning behind this extreme assumption, which unfortunately biases the results for black women, is that it is essentially impossible to determine why certain payments are given. If one examines the list in footnote 13, it should be clear that any type of payment could be directly or indirectly related to a disability or its consequences. Thus, we chose to attribute as much as possible to disability-related payments and still found them effective for only 40 percent of the affected group.

18. It is difficult to directly compare these data with usual measures of income distribution for several reasons. First, they are limited to people aged eighteen to sixty-four. Second, each adult in the family is identified and counted once in the distribution, although total family income is used each time. Thus, the distribution is based on families weighted by the number of adults per family. Third, some extreme assumptions are made with respect to transfer payments, as discussed above.

19. A second source of bias is introduced in the well family distribution, some of whose families include other persons who are disabled. This will lead to an underestimate of the proportion of the poor who are so because of disability.

THE ECONOMIC CAUSES AND
CONSEQUENCES OF HEALTH
PROBLEMS OVER TIME

All of the analyses in this book are based on cross-sectional data—
that is, the behavior of a given sample of people at a given time, or
at best, over a period of a few years. Questions may be asked about
the stability of the relationships over time and whether our results
are sensitive to the particular years for which there are data—1966
to 1967. The two parts of the problem—the causes and the consequences—are more difficult to disentangle, and there are only frag-
mentary data available.

Business Cycle Factors and Health Problems

There is some evidence that broad economic factors have a substantial influence on the causes of health problems. For instance,
increases in employment lead to the hiring of an increased proportion of inexperienced workers and thus an increase in the work-
injury rate (U.S., Office of the President, 1972: 59). The boom part
of the cycle also leads to putting older and more marginal equipment
in service which may also result in higher accident rates. Recessions
also take their toll. Cyclical changes in unemployment are likely to
alter the mix of job types (e.g., blue versus white collar) and thus the
interactions of job opportunities and impairments.

M. Harvey Brenner has undertaken a number of studies linking
various health problems to economic fluctuations. For instance, in a
major investigation of admissions to mental hospitals in New York
State over a 127 year period, he finds that there are significant correlations between economic fluctuations and almost all categories of
admissions (Brenner, 1973). Brenner argues that there are at least
two causal relationships between economic fluctuations and mental
hospital admissions (Ibid., 239). The first is that economic downturns bring about increases in psychiatric symptoms, largely through
an increase in social disorientation. The second is that downturns
bring about increases in intolerance of mental illness. While there
may be some questions raised about Brenner's statistical methodology and conclusions, there appears to be little doubt that macroeconomic factors do have an influence on individual health.[20]
Furthermore, given the influence of psychological stress on other
health problems, it is not surprising that relationships are found

20. See, for instance, Eyer, 1976A: 139-48; Brenner, 1976: 149-55; and
Eyer, 1976B: 157-68.

between periods of economic downturns and distilled alcohol consumption and subsequent mental hospitalization and, with a two year lag, mortality due to cirrhosis of the liver (Brenner, 1975B). Brenner (1975A) has also found that cardiovascular-renal diseases tend to be related to general economic activity: recessions are followed one to three years later by peaks in hospital admissions and three to five years later by peaks in mortality.

Business Cycle Variables and Estimates
of Disability

An impressive amount of evidence is beginning to accumulate that indicates an influence from the general state of the economy on health problems. But, it is unlikely that these results will seriously throw into question the findings of cross-sectional studies, for two reasons. The first is that the business cycle seems to affect different health problems with different lags. Thus, while there may be some differences in the relative distribution of problems from year to year, it is unlikely that the overall rate of illness or disability varies very much. Second, the analyses of Brenner and others have been focused on the extent to which deviations from the average or trend are correlated with changes in economic activity. In some ways this is like focusing on the dog's tail because it moves around a lot while ignoring the total body mass. If one is interested in what varies, then Brenner's type of analysis is appropriate. If we are concerned with the overall magnitude of health problems and their effects, then we must also consider the much larger, invariant mass.

Figure 6–1 presents some data drawn from the annual Health Interview Survey concerning the prevalence of chronic conditions since 1957 and the unemployment rate for those years. The unemployment rate varies from 3.5 to 6.8 percent around a mean of about 5 percent, or about ± 30 percent. The proportion of people unable to carry on their usual major activity varied less than ± 7 percent. In fact, changes in interviewing procedure account for a break in the series in 1967 that is equivalent to a 38 percent increase. There is substantially more variation in the proportion of people who are limited in the amount or kind of major activity, but here, too, there is reason to suspect that interviewing changes are probably as important as real changes in chronic health problems.

The difficulty in interpreting anything but the "hardest" clinical data was discussed in some detail in Chapter 3.[21] One major concern

21. In fact, there is substantial evidence that "hard clinical data" are subject to very high rates of differential interpretation, or inter- and intrarater variability. See, for instance, Spodick (1975: 592–96), who also points out some of the biasing effects of external information.

is that in periods of economic recession, people who are unemployed for reasons entirely unrelated to health will claim that their health problem is the reason for their not working. The data in Figure 6–1 suggest that this is not an important problem in the overall estimates. If there is a relationship, it would be expected to appear rather rapidly and not with any substantial lags. In any case, the cross-sectional data used in this study are from 1966–1967, years of extremely low unemployment in the postwar period.

It is likely that the economy plays an important role in altering the effects of a given set of health problems. There are two aspects to this: the demand and supply of labor. On the demand side, it is reasonable to expect that in periods of economic recession, employers will hire and try to retain only the most productive workers. This will tend to make it even more difficult than in stable periods for people with some health problem to maintain their earnings. When the economy is undergoing a boom, some of the disabled who would normally not be working or only be working part time may be drawn into the full-time sector. This phenomenon has often been described in terms of the "discouraged worker" and is especially used to explain the behavior of married women and others who are not "required" to work full time (Rosett, 1958; Mincer, 1962). The parallels between the disabled and the married woman stem largely from the supply response. In both cases there are at least partially viable alternatives to full-time work in the labor market. For the married woman, it is providing more services at home while her husband provides the cash income. For the disabled person, it is subsisting on the income transfers available to disabled people. During a recession, the expected value of potential earnings falls and the relative attractiveness of the fixed rewards from household work or disability payments rises. There is some evidence for the disabled population supporting this hypothesis. Using quarterly data from 1964 to 1971, Hambor (1975) has found that there was a positive and highly significant response of the rate of applications for Social Security disability benefits to the unemployment rate. Thus, if one relies upon data based on benefit payments, there may be some bias introduced by the changing relative attractiveness of disability benefits during the business cycle. However, there is little evidence that this bias affects self-classification of disabilities that include being able to work but with some difficulty. In any case, if there is some bias, it will be to make our figures an underestimate of the effects of health problems when the economy is at less than full employment.

Figure 6–1. Measures of Chronic Conditions and the Unemployment Rate, 1957–1974

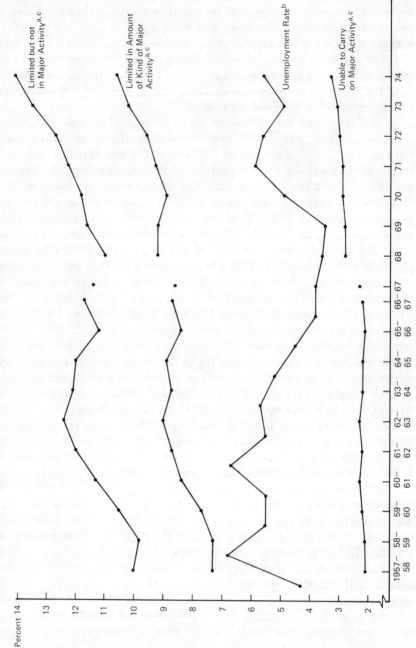

[a]USNCHS "Limitation of Activity and Mobility Due to Chronic Conditions, U.S. 1972," *Vital and Health Statistics*, Series 10, no. 96, DHEW Pub. No. (HRA) 75–1523 (Washington, D.C.: USGPO, November 1974), p. 3. For the period until July 1967, these data are on a fiscal year basis; thereafter, a calendar year. A major change in questionnaire design took place in 1967.

[b]U.S. Department of Labor, *Manpower Report of the President* (Washington, D.C.: USGPO, 1975), p. 203.

[c]USNCHS "Current Estimates From the Health Interview Survey, U.S., 1974," *Vital and Health Statistics*, Series 10, no. 100, DHEW Pub. No. (HRA) 76–1527 (Washington, D.C.: USGPO, September 1975), p. 3.

SUMMARY

This chapter has attempted to bring into perspective the results of our analyses concerning the economic effects of health problems. These effects may be considered at various levels: the individual, his or her immediate or extended family, or the nation as a whole. The greatest relative economic losses are found by focusing only on the earnings of the disabled person whose actual earnings are 35 percent below the expected or predicted levels. These losses are cushioned, to some degree, by adjustments within the family. Other family members increase their earnings and chores, and family roles are altered. There is also some evidence that disability leads to somewhat atypical family structures with more adult children and dependent adults than is usual for the United States. It is impossible to set a value on the psychic costs associated with such family adjustments. On the aggregate level, it is much easier to approximate the productivity loss associated with disability by the earnings that would have been received by the disabled had they been well. While such aggregate measures are of limited usefulness, they do allow comparisons with other studies that indicate rather close agreement in magnitudes.

There are many different ways of measuring the effects of disability on poverty, and all point to a rather substantial influence. As is well known, a great many of the nonaged poor are disabled. What is surprising is that among poor, husband-wife families, well over half include a disabled adult. While the poor have a somewhat higher probability of disability, this accounts for only a small part of the observed difference. Disability causes such a large loss of earnings that 18 percent of all disabled families would be moved into poverty, if not for transfer payments. Furthermore, almost all of the shift is to the very lowest level, which is earnings less than half the poverty line. Transfer payments help somewhat, but their primary effect is to remove families from the very lowest levels while still leaving them below the poverty line. As has been seen in Chapter 5, the effects of disability are different for each race-sex group, partly because of the direct effects of the disability, and partly because of the general socioeconomic environment which results in very different poverty rates among well people of different races and sexes.

A final perspective on the question of the economic causes and consequences of health problems is from the viewpoint of cyclical changes with respect to the economy. Very little research has been undertaken in this area, but it appears that at least some health problems are both theoretically and empirically causally related to the business cycle. The effects of given problems on labor force behavior also appear to be related to the general demand for labor and the relative attractiveness of market-oriented work. In any event, these cyclical patterns seem to affect only a small fraction of the people involved, and since our data come from a period of full employment, they probably represent lower bound estimates.

In addition to these general findings, some of the specific results of this chapter are:

1. There are substantial changes among disabled adults in who performs various household chores. Depending upon the activity, between 15 and 56 percent of the disabled adults change roles.
2. There is some evidence that the family living arrangements of the disabled change so as to provide additional sources of income to substitute for that lost by the disabled earner.
3. The average disabled person earns $1,445 less per year than would be expected if well. This ranges from $575 per disabled black woman to $2,208 per disabled white man. The range largely reflects the wide variation in normal or expected earnings levels; the losses represent from 33 percent to 45 percent of expected earnings. A little more than half the total earnings loss is accounted for by the 19 percent of the disabled who have dropped out of the labor force for the whole year—their average earnings loss is $4,026.
4. While disability results in a 35 percent reduction in the earnings of the disabled, the family earnings of the disabled fall "only" 16 percent, reflecting the activity of other family members. This is still large enough to shift at least 18 percent of all families with a disabled adult below the poverty line if transfer payments are not taken into account. All of this estimated shift is into the very lowest group—families with incomes more than 50 percent below the poverty line.
5. Transfer payments of all types are primarily helpful in removing the impoverished from the very lowest income levels. Among the disabled, there is still at least a 43 percent increase in poor families over what would be expected had they not been disabled. In fact, only 40 percent of the nonaged families impoverished by disability were lifted back out of poverty by transfer payments.
6. The absolute and relative effects of disability vary substantially by race and sex. A quarter of the families of disabled white men would be shifted into poverty based on their earnings alone, and 14 percent are still impoverished even after transfer payments are included. Thus, even with transfers, the proportion of disabled white men who are poor is four times what would have been the

case had they been well. An even larger proportion of black men are shifted below the poverty line by their disability, and fewer are helped by transfers. Because of the normally higher poverty levels of blacks, however, disability accounts for less than a doubling of the proportion in poverty. While disability has a substantial impact on women's earnings, only a small fraction of them are shifted into poverty by their disability. This is due to a combination of the availability of their spouse's earnings in some instances and their normally very high levels of impoverishment in others.

7. Overall, it may be conservatively estimated that 30 percent of all poor families with a disabled adult aged eighteen to sixty-four are poor because of the disability. For families with a disabled white man, the proportion who are poor because of disability rises to 75 percent.

8. In the aggregate, disability among noninstitutionalized adults aged eighteen to sixty-four accounted for a $22.2 billion earnings loss in 1967. This is about 6 percent of all earnings in that year.

9. Even with transfer payments, disability is responsible for at least 9 to 18 percent of all poverty among the nonaged. Similarly, at least 23 to 31 percent of all nonaged poor white men are poor because of their disability.

Chapter 7

Conclusions and Policy Proposals

The three primary foci of this book have been (1) the investigation of socioeconomic factors leading to health problems, (2) the identification of the magnitudes of the effects of health problems, and (3) the factors that help alleviate the impact of health problems. This concluding chapter will move from the empirical discussion to policy proposals. These proposals go substantially beyond most existing policy discussion. It is hoped, however, that the basic concepts may be helpful in the subsequent design of policy.

This chapter begins by reviewing some of the results of the preceding chapters. The first section summarizes the magnitude of the effects of health problems. The second section examines different causes of health problems: genetics, specific external agents, and psychosocial stresses. These causes may also be classified by two major behavioral environments—occupational and lifestyle. Viewing health problems as having different primary causes and behavioral environments leads to a multifaceted approach to health promotion. Before outlining the policy recommendations, however, the third section sets the stage by presenting two polar approaches—the interventionist and the market strategy. Each has advantages and disadvantages, and I present my preferences for a balance of the two. The fourth section suggests policies aimed at the specific problems outlined in the preceding chapters. It has three subsections dealing with (1) reducing the incidence of health problems, (2) reducing the severity of health problems, and (3) reducing the impact of disability on family income. While the fourth section focuses on relatively independent policies, the fifth offers a sketch of how the various policies may be integrated to provide the appropriate feedback and incentives.

THE MAGNITUDE OF THE PROBLEM

The focus of this book has been on the health problems of the nonelderly. Between 15 and 17 percent of the noninstitutionalized population aged eighteen to sixty-four report health problems severe enough to affect the ability to work. These estimates are based on self-reported limitations, but numerous studies using various other types of data strongly support them. Furthermore, the available data with respect to specific pathologies, impairments, and chronic conditions are all consistent and suggest that the overall disability estimates may, in fact, omit many health problems that are either embarrassing or relatively minor, but nonetheless troublesome.

More important than the sheer magnitude of the number of people with health problems is the nonrandom nature of their occurrence. In Chapter 3 I examined the extent to which various socioeconomic variables were causal factors in different types of health problems. At the level of pathologies, there is some evidence that the poor are subject to somewhat higher prevalence rates. As the focus shifts to measures more related to outcomes, such as impairments and activity-limiting chronic conditions, the negative relationships between prevalence and income-education become more clear. Two approaches to measuring the effects of socioeconomic characteristics upon the incidence of disability both show substantial relationships between poor education, low income, and certain job characteristics on the one hand and higher incidence rates on the other.

Not only are a great many people directly affected by health problems, but these problems account for substantial economic losses. The average disabled person received about 35 percent less than what he or she would be expected to earn; this amounted to about 6 percent of all wage and salary earnings in the United States, or $22 billion in 1967. This earnings loss is only partially compensated for by income transfers and extra earnings by relatives. About 30 percent of all poor disabled families are poor because of their disability. Disability was the cause of between 9 and 18 percent of all poverty among the nonelderly, whether disabled or not, a rather substantial fraction considering all the other forces that account for poverty. All of these estimates are limited to the noninstitutionalized population aged eighteen to sixty-four. The prevalence and severity of health problems is much greater among the aged, and almost all the institutionalized population is severely disabled. In addition, one may also choose to include the effects of short-term health problems which account for more disability days (although spread over a much larger population) than do long-term problems.

Considering all of these effects of health problems, it seems only logical that more attention be paid to means to prevent the conditions from occurring and to alleviating their effects so that the outcomes are less serious. The shift from a purely medical care orientation to one that emphasizes causation and prevention has just begun to become more accepted in recent years.[1] What is necessary now is the development of a well-integrated set of policies to begin moving in that direction.

THE CAUSES AND CONSEQUENCES OF HEALTH PROBLEMS

The primary concern in the first part of this book was on the relatively narrow question of whether there are economic variables that have a causal effect, at least in part, on health problems. For instance, the much higher disability rates for black men are entirely explained, in a statistical sense, by the income and education differences between black and white men. Yet it is unlikely that merely providing black men with as much income and education as white men, and doing nothing else, will result in identical disability rates. In other words, the socioeconomic factors that have been included in this study, such as income and education, probably serve primarily as proxies or variables related to other factors that have a true causal effect on the incidence of health problems. To illustrate the necessity for understanding the true causes, consider two hypothetical situations. In one, low income people do not have enough money to buy the food necessary for a nutritious diet that helps prevent disease. In the other, low income people choose an inappropriate mix of foods that does not provide the proper nutrition even though they could afford a "proper diet." In the first example, income supplements would lead to better diets and health; in the second example,

1. Prevention may be less expensive than curative medicine, but the evidence is far from conclusive (see, for instance, Lave and Lave, 1977). A more subtle point, however, is that much of medical progress has served to eliminate the acute but deadly illnesses that often killed the old and weak. For instance, pneumonia has long been termed the old man's friend. Now we are "left" with many chronically ill people who require costly, long-term treatment. Their longer lives may be worthwhile, but they are expensive (see, for instance, Gruenberg, 1977).

diets would not change. One would have to discover what caused the choice of poor diet and, perhaps, try to alter that behavior.[2]

There seem to be three major groupings of the causes of various health problems: genetics, specific external agents, and psychosocial stresses. Some diseases, such as hemophilia, have very clear genetic causes; for others there is evidence that the likelihood of developing the disease is genetically related, but that the "trait" doesn't cause the disease, it only predisposes to it, or results in lowered resistance. Specific agents, such as bacteria and viruses, have long been identified as the causes of certain conditions such as infectious diseases. Finally, psychosocial factors are increasingly being recognized as having an influence on health problems (Cassel, 1974; Mechanic, 1968). The mechanism by which all three factors interact can be described in the following way. Every organism has certain built-in defenses against external agents, and the effectiveness of some of these defenses varies with genetic heritage. Furthermore, it appears that these defenses are less effective when the organism is subject to various external or internal stresses (see, for instance, Riley, 1975; Hinkle, 1973). Of course, the relative importance of the three factors varies with the disease, and researchers are only beginning to view the causes of disease in this multivariate way.

Viewing health problems as resulting from the interactions of these three groups of factors helps identify appropriate areas for public policy intervention. There is little that can currently be done about genetic predisposition to disease susceptibility or resistance aside from genetic counseling and amniocentesis to identify certain types of severe birth defects. More direct intervention through "genetic engineering" may be on the horizon. The ethical issues of genetic policy are of tremendous importance, but are beyond the scope of this book. When the causal role of specific external agents is large, there is often much that modern medicine can do to prevent or reduce the effects of disease through vaccination or antibiotics. In addition to such measures that are aimed at specific individuals who may be exposed to the agent, preventive measures may also be taken. For instance, a large fraction of cancers are environmentally caused by carcinogens such as cigarette smoke, industrial pollution, and radiation (Fraumeni, 1975). Various measures can be taken either to protect individuals from exposures to such carcinogens or to substantially reduce their prevalence. The role of psychosocial stresses is the least well understood. Many studies indicate that per-

2. The ethics of such attempts at changing behavior will be discussed in the next section.

sons under various stresses and life changes increase susceptibility to a wide range of diseases and accidents (Dohrenwend and Dohrenwend, 1973; Rahe, Mahan, and Arthur, 1970; Holmes and Masuda, 1972).

In addition to the above classification of "causes," two related categories are useful: occupational and lifestyle-related problems. As was seen in the first part of this book, occupational factors play an important role in the development of health problems. Over a fifth of the disabled adults who had worked prior to their disability reported that their condition occurred on the job. While there are sometimes incentives to overestimate the degree to which problems are occupationally caused (because of worker's compensation), our ignorance as to the various ways in which industrial products and processes affect health probably leads to an underestimate of the true effects. The importance of the existing worker's compensation system and the combination of public and private choices in the area of occupational health and safety makes this a particularly critical subject. Furthermore, the recent federal legislation in occupational health and safety (the Coal Mine Health and Safety Act of 1969 and the Occupational Safety and Health Act of 1970), as well as increasing action in environmental protection, have brought these issues into the public view.

Nicholas Ashford makes the important distinction between the two areas in terms of who bears the risks. General pollutants in the environment, such as sulfur dioxide from fuel oil, put everyone equally at risk, so that a social decision to save money by burning high sulfur oil is equitable in that everyone has an equal chance of suffering from the pollution. Occupational hazards, on the other hand, tend to be inequitable because the "savings" from using more dangerous processes are passed on to consumers, owners (and to some extent the workers), while the costs, in terms of increased risk, are borne largely by the workers and their families (Ashford, 1975: 43). While this distinction is very important in many cases, there are also many instances in which nonoccupational hazards differentially affect certain groups of people, such as smokers of high tar and nicotine cigarettes, users of certain chronic drugs, and people living downwind from a pollution source. Thus, it is important to distinguish occupational and product health and safety problems and to provide special incentives to deal with them.

The second important group or classification of health problems are those that are substantially influenced by people's behavior or lifestyles. It is difficult to determine the precise role of lifestyle, but there is increasing evidence that overeating, lack of exercise, excessive drinking, excessive stress, and cigarette smoking all have some influence on a number of diseases such as heart conditions, cancer, hypertension and stroke, emphysema, cirrhosis of liver, and peptic ulcer (Fuchs, 1974; Fogarty International Center, 1976). If one also includes accidents, suicide, and homicide as having a substantial behavioral component, then 79.5 percent of all deaths in the United States occur in "diseases" influenced by lifestyle (see Table 7–1). If the "behavioral" hypothesis is substantiated for even a fraction of the listed diagnoses, then a large number of deaths in the U.S. can be postponed. Identifying those behavioral characteristics that affect the incidence of health problems is important so that policies may be designed to alter such behavior or at least to make more clear to the individuals the potential consequences of their actions.

The ethics of such policies are discussed in more detail below, but the identification of lifestyle factors is not meant to imply that all or even part of the blame for such behavior must rest with the individual—often described as a case of "blaming the victim." For instance, there is substantial evidence that cigarette smoking causes lung cancer (as well as other health problems) and smoking is clearly an individual action. But it is difficult to accept the argument that some people are born to be smokers and that cigarette advertising is merely designed to inform smokers about their taste options. In addition to such "institutional" pressures, social norms also influence behavior patterns. Both factors have a substantial role in lifestyle decisions and must be carefully considered in designing an effective and equitable policy.

Chapter 5 focused on the factors that intervene to reduce the severity of the effects of a given condition. Various characteristics of the person and his or her job were important in predicting who would be able to return to work and suffer relatively little in the way of income losses. The interactions between the specific requirements of the job and the person's functional limitations were as important as expected. Moreover, a number of findings emerged from the analysis that lead to potential policy actions. For example, when the various functional limitations and job requirements are controlled for, there are substantial effects from variables such as education, job tenure, race, and sex. It appears that these factors represent different sets of labor market conditions and job flexibility. The poor, blacks, and women seem at a particular disadvantage when disabled, and specific characteristics, such as education and job security, are much more critical to them than to white men initially in well-paying jobs. These findings suggest that specific poli-

Table 7–1.   Deaths and Death Rates for the Fifteen Leading Causes of Death—United States, 1969
(rates per 100,000 estimated population)

Rank	Cause of Death (Eighth Revision, International Classification of Diseases, Adapted, 1965)	Number	Rate
	All causes	1,921,990	951.9
* 1	Diseases of heart 390–398, 402, 404, 410–429	739,265	366.1
* 2	Malignant neoplasms, including neoplasms of lymphatic and hematopoietic tissues 140–209	323,092	160.0
* 3	Cerebrovascular diseases 430–438	207,179	102.6
* 4	Accidents E800–E949	116,385	57.6
	Motor vehicle accidents E810–E823	55,791	27.6
	All other accidents E800–807, E825–E949	60,594	30.0
5	Influenza and pneumonia 470–474, 480–486	68,365	33.9
6	Certain causes of mortality in early infancy 760–769.2, 769.4–772, 774–778	43,171	21.4
7	Diabetes mellitus 250	38,541	19.1
* 8	Arteriosclerosis 440	33,063	16.4
* 9	Bronchitis, emphysema, and asthma 490–493	31,144	15.4
*10	Cirrhosis of liver 571	29,866	14.8
*11	Suicide E950–E959	22,364	11.1
12	Congenital anomalies 740–759	17,008	8.4
*13	Homicide E960–E978	15,477	7.7
14	Nephritis and nephrosis 580–584	9,417	4.7
*15	Peptic ulcer 531–533	9,312	4.6
	All other causes Residual	218,341	108.1

*Indicates a cause of death potentially influenced by behavioral or lifestyle factors.
Source: USNCHS 1974: 20/16: 1

cies may be aimed at such groups to help them obtain alternative jobs and/or to cushion the income losses that they suffer.

This section has set the stage for a consideration of policy alternatives by very briefly summarizing the key issues that have emerged from previous chapters. There is substantial evidence that the incidence of health problems is not random and that, in fact, the poor and less well-educated do have higher rates of disabling conditions. It is impossible to identify the specific causal factors more clearly at this time. Future investigations may determine the relative importance of genetic heritage, external agents, and psychosocial-psychological stresses. In addition to thinking about these three broad classifications of the causes of health problems, it is useful to consider two other dimensions—occupational factors and lifestyle factors. For instance, some occupations may selectively recruit certain people such as blacks or women who happen to be particularly predisposed or resistant to specific diseases, the working environment may include a number of health and safety hazards, and the work situation may produce substantial amounts of stress. Similarly, certain lifestyles may be particularly attractive to specific groups with relatively common genetic traits, involve more or fewer hazards, and have different levels of stress.[3] While policies may be designed along the dimensions of occupational and lifestyle factors, they must recognize the underlying causal variables. With these distinctions in mind, the next section will explore the appropriate role of public policy.

CHOOSING THE APPROPRIATE ROLE FOR PUBLIC POLICY

Public policy statements always reflect the author's preferences concerning the appropriate role of such policy and the weights to be given such conflicting goals as equity and efficiency. Unfortunately, the range of available options is rarely discussed. In this section, I will outline two polar approaches to the possible public role and then state my own position. Hopefully, those who disagree with my value judgments will find the analysis helpful in developing their own policy positions.

Two Polar Approaches

The two polar approaches to public policy may be labeled "interventionist" and "market strategy." In an extreme interventionist

3. Fuchs (1974: 52–54) provides a beautiful example of this in which age-sex-specific death rates are 40–50 percent higher in Nevada than in Utah.

strategy the government, acting as the agent of the public, takes an active role in eliminating health problems through medical research and regulations concerning safety and health hazards, both of a public nature, such as pollution, and of a private nature, such as cigarettes. Medical care would also be provided through a national health insurance scheme for all who are expected to benefit from it, and income transfers would compensate people for their losses.

In an extreme market strategy most, if not all, actions would be left to the market place, and the role of government policy would be only to help the market work better in those situations in which there are inherent imperfections in the market. People would be left to make their own choices about risky occupations and lifestyles. They could buy insurance against uncertain events such as disability and medical costs if that would result in an increase in their expected welfare. The government might produce some purely public goods. If certain rather stringent conditions hold, the market strategy offers the most efficient allocation of resources given people's initial endowments. Such an analysis is common in purely economic models of behavior. Among careful analysts, however, it is usually taken as a discussion of tendencies, rather than as a description of reality.[4]

Although few people would argue for the adoption of either pure strategy, it is useful to examine the strengths and weaknesses of each to help choose the intermediate position that best fits the decision-maker's values. The primary advantages of an interventionist strategy are equity, potential for rapid action, and the provision of public goods. The major arguments for the market strategy are individual choice and efficiency. When evaluating each strategy, one must also decide the extent to which its practical implementation approximates the ideal model.

The Interventionist Strategy

The strongest argument for intervention is equity—the costs of preventing health problems, treating illness, and compensating the disabled are borne by those who can best afford to pay. A second argument is that there are so many health hazards that it will take too long for the market to eliminate them, while people needlessly become ill. Specific actions are also preferred when it is feared that individuals may make the wrong decisions, because of either lack of information, faulty markets for capital, or simple myopia.

The third major argument for intervention is based on the pro-

4. The economists involved in public policy discussions usually realize that there are a great many political and social constraints that prevent a theoretically appropriate strategy from reaching fruition (see, for example, Nelson, 1974).

vision of public goods that will not be offered by private market forces. One instance of this is the development of new information, say, concerning the causes of various health problems. While the research itself may be undertaken on a relatively small scale, the information is of value to everyone, and it is difficult, if not impossible, to make people pay for it. This is not true for all research; studies of the influence of diet on heart disease would fall under the public good heading, while research into the effects of certain industrial chemicals is of interest to, and could be purchased by, the users, workers, and producers of the suspect materials. But a second important point is the availability of information. In theory, government-sponsored research results are equally available to all, while the private funding of the health effects of chemicals, as mentioned above, may result in information available to employers but not to employees. This has recently come to the fore concerning occupational exposure to drugs causing sterility (Associated Press, 1977).

Another aspect of the public good argument for intervention is externalities. The market often doesn't perform optimally because of transaction costs, making public, nonmarket, intervention necessary. For instance, such difficulties may occur through the air pollution of an industry that affects everyone downwind. Another example is that of interdependent utilities (or altruism), whereby everyone feels better off knowing that other people are healthier.

The Market Strategy

The primary arguments against an interventionist strategy are its implications for individual choice, efficiency, and the extent to which the realities of intervention diverge from the ideal. The first two are the major points in favor of the market. Obviously, social choices and rules impose restrictions on individual behavior and responsibility. For some, rugged individualism is a paramount value. Others point to a more subtle implication of social responsibility:

> In the 1920s R.H. Tawney, surveying the eighteenth- and nineteenth-century attitudes toward poverty, wrote that "the most curious feature in the whole discussion . . . was the resolute refusal to admit that society had any responsibility for the causes of distress." Some future historian, in reviewing mid-twentieth-century social reform literature, may note an equally curious feature—a "resolute refusal" to admit that individuals have any responsibility for their own distress.
>
> From the idealization of individual responsibility and the neglect of social responsibility we have gone, in some quarters, to the denial of individual responsibility and the idealization of social responsibility. The rejec-

tion of any sense of responsibility for one's fellow men is inhuman, but the denial of any individual responsibility is also dehumanizing. (Fuchs, 1974: 27)

When all goods and services are appropriately priced and a few other (often nontrivial) requirements are met, the market solution to the allocation of resources will be the most efficient. In particular, the price system is a highly effective and infinitely subtle means of transmitting both information and incentives. For instance, if people suddenly want more wheelchairs, they will begin to bid up the price of the existing supply, indicating to manufacturers that they should build more. The price of secondhand wheelchairs will also rise, more people will become interested in refurbishing old ones, and enterprising individuals may develop acceptable substitutes for wheelchairs. The reaction of a highly structured nonmarket economy would be much more cumbersome and, importantly, would probably not include the incentive to find wheelchair substitutes. Furthermore, the "transactions" cost of transmitting price information is a small fraction of the cost of writing and disseminating government regulations to increase the supply of wheelchairs.

Model Strategies Versus Real Implementation

Both models suffer when one compares their assumptions with practice. The interventionist must face the problem of regulatory agencies that fail to do what they were supposed to do. The free marketeers must recognize problems of market failure and political power.

In general, two difficulties have been identified with strategies requiring active government regulation. The first is that regulatory agencies often serve the industries they are designed to regulate. (Stigler, 1971; Noll, 1971). Among the many reasons for this are bureaucratic survival, inequality of information between the regulator and industry, personnel interchange, and so forth. The second difficulty arises when designing laws or specific regulations. There is often a large group (e.g., the public) in which each member obtains a small benefit that is collectively quite large. The costs of the proposed changes, in contrast, are likely to be borne by a relatively small group, each of whom bears a substantial fraction of the cost. The same difficulty occurs when the change is expected to result in small costs for many and large benefits for a few. The political power and influence of a small group of aroused people and organizations is very impressive, and broad interventionist schemes are likely to be subverted and altered to meet the needs of such special interest groups (Marmor et al., 1976; Alford, 1972; Luft, 1976).

Assumptions crucial to the market strategy are also often unten-
able. For instance, the market solution is independent of the distribution of wealth and power. It is assumed that equity can be achieved
by an independent redistribution of income which is, therefore,
eliminated from the discussion. Such redistributions rarely occur.
Unfortunately, not only is wealth unequally distributed, but so is
information, and it is generally assumed in market models that both
the buyer and seller have essentially equal information about the
costs and benefits of the product. This is frequently not the case,
and in such instances the cost of obtaining the information is often
too great to expect a balance to be worked out without intervention.[5]

When public goods exist, the market deals poorly with them. In
addition to the arguments already presented concerning public
goods, it is not unreasonable to think that people may obtain some
utility from knowing that other people are healthy. If this is the
case, then those who feel that way would be better off if they used
the government to enforce (encourage) a somewhat higher level of
health-inducing behavior than each would choose individually. In
other cases, the necessary submarkets do not exist to allow the
market solution to really work. The absence of a comprehensive
market for risk has already been mentioned (Arrow, 1963). In addition, some people may wish to "invest" in human capital by avoid-
ing hazardous behavior. In the absence of slavery, capital markets
do not exist for such people to borrow money for such investments.

A final problem of some importance is that the advantages of the
market solution are all based on equilibrium conditions—that is,
when all the adjustments have been made and the situation is stable.
Little can be said about the relative efficiency of the market strategy
while in the process of reaching that long run equilibrium, nor how
long it may take to get there. Furthermore, if the external environment is always changing, then the market may never be in equilibrium, and some other strategy may well be better.

Whether by training or by self-selection, economists tend to favor
market solutions, and I am no exception. But, considerations of
equity and the many disadvantages of the market approach lead me
to include certain very important qualifications in the specific policies to be discussed below. In essence, I think we should try to
whenever possible make use of the advantages of the information
transfer and incentives offered by the price system. When there is a
choice between direct regulation and indirect intervention through

5. This is often the case in the medical care situation in which the patient
can almost never know as much about the technical aspects of the problem as
the physician (see Arrow, 1974).

changes in prices, we should choose the latter. But, in making that choice, we should give heavy weight to equity and to whether the policies will be best in practice, not just in theory. This will often result in a preference for intervention.

It should be clear that I prefer a strategy quite unlike either of the two extremes that have been discussed. The market, if left alone, has far too many imperfections. Some can be partially remedied through government action to improve the market. In many cases, this will involve schemes to "internalize externalities" or to eliminate situations in which one party is able to shift costs to another without compensation. The important point in this case is not just improving equity, but establishing the correct incentives. Government intervention is also necessary to offset concentrations of political or economic power that render "market bargaining" paradigms ludicrous. An example is when only one party has the relevant information. Furthermore, whenever possible, I prefer a system that forces two private sector groups, such as labor and management, to deal directly with each other, with the government as a referee rather than relying upon the government to extract penalties from one party to give to the other. My suspicion is that the direct government role is more easily subverted. Government health programs also may have "too much" appeal. Medical care already accounts for 8 percent of the GNP and is likely to further increase if it appears to be free. As is often the case with such programs, each taxpayer loses a little and each provider gains a lot under the current schemes. More direct consumer involvement will result in a more carefully considered decision as to how much health care is enough relative to other expenditures.

SPECIFIC ISSUES IN DESIGNING POLICY

In designing my policy recommendations, I will focus first on specific steps that should be taken to reduce the incidence of health problems, then on those to reduce their severity, and finally on efforts to reduce their impact. These recommendations are far from all-inclusive and represent largely economic policies and incentives. Other investigators are better at arguing the specific cases for education, preventive medicine, and so forth. After these specific policies are outlines, the following section will sketch a program to increase their interdependence.

Reducing the Incidence of Health Problems
The rationale behind the proposals in this subsection is that the current incentives to adopt healthy behavior patterns are insuffi-

cient in the sense that people would like to do more but feel they need a little help. This is an important point. One could argue that the current situation is optimal because if people wanted to be healthier, they could do something about it now. I believe that additional programs are necessary because of public good aspects ("we all gain by knowing that others are healthier"), indirect self-protection ("I know I respond to advertising, so I should be protected from cigarette ads"), or a socially agreed upon decision to induce people to be healthier than they otherwise would want to be ("because the rest of us pay the medical and disability bills").

Research and Information Gathering. Research to increase our knowledge of the causes of health problems and how to prevent their occurrence is the most critical need. Medical schools and medical research should sharply redirect their efforts toward more emphasis on prevention and health maintenance rather than sophisticated treatments and techniques that seem only to marginally prolong dying (Fuchs, 1976). It is also necessary that the results of such research be made available to the public and that the appropriate incentives be designed to encourage both the dissemination and the public and private application of health maintenance information.

Much is already known about health problems caused by occupational factors. Recent legislation has been designed to reduce health and safety hazards in the workplace through regulations and other incentives. Ashford provides an excellent evaluation and critique of the existing situation. He recognizes that the problems are complex and, therefore, argues for a multifaceted approach:

> I have sought throughout this work to demonstrate that occupational health and safety problems will not yield significantly to simplistic strategies based on single approaches. "Enforcing the law," as is argued by some, will not suffice; nor will "research" to determine "safe levels" of exposure or "hypersusceptibility."* Rather, the design of policy to bring about improvements in occupational environments must rely upon four sets of policy instruments: (1) the law, (2) market incentives, (3) the generation, dissemination, and utilization of knowledge, and (4) the development of personnel in the various professions, in labor unions, in management, and in government with the requisite knowledge of the issues.
>
> While the policy instruments cited above must be further developed and

---

*Contrary to popular belief, the best evidence does not support the thesis that the worker who is "accident-prone" or "hypersusceptible" to disease accounts for a significant amount of job-related injury or disease. However, the continuing adherence to this belief prevents more progressive and innovative measures from being taken to reduce job illness and injury. (Ashford, 1975: 34n) aggressively wielded, they will nonetheless be insufficient even when working in concert. In addition, workers themselves must assume a greater role in self-monitoring the quality of their own work environments. It is true that both law and tradition place ultimate responsibility for job health and safety on the employer. But full reliance on law or market incentives to encourage fulfillment of this obligation is impossible in any practical sense. While some progress can be expected through the courts and hearings—and in laboratories and classrooms—much more progress is likely if workers and their representatives are enabled to function responsibly and effectively in fruitful interaction with, and as a necessary check on, employers.

This latter conclusion is based on the fact that too little is now known—or even, at least in the short run, knowable—about health hazards for scientific proof and definitive standards to be widely forthcoming. Rather, most decisions regarding workplace environmental quality must be worked out in other forums on the basis of existing, often underutilized knowledge. In part these forums will be the courts or administrative agencies, and in part they will be the arenas of politics and public opinion. In the main, however, these issues need to be addressed in the day-to-day relationship between informed employers and employees—and in a deepening of the trend toward placing a higher priority on job environment issues in collective bargaining. (Ashford, 1975: 34).

Perhaps the most important aspect of both Ashford's discussion and my proposals is the necessity for more emphasis on information gathering and action at the local level—in the workplace. There is no way in which specific regulations and government inspectors can deal with the multitude of "little" factors involved in health and safety hazards. Unfortunately, workplace conditions have traditionally been seen as the responsibility of management, not the employees. Only a handful of unions have specific programs related to health and safety and these are all relatively recent (see, for instance, Urban Planning Aid, 1966; MacLeod, 1975; Oil, Chemical, and Atomic Workers, 1973; Mossberg, 1974).

The major problem with the current situation is that the effect of more information is almost always seen as being biased. Currently, the employer bears some responsibility for identifiable workplace-caused problems through experience-rated workers' compensation payments.[6] Occupational diseases are not covered, in general, nor

6. Experience rating means that the employer's premium for workers' compensation insurance bears some relationship to the claims experience of the firm's workers. In general, the degree to which premiums are experience rated depends on the number of employees in the firm. Very small firms pay premiums based on the average cost in their industry, with no responsiveness to their own experience, while firms of 2,500 or more employees essentially have premiums that completely reflect their own experience. In fact, many large firms essentially self-insure and only purchase insurance against catastrophic losses.

are many other things likely to be discovered as the result of further research. Thus, employers resist such investigations because they may increase their insurance costs. There may be no change in costs, however, if the employer also pays for "general" medical care through medical care insurance and general disability, pension coverage, and life insurance that are experience-rated for the employees in the firm. This is generally not the case. In addition, employer payments for the other forms of insurance are usually considered part of the overall compensation package subject to collective bargaining, while workers' compensation is not. It may be difficult to convince labor and management that health and safety issues are all interrelated, regardless of who bears legal responsibility for the payments.

While occupational diseases often require long-term, multiplant surveillance, preventing job hazards often depends upon the intimate knowledge of a specific plant. It appears that additional incentives must be given to employees to encourage the development of such knowledge. For instance, federal funds may be made available on a matching basis to encourage union efforts in occupational health and safety. Special training programs may be designed to increase the level of technical expertise that is avialable. Currently, there is a great shortage of trained personnel, especially with backgrounds in health hazards rather than the traditional safety orientation (Ashford, 1975; Koris, 1977). (Most of my emphasis is on encouraging workers to challenge their employers on safety issues. The knowledge generally exists at the shop floor, but the power relationships are such that the status quo is maintained.) Tax incentives for employers may be used for new equipment purchased to reduce hazardous conditions.[7]

It is important that as new information is developed, it be widely disseminated and put to use through national information systems and incentives. Thus, firms and employees will not have to reinvent the wheel. It also implies that once a health hazard is identified in one place, it can be attacked everywhere. This reduces the protection offered an employer by foot dragging—only if no one else is tackling the problem is the firm "safe." Such an emphasis is designed to offer partial protection to the vast majority of American workers who are not unionized and thus are at an even greater disadvantage vis à vis their employers. Perhaps the most hopeful point that can be made is that greater emphasis on health and safety issues may lead to either

---

7. At best, this should be a short run subsidy, and even then it is likely to be abused. The suggestion is made partly out of completeness and partly because it is one idea most likely to be favorably received.

employer action to improve the situation or to issues around which unions can more effectively organize the workers (Ashford, 1975: 373−80). This requires that much more attention be given to making information available to unorganized workers.

Current Workers Compensation Incentives. Health and safety come at a price except in a few rare instances. The question then becomes, Who should pay for the improvements in working conditions—the employees, through an offsetting wage reduction; the employer, through a decrease in profit; or the consumer, through higher prices? A precedent was set at the turn of the century concerning workers' compensation laws that the employer should be required to compensate an injured worker. Such compensation is considered a cost of production. Thus, riskier firms and industries would be at a competitive disadvantage and would have the incentive to either improve conditions or be driven out of business. It seems reasonable that this should continue to be the case with health hazards that have not yet been identified. (A crucial factor in the occupational setting is that by far the major focus is on safety issues, while there is little emphasis on occupational diseases and other health problems aggravated by the work environment. In large part, this has been because the workers' compensation system requires proof that the health problem was caused on the job. I will return to this issue later.)

The primary focus of these proposals is to design and improve incentives for health maintenance; thus it is important to consider the incentives within the existing workers' compensation system. Louise Russell (1974) has demonstrated that the existing formula for adjusting a firm's premium to reflect its experience does not offer much incentive for reducing risks. This is especially true for smaller firms, and increasing the benefit levels will not markedly improve the situation. The problems stem from the specific formula used, not the basic ideas behind experience rating. Russell suggests an attractive scheme based on a large deductible about equal to the average level of claims for a firm of that size in that industry. This is supplemented by a coinsurance rate with the amount of risk increasing with the size of the firm, perhaps with an upper limit on the total liability (Russell, 1974: 373). This idea is based on Martin Feldstein's (1971) proposal for major risk insurance for medical care but, because of the differences between workers' compensation and medical care insurance, it avoids many of the problems of the latter. Any scheme that increases the responsiveness of the firm's costs to its own health and safety programs is a step in the right direction. This is especially true for small firms which tend to have more hazardous working conditions (Ashford, 1975: 369–70).

Nonoccupational Health Problems.   Although occupational health and safety hazards have been the prime focus of most policy schemes, health is probably much more influenced by nonoccupational factors. For instance, of all accidents that caused an injury either restricting activity or requiring medical attention, 38 percent occurred at home and only 14 percent at work (USNCHS, 1976: 10/105: 19). The difficulty, of course, is that so little is known about the causes of most health problems. In some cases there is substantial evidence as to the causes, and it seems reasonable to do what can be done now, rather than waiting until all the evidence is in for everything. Two qualifiers must be added to such a proposal. First, the scheme must be flexible, so that as new evidence is acquired, incentives can be changed. Second, it is desirable that things be designed so that small changes do not result in major disruptions. Thus, taxes are generally to be preferred to prohibitions, if only because the former can be varied continuously, rather than being on or off.[8] As an example, the steady rise in cigarette taxes in the period 1964–1972 seemed to be at least as effective in stopping the rise of cigarettes per capita as were the antismoking campaigns (Warner, 1977). The latter drew much resistance from the tobacco industry while the former seems to have gone relatively unnoticed, although the antismoking campaign was partly responsible for the increased taxes.

The list of well-established behavioral factors is not very long at present, probably because of the lack of research rather than the lack of true relationships. Cigarette and alcohol consumption come immediately to mind, as do automobile safety devices and speed reduction schemes. The difficulty, of course, is in designing suitable incentives to change behavior if the mere dissemination of information is insufficient. Not all information is comparable. Tobacco and

---

8. It must be recognized that although taxes may be relatively efficient incentive schemes, they do impose an equity burden by bearing more heavily on the poor than on the wealthy. Excise taxes that are imposed to change behavior may be offset by income tax credits. This will not entirely remove the equity problem, because the poor who do not change their behavior, say to stop smoking, may still suffer a net loss of income while those who do not smoke receive a windfall gain. On the other hand, it is likely that during prohibition, the wealthy were able to continue their drinking habits, although with an income transfer to the bootleggers, while the poor suffered without drink or from the dangers of moonshine. It is probably the case that regardless of the incentive scheme, the poor suffer more.

alcohol advertising goes far beyond information dissemination; it is designed to convince people to consume. The countersmoking advertising on television appeared to be rather effective and could be reintroduced. Similarly, advertising for dangerous substances could be banned or limited to specifics such as tar and nicotine content, prices, and so forth.

In some cases, such as cigarettes and alcohol, it is possible to tax the consumption of the substance. It would be disirable, however, to adjust the taxes to approximate the expected costs imposed by the health problems they cause and to identify this for the potential consumer. Taxes on cigarettes could be made a function of the tar and nicotine content. In essence, the cigarette tax would be seen as increasing the effective payment that the smoker makes to the disability, life, and medical insurance funds whose premiums otherwise do not differentiate among smokers and nonsmokers. Current excise taxes on these substances are substantial, but are used by state and federal governments as general revenue. Thus, there is a disincentive on the part of the government to reduce the source of income (Bauer, 1974). Tying the funds to health programs would remove some of those perverse incentives.

In other cases the mechanisms may be more complicated. For instance, the premiums for automobile insurance to cover medical, life, and disability payments could be reduced for drivers of safer cars. In some cases, this is already done, although usually the differentials are based on cost differences for car repair. The Travelers Insurance Company (1977), however, has recently offered a 30 percent discount on personal injury and medical coverage premiums for cars equipped with airbags.

Other behavioral changes are even more difficult to enforce on an individual basis, but group incentives and reenforcement could be utilized. This is clearly the case in workers' compensation and company programs to reduce on the job problems. One study of matched pairs of plants with high and low rates showed that firms with low accident rates were more likely to use community efforts, varied incentives, and more informal safety inspections (Cohen, Smith, and Cohen, 1975). In this case, the firm reaps the direct benefit of the lowered insurance premiums, but it could just as well be the employee group. Seventh Day Adventists who maintain a lacto-ovo-vegetarian diet and abstain from alcohol, tobacco, tea, and coffee have a substantially reduced rate of cancer and coronary heart disease (Wynder, Lemon and Bross, 1959; Phillips, 1975). It is reasonable that they can buy insurance at rates substantially below that of the general population. Enforcement is not too difficult because one must really be a church member to be eligible, and it is likely that backsliders are eventually cut off from the insurance coverage.

What about nonreligious organizations composed of joggers or of agnostic vegetarians? In such instances, one could set up small associations to provide the social pressures for conformance to the regimen. Some enforcement scheme is necessary to prevent the development of dummy organizations that people join to save on insurance premiums without a behavior change. Perhaps the best enforcement is to put the organization itself fully or partially at risk for the cost reductions it claims to achieve. Thus, the joggers organization may take on responsibility for the coverage of coronary heart disease problems and, if their costs are truly lower, the members will benefit both through better health and lower premiums.

Even this form of experience rating may be impossible to administer, or more precisely, administrative costs may far exceed the benefits of the program. Active policies are much more feasible at the community level. The Stanford Heart Disease Prevention Program has demonstrated substantial success in changing smoking and eating behavior through the use of targeted communitywide media campaigns (Farquhar et al., 1977). Various communities can develop the methods most suitable to their environment and tastes. This is probably the best compromise between the inflexibility of a single national program (or nonprogram) and individualized incentives. People will tend to locate in areas that suit their tastes and reenforce their goals. This model already partially exists in local control of education. The suggestions in this chapter are designed to encourage the development of more efforts in this direction for health.

The administration of such programs is conceptually simple, although the details are well beyond the scope of this book. The community no more needs to be an insurance company than does an employer who has partially experience-rated workers' compensation insurance. The insurance bookkeeping and the risk bearing, both for catastrophic losses and for non-experience-rated risks, can be borne through rather simply designed insurance coverages. Whether this would be administered by a federal agency such as the Social Security Administration, entirely by private firms, or with federal standards and basic rate and risk setting but with private firms doing the day-to-day administration (as in the Medicare case) is largely a matter of choice. The strongest role for private firms is in the day-to-day administration and data processing to encourage innovation and efficiency in carrying out the program (Vogel and Blair, 1975). The best argument for a national program is having a universal data base so that all risks are included. Furthermore, by examining all these risks and having to bear the costs for morbidity, mortality, and medical care, the agency would have an incentive to direct research toward understanding the causes of health problems, how to prevent them, and how to reduce their severity. The current fragmentation of responsibility among medical, disability, life, and worker compensation insurers on the one hand, and the National Institutes of Health on the other, leads to much less focused research.

One wonders why existing insurers have not been more active in encouraging research and prevention. Two explanations come to mind. One is that by training, insurers tend to think in terms of fixed, immutable risks. In fact, recognizing that people have some control over risk threatens actuarial certainty. But, a few firms do provide consultation and programs in accident prevention for workers' compensation insurance (see, for instance, Ashford, 1975: 449). This leads to a second explanation: nonappropriability. Consultation to an industrial client benefits only that firm and the insurer. Research into the causes and prevention of heart disease would benefit not only the insurers' policyholders, but also those of other companies, who would be freeriders. Industrywide research efforts could be effective, but have not been forthcoming, with the notable exception of the Insurance Institute for Highway Safety. A national insurance program would internalize all of those benefits and should be given authority to allocate research funds.

This subsection has opened and closed with discussions of the need for more research into the causes of health problems and how to prevent them. Our ignorance severely hampers the design of appropriate policies to reduce the incidence of health problems. I have also focused on the problems of fragmented and conflicting incentives. Because of fragmentation, there is no organization that even has access to data concerning the whole range of health problems and their effects, let alone incentives to do something about them. The major thrust of the proposals in this section is to pull all the possible risks together and to provide financial incentives and moral suasion to change behavior. A primary focus was on occupational health and safety problems because more is known about them and there are existing insurance programs with incentive schemes that can be built upon. The problems in designing nonoccupational policies are more substantial, but the rewards are likely to be even greater.

Reducing the Severity of Health Problems

As has been discussed in previous chapters, the severity of a health problem is dependent on two major factors—the "clinical severity" and the ways in which its limitations interact with the person's skills, environment, and opportunities. The clinical aspects are often the major concern, and the policies that stem from this concern deal with the medical care system. Changes in the financing of medical care over the past decade have resulted in substantial improvements in the ability of the poor and the disabled to obtain treatment. The current system, however, is still far from perfect in terms of equity of access (Davis and Reynolds, 1976; Andersen, Lion, and Anderson, 1976; Lerner and Stutz, 1977; Wilson and White, 1977).

Preventive Medical Care. Of more concern now are the incentives emphasizing intensive inhospital treatment rather than ambulatory care and prevention. Medical care insurance tends to be much more widely held and is more comprehensive in its coverage of inpatient care than outpatient care (Andersen, Lion, and Anderson, 1976: 110–12). More importantly, the primary focus of medical education and research has been on inhospital care, at least in part because of the more readily available funds for such work. It is difficult to imagine physicians trained in that manner and large teaching hospitals, which also operate on a fee for service basis, devoting major efforts to preventive medicine, ambulatory treatment, and rehabilitation.

Financial incentives are only part of the problem. But they reinforce instead of countering the usual biases of the physician's training to act against the visible problem rather than take precautionary measures against the possible. Physicians are generally not trained to identify and deal with occupational hazards and the various stresses that may lead to a substantial fraction of health problems. Primary prevention in such instances may require a restructuring of the work and living environment. This should not be taken as an argument to expand medicine; if anything, there is probably an overmedicalization of problems that can be better dealt with through other means (Illich, 1976).

A major effort must be made to educate consumers about their health and about how to recognize problems when they are beginning and are still easy to treat successfully. Early detection and identification of diseases are best done by the individual. The available studies of mass screening programs have often shown them to be costly and ineffective (Cochrane and Ellwood, 1969). Involving the consumer will require not only education about the warning signs, but also some sense of false signals and minor problems that really do not require medical attention (Vickery and Fries, 1976). This is important for two reasons. The first is so as not to flood physicians' offices with trivial problems that are likely to result in the physicians discouraging self-examination. Second, the potential identification of health problems often arouses a great deal of anxiety. The fear of finding such a problem may keep people from looking. If they are reassured that most cases are trivial and that they can easily distinguish such cases, then they may be more willing to check out symptoms and to seek medical advice when appropriate.

Internalizing the Incentives: Health Maintenance Organizations and Health Maintenance Insurance. Shifting some of the current financial incentives in the medical care system could help to encourage such consumer behavior. Health maintenance organizations (HMOs) reverse the usual incentives—the consumer pays a fixed amount per year to the organization which agrees to provide the necessary medical care. Thus, in theory, the HMO has the incentive to reduce expensive medical treatment and to encourage preventive care. There is substantial evidence that HMOs have lower hospitalization rates, but there is mixed evidence concerning an increased emphasis on prevention. The greater use of preventive services by HMO enrollees is explained by their more comprehensive ambulatory coverage, not any "health maintenance philosophy" (Luft, 1977). In part, this may be attributable to criticisms from the "medical establishment" that HMOs practice second-class medicine; thus, they have not been as innovative as they could be or as would be indicated by their financial incentives. (In contrast, a consumers' health cooperative that currently operates on a fee for service basis but plans eventually to become an HMO encourages its members to purchase and use the Vickery and Fries (1976) book, *Take Care of Yourself: A Consumer's Guide to Medical Care* (Mid-Peninsula Health Services, 1977: 5).)

The financial incentives of the HMO, while a step in the right direction, are still not complete. The HMO is only responsible for providing medical care, not for maintaining health, as its name seems to imply. If its members die or are disabled without requiring excessive medical attention, there are no extra costs to the program. In fact, there are theoretical incentives not to provide medical care in such instances which are offset by the physician's training and sense of ethics.[9] While financial incentives probably play a secondary role, it would be worthwhile to experiment with a new type of health maintenance insurance combining medical care, morbidity, and life insurance payments.

9. Warner and Chadwick (1976) have independently arrived at the same conclusions regarding the combination of incentives.

Such a scheme would place all the financial incentives in the same direction. It is not difficult to identify situations in which the non-internalization of incentives can lead to inefficiency. For instance, based on the usual clinical evidence, about two-thirds of the patients who survive the first week after a myocardial infarction have a relatively mild form of the problem. The standard treatment for all such patients is to remain away from work for seven to twelve weeks. Procedures do exist, however, to evaluate their functional abilities and to identify those who can be sent back to work within four weeks and those at substantially higher risk who can be aggressively treated (DeBusk et al., 1977). The conventional health insurer or HMO would have an incentive to avoid the extra costs of the test and potential treatment. A disability insurer might prefer to use the test and send most of the patients back to work, but it has no control over the situation. Allowing transfers among the insurers or providing combined coverage would improve the financial incentives.[10]

One particularly unfortunate set of incentives occurs in some cases when a workers' compensation claim is at stake and the patient, in order to obtain benefits, has the incentive to maximize the apparent damage and disability until such time as the case has been settled. This sometimes leads to the refusal of prompt treatment and rehabilitation (Gulledge, 1963: 398–401). It is impossible to determine how frequently such situations occur, but their incidence could be reduced by diminishing the differential financial outcomes between "winning" and "losing" the case. Some of the disability payment schemes discussed below would have such an effect.

Vocational Rehabilitation. Prevention, health education, and prompt and effective medical care deal with only some of the factors influencing the severity of health problems. Attention must also be given to improving the skills of the disabled person and how he or she interacts with the labor market. One of the key empirical findings of Chapter 5 was the importance of education in reducing the severity of given functional limitations. It is unlikely that anything specific is associated with more schooling that helps a person cope with a disability. Instead, schooling is probably a proxy for general

10. Just providing combined coverage in this case would not be enough to assure a fair "test" of the evaluation unit because of the key role of the physician. It is likely that the predominant influence in the decision to order a new test is the change in medical practice and the consequent fear of malpractice claims should there be an adverse outcome (see Luft, 1976). The question of medical malpractice is beyond the scope of this book, but it is a subject that must be considered when attempting to implement substantial changes in medical care delivery.

educational skills and human capital that allows a person to consider a broader range of jobs and be able to find an occupation that does not interact adversely with his or her limitations. This suggests that more emphasis be given to general skills development and related educational programs. The generalist, in essence, acquires insurance that may be used in the event of a future disability.

One clear implication of these findings is that more effort should be put into vocational rehabilitation programs of various types. These may range from efforts to better match people with jobs that they can do to much more extensive programs to retrain the disabled. Various evaluations of existing vocational rehabilitation programs have produced very high benefit-cost ratios, in the order of 7:1 to 35:1 (Conley 1969; U.S. Vocational Rehabilitation Administration, 1967). It may be anticipated, however, that a substantial expansion of rehabilitation programs will be accompanied by a fall in the marginal and average benefit-cost ratios. This is a natural phenomenon that can be expected with any program because the initial focus of program managers is on those who can show the greatest benefit per program dollar. Unfortunately, this has often meant directing efforts toward people who are likely to have gone back to work even without rehabilitation. The incentives have been to show the greatest number of closed cases with high earnings. This leads to the exclusion of difficult cases and those who would have low earnings even if rehabilitated.

The incentives facing the vocational rehabilitation program can be changed in two ways. One change is relatively simple and would alter the incentives faced by the vocational rehabilitation personnel; the second is much more sweeping and would require a major restructuring of the system. The current incentives toward showing a high rate of people back at work in well-paying jobs are often met by selecting people most likely to succeed. The incentives could be changed to reward the program for the *change* in the client's outcome relative to what would be expected had he or she not been in the program. This is intended to reward the improvement attributable to the program itself. It may be taken a step further by keying the incentives to the *relative* improvement rather than the absolute level. Thus, a $2,000 improvement in earnings for someone who would be expected to earn $2,000 without rehabilitation could be "worth" substantially more than a $2,000 improvement for someone expected to earn $8,000.

A more substantial restructuring of vocational rehabilitation would incorporate it into the true health maintenance insurance system outlined above. The same system of medical care, disability, and life insurers would have the responsibility for providing vocational rehabilitation services. They would have a strong incentive to do so because of their liability for disability payments. The linkages with medical care coverage would help in identifying people with different degrees of functional limitations. One example where this system has been partially implemented is the program of Liberty Mutual Insurance Company, the largest underwriter of workers' compensation insurance. Liberty Mutual operates several rehabilitation centers of its own and a research laboratory (Ashford, 1975: 490). Its aim is to reduce the long-term losses attributable to workers' compensation claims, and to do so, it provides more effective programs for some of the most seriously disabled (and therefore most costly) workers.

Improving the Labor Market for the Disabled.   Appropriate treatment and vocational rehabilitation for the disabled will still be of only limited effectiveness if labor market conditions preclude their getting jobs. At the macroeconomic level, policies designed to lower the general rate of unemployment will almost certainly have an especially salutary effect on the disabled. Because people with various functional limitations are less flexible and less efficient than those who are well and because they are more likely to have changed jobs and to thus not have tenure, the disabled have particular problems during economic downturns (Levitan and Taggart, 1977). However, when the labor market is tight, employers are more willing to hire the disabled worker. Employment problems among the disabled are even greater for women and minority groups.

A number of specific policy steps should be taken to help the disabled get and retain jobs. Two broad categories of policy problems must be addressed to help the disabled get and retain jobs. The first includes problems that interfere with employers hiring as many disabled workers as would be optimal for them in a perfect world. The second includes those that prevent the hiring of as many disabled workers as is socially optimal.

Suppose that a disabled woman is able to work. Even if she is as productive as other workers, she may have more difficulty being hired. It has long been recognized that employers are afraid to hire disabled workers because they fear that such workers are more likely to have a subsequent accident leading to a workers' compensation claim. Most states, therefore, have a "second injury fund" to make sure that the employer is only charged with the benefits associated with the second injury, while the fund pays the remainder of the full compensation due to the worker (Ashford, 1975: 418). While not perfect, the "second injury fund" is a step in the right direction. It is more difficult to apply this concept in the case of diseases than to injury because the role of causation is so much less clear in the former. Much less obvious than workers' compensation, but probably more important, is the role of experience-rated "health insurance" in denying jobs to workers whose health problems are fully controlled (Kwitney, 1976). In such cases, employers are afraid of medical costs, not compensation claims, that will eventually increase their premium costs. Although an obvious solution is to remove medical care insurance from company experience rating, through a national "health" insurance scheme, such a program reduces the efficiency incentives of experience rating. This is but one example of the equity-efficiency conflict.

A second set of problems arises if the disabled person is not as productive as the average employee but is still able to do some work. In theory, an employer might be willing to hire such people if they would be paid their marginal revenue product. Thus, if a disabled worker was half as efficient as the average employee, he or she would be paid half as much per hour. There are obviously several problems with such a scheme. For instance, half the going wage may be less than the legal minimum wage or than what is available through welfare. The first problem may be handled with legal exemptions to the minimum wage. The second depends on the extent to which people want to work, in spite of the available income supports. The evidence is that most people do want to work (Watts et al., 1974; Goodwin, 1972). The potential also exists for employers to exploit disabled workers by taking advantage of their poor bargaining position and offering them less than they are truly worth. Sheltered workshops have often been used in such situations, but the job opportunities are too limited and the workshops are best designed for those who are rather severely disabled, not those with more moderate limitations.

Even if all these problems could be eliminated, society may prefer that more disabled persons be hired than would otherwise be the case. In essence, the social benefits of employing the disabled worker may exceed the private benefits. Society should then subsidize wages for the disabled. This may occur because it is considered better to subsidize people's work rather than just give them income support payments. Alternatively, it may be recognized that the current social structure places a high value on work and that the disabled themselves would prefer to work (Levitan and Johnson, 1973). Wage subsidy schemes have been used in various instances when a person's market production is expected to be worth less than society feels the person should be paid—for instance, in training programs for veterans. Wage and/or earnings subsidies have also been discussed as alternatives to the current welfare system (Haveman, 1975). Such a program would offer significant benefits to the disabled who are able to work and yet cannot earn enough to avoid a substantial reduction in earnings.

A wage subsidy for the disabled should be designed to provide work incentives and avoid sharp distinctions in eligibility. The disability evaluation would assess the proportionate wage reduction caused by the person's limitations. To reduce administrative costs, people with a moderate reduction in earnings capacity—for example, less than 20 percent—would not be eligible, while those who have greater incapacities would receive a subsidy in proportion to their limitations.[11] The use of a percentage adjustment allows the dollar amount of the subsidy to grow with inflation, rather than being fixed at an initial level as is often the case with compensation payments. If the worker recovered and was able to increase his or her responsibilities and earnings per hour, the subsidy rate could be gradually reduced until it was eliminated. The important feature is that, for all but minor disabilities, there are no cutoffs. Thus, there is little to be gained from making an ailment appear somewhat worse, as in the case currently when someone either is or is not disabled, with large subsidies dependent on the determination.

The disability evaluation system is unlikely to be much more complex than the current evaluation schemes and could be a substantial improvement by including detailed information on actual functional limitations and job requirements. The very crude estimates in Chapter 5 explained between 23 and 50 percent of the variation in relative earnings levels among individuals. More detailed models using individual-specific data rather than group approximations for job requirements would surely do much better.

The earnings subsidy scheme, while not perfect, is likely to be substantially better than proposals that require employers to hire a quota of disabled workers (Haber, 1973: 52). The enforcement problems of such a scheme appear to be enormous. Employers would want to hire the least disabled, while little would be done for those who are more handicapped. Employers would have no incentive to help rehabilitate workers. In fact, it might be to their advantage to hire the minimum number of handicapped workers and to keep them in menial jobs. Quota schemes are often politically attractive because

11. The use of a 20 percent, or any other such arbitrary cutoff, requires a careful weighing of the administrative advantages of eliminating a large number of relatively low subsidy people against the problems created by having a very high marginal tax rate near the cutoff point.

they appear to be cost-free from the taxpayer's point of view. Unfortunately, they rarely work.

The multifaceted approach required in policies to reduce the severity of health problems mirrors the complexity of the causal factors outlined in the empirical work. Part of the approach must be directed toward a reduction in clinical pathology and its sequelae. Although improved access to medical care is important, greater emphasis must be placed on teaching people to recognize symptoms and to come in for early treatment. A shift in medical care from intensive hospital treatment to prevention, ambulatory care, and rehabilitation is also necessary. Such a shift requires changes in both medical education and the financial incentives faced by medical providers. A second part of the approach is the development of general skills and effective vocational rehabilitation of people with functional limitations. People with skills and job flexibility are best able to remain in the labor force and to experience relatively small earnings reductions. New incentives must be designed for vocational rehabilitation programs that emphasize improvement in skills and direct attention to those people who need it the most. The third part of the approach must be on increasing labor market demand for disabled workers. This entails reducing the employer's fear of higher workers' compensation and medical care insurance claims and of specific wage subsidy programs. Efforts to reduce the general level of unemployment will have an especially positive effect on the disabled.

Reducing the Impact of Disability
on Family Income

Even if all the aforementioned programs worked as well as one could hope, there would still be a great many disabled persons unable to work; or even if they could work, they would be impoverished. Income transfer programs were shown to replace only 40 percent of the earnings loss attributable to disability. They only removed from poverty 40 percent of the families that are impoverished by disability. More importantly, existing income transfers for the disabled have strong disincentive effects concerning rehabilitation and return to work. For instance, Social Security disability benefits are based on the person's inability to undertake any "substantial gainful activity"— earnings above $140 per month eliminate the person from the program (U.S. Congress, 1974: 9). There is also a wide range of different programs with conflicting requirements: Social Security, disability insurance, supplemental security income, veteran's pensions, veteran's disability benefits, black lung program, workers' compensation, and a whole range of private disability programs.

The primary objectives of a disability income maintenance program should be twofold: guaranteeing a reasonable minimum income level for those unable to work, and providing work incentives for those able to work. Any such scheme should be all-inclusive and should not have differential benefits for veterans, workers in certain industries, and so forth.[12] From the previous discussion in this chapter, two design criterial are important—maintaining smooth transitions across categories to eliminate notch effects, and reducing the number of supplemental benefits tied to income maintenance. For instance, Social Security disability benefits are valuable for more than just the cash transfers because Medicare benefits are often available to disability recipients. A key factor in the design of any income maintenance program for the disabled is the structure of income support programs for others. Obviously, the two must be integrated, and it is important that there be no sharp distinctions in benefits between the two programs, so that disincentive effects are minimized. (I will briefly discuss the disability program assuming that a general income support program will be compatible. Obviously, much more work needs to be done on the specific design of such programs.)

The basic outline of the program was sketched in the preceding subsection. The disabled person would be evaluated as to the extent of his or her loss of functional capacity. The evaluation of functional limitations should include consideration of the person's skills and occupational options. A mathematician with a back injury would have a smaller functional loss than a longshoreman with the same injury. These evaluations would be on a continuous scale. While the inherent arbitrariness in such an evaluation cannot be avoided, the implications of differences of opinion are substantially reduced because there is less at stake than in a decision as to whether the person is disabled or not disabled.

The degree of disability then determines a base level of flat income support and the extent of earnings subsidy. For any given level of disability, the earnings subsidy rate falls with total earnings, but there is still an incentive to work. Over time, if a person demonstrates that he or she is able to work at levels substantially above what would be predicted, as shown by their earnings levels, then their degree of disability may be reevaluated. In all cases, the changes in disability evaluation (and implicitly the benefit and subsidy levels) should be made in increments comparable to those of the actual change in status. The only desirable discontinuity may be at the very

---

12. An exciting example of comprehensive coverage is the accident compensation scheme in New Zealand that provides for compensation, medical care, and rehabilitation for all persons and all accidents (see, New Zealand, Accident Compensation Commission, 1976).

low end of disability level, so that the administrative system is not overwhelmed by the large number of people with minor limitations.

Rehabilitation programs should be incorporated in such a scheme, as is often the case now, but with different incentives. Currently, disability benefit recipients are often required to accept rehabilitation services as a condition of receiving benefits. But the rehabilitation may suceed only in placing them in low-paying jobs, which will consequently disqualify them for disability benefits. Earnings subsidies provide a positive incentive for the disabled person to improve his or her earnings capacity through rehabilitation. In fact. as such programs become desired, rather than required, the government could provide vouchers or otherwise pay for rehabilitation services offered by various providers rather than offering the services directly. The disabled beneficiaries will seek out the most effective ways to improve their earning capacity and to increase their income.

The key to my proposal for income support is integration and the maintenance of appropriate incentives for the disabled. The next section offers a brief sketch of how to complete the circle and tie together income support, rehabilitation, medical care, and hazard reduction programs.

DESIGN OF ECONOMIC INCENTIVES TO DEAL WITH HEALTH PROBLEMS

In the preceding section I have outlined various policy proposals to deal with some of the economic causes and consequences of health problems. None were described in much detail because a careful working out of any one of the policies would be a major undertaking. Instead of focusing on the specifics, I have emphasized broader issues and patterns of incentives. In this section I consider how all of these proposals may be woven into a grand scheme of incentives. There are many flaws and problems in this scheme. It is not a blueprint, but rather an attempt to generate discussion.

Premises and Assumptions

There are a few general ideas that underlie both the specific proposals and the "grand scheme" that bear reiteration: (1) At issue is a system of interlocking parts and it is a mistake to act as if they were separable—many of the current problems are due to such fragmentation. (2) The system is evolving under internal and external pressures—feedback loops must be incorporated to allow for such pressures and to encourage change in the appropriate directions. (3) People and organizations probably respond more strongly to microincentives—the little day-to-day choices and decisions—than to broad goals and ideologies (Schelling, 1971). (4) The emphasis should be on outcomes, not on rigidly specified process measures. (5) Major changes in social institutions involve adjustment problems with huge potential gains and losses for various parties. The transitions must be eased, and if groups in power stand to lose, unless they can be "bought off," nothing will happen to change the status quo.

I assume the existence of three major social programs as part of the context for the proposals. The first is some form of universal basic income support for the poor, either through a negative income tax, demogrants, or some other scheme. The second is a basic commitment to maintaining a full employment economy so that people will not be faced with the choice of hazardous work or no job at all and the disabled will have some chance of being hired. Obviously, full employment allows some frictional unemployment through job changing and labor market entry, but it should be more like the situation of the late 1960s than the mid-1970s. The third assumption is that there is some form of national health (medical care) insurance so that eligibility for coverage is not dependent on employment status or separate programs such as Medicare and Medicaid.

Within this context, the scheme should integrate medical care insurance, disability insurance, accident and hazard insurance, rehabilitation, and life insurance. The purpose of this integration is to internalize the currently existing externalities and to improve the incentives for people to stay healthy and to recover from their health problems. Two sets of incentives are involved, financial and informational, and both revolve around the development of a health status index that includes not only current status but the person's prognosis and life expectancy. Much work has been done on such health status indexes, and their refinement does not appear too difficult.[13] Furthermore, a number of organizations are already computing a person's predicted age or life expectance on the basis of various risk factors such as weight, exercise, smoking, drinking (McQuade, 1977). Thus, it is likely that with reasonable effort, valid and reliable predictors can be developed for life expectancy and for various degrees of disability that incorporate known and suspected genetic, environmental, and individual factors.

Applying Information and Incentives

The mere knowledge of one's predicted health status and how it might change with certain actions may in itself lead directly to the appropriate behavior change or induce the person to join a social

13. See, for instance, Berg, 1973, and the entire Winter 1976 issue of *Health Services Research*.

support system, like Alcoholics Anonymous, to help in the change (LaDou, Sherwood, and Hughes, 1975). An increase in healthy years is of greatest significance to the individual and his or her family. The financial implications of improved health are significant for others, such as the social insurance system. (It is important to note that the integration of insurers can be achieved either through a government takeover or through coordination of activities among private carriers operating under contract to the government, much as in Medicare.)

At this point, a distinction must be made between how some of the risk factors are to be used. When computing the expected life and health status for informational purposes, all the relevant information should be used, including data such as genetic heritage and medical history. Each individual must have access to the data to insure its validity. When performing calculations for setting risk premiums, it is appropriate and perhaps desirable that some variables be excluded (or set at their mean values). This implies that those people who are at low risk with respect to the variable in question are subsidizing those at high risk. Whether or not this should be the case is a social policy question, but there are good reasons for not penalizing individuals for things not under their control.[14] For instance, race and other variables may be predictive of certain health problems, but they should not be used to set premiums at the individual's level.

A second safeguard is necessary to prevent insurers and others from attempting to select only the good risks. It is often argued that this is even a problem now with the rather limited experience rating present in workers' compensation and medical care insurance programs. The incentives to select good risks can be substantially reduced, if not eliminated, by basing experience rating on a predicted risk level. This predicted risk uses as its norm not the population average but, instead, the risk level for the people in question, abstracting only from those variables that the firm should be able to influence. For example, currently a company can demonstrate a low rate of health problems merely by having a relatively young labor force. The working conditions may, however, cause a rate of disease substantially higher than would be expected given the worker's age. This difference would be captured in the proposed

14. A current example of this is the controversy over the "fair" level for annuity payments for men and women. Women live longer, so that for any given sum of money their "actuarially fair" annuity is less than that of a man the same age. But one may argue that the cost of living is the same for men and women and, therefore, that monthly payments should be equal. In the first case the total annuities are equal and women get less per month. In the second case the monthly payments are equal and men get less in their lifetimes.

scheme. Similarly, if a firm selectively hired people who had heart attacks, it would start off with an expected heart attack rate substantially above the average and not be penalized unless its experience was actually worse than expected.

Although using the difference in outcome between actual and predicted levels as an incentive for changing behavior is an apparently new idea, it has some precedent in the experience-rated workers' compensation schemes. The concept may be extended to provide additional incentives to changing private behavior. As discussed in the preceding section, if people choose to get together to change their diets, exercise more, and stop smoking, they should be able to capture some of the savings attributable to that behavior—otherwise, they are implicitly subsidizing those who do not make such changes. Note that the discussion is limited to factors over which people have control and that the savings to the group should be limited to those attributable to such factors. Thus, if an organization claims to reduce the incidence of heart disease, then it can be put at risk (partially or wholly) for the outcomes and costs associated with heart disease. The risk calculation should take into account the other risk factors, so that they won't appear to reduce their risk when, for instance, they merely select younger people. Various types of organizations may choose to undertake such risk reduction programs. Religious groups and other voluntary organizations with special behavioral requirements are natural candidates. Other social groupings such as unions and employee-employer groups may decide to try to alter behavior such as smoking and diet. Medically oriented groups, such as HMOs, may not have the constant social contact to reenforce behavior change, but they do have more readily available objective medical measures. Even more remote, but perhaps the most feasible level, is the community. A number of national health insurance schemes such as those of Corman-Kennedy and Enthoven already envision a regional medical care budget (U.S. Congress, House, 1977; Enthoven, 1977). In Enthoven's plan, the per capita payments are adjusted for age, sex, and disability status. Clearly, some of those funds might be better spent on prevention and behavior change, with the savings distributed as a dividend to the residents.

The focus on behavior change and incentives does not imply that all the responsibility rests with the individual. That may be blaming the victim. Pulling everything together, however, should help society make some important choices about responsibility. For instance, the absurdity of spending billions for the treatment of lung cancer while allowing cigarette advertising may become more apparent. People do make choices about their lifestyle, but they are also swayed by their social environment. The increased concern about the hazards of smoking is probably responsible for the decline in cigarette consumption and reduction in tar and nicotine levels over the last two decades (Wynder and Hoffman, 1976; U.S. Center for Disease Control, 1977). But further action may be warranted. It seems perfectly reasonable for a significant fraction of a national health agency's budget to be allocated to advertising healthy behavior.

Taxes may be levied on industrial polluters whose emissions affect not only their workers, but people in the surrounding region. In essence, such polluters would then be paying a surcharge that should cover the extra health costs being borne by their neighbors (Schultze, 1977). The basic objection to such proposals is that they appear to give the producer a license to generate health hazards. Instead, the argument goes, such hazards should be banned. The major difficulty is that most things that people produce or consume entail some risks to themselves or others. Although the abstemious life of a monk may be healthy, many people would rather have some extra risk than do without the products of modern industrial society. The taxing of producers of health hazards does, in fact, give them a license to do so. The problem arises when the cost of the license is far less than the damage done.[15] Raising taxes to approximate the social costs may force some firms out of business if the public is unwilling to pay the price, or it may lead them to discover safer means of production.

The implementation of such a broad program will require careful planning and phasing. When risks are not specifically identified, they are implicitly borne by society at large. Internalizing responsibility for medical care, disability, and mortality costs within a single agency or group of insurers will make it possible to collect data concerning the effects of health hazards and the effectiveness of medical treatments. Although the data requirements for risk factor calculations are large, they are manageable. The potential savings through changing behavior are substantially larger.

A fraction of the funds cycling through this social insurance system should be allocated to identifying ways to reduce health problems. Incentives can then be designed to begin to change behavior and risks. This research should be undertaken both at the level of basic research into the causes of certain diseases, and at a much more

15. It is quite clear, although he does not make his argument explicit, that Ashford's criticism of tax incentives is based on the assumptions that firms can avoid them through the screening of workers and that the taxes do not reflect the true social costs involved (Ashford, 1975: 334). My proposal is aimed at eliminating both escape routes.

applied level concerning specific hazards at the plant level. As was discussed above, efforts must be made to help employees counterbalance the information advantages held by the employers. If causal relationships are discovered but some uncertainty remains, the incentives may be appropriately modified to reflect the uncertainty.

This grand scheme is not a blueprint. Instead, it is offered as a framework for the discussion of a truly comprehensive health-promoting social insurance system. Its major goal is to foster an understanding of the importance of incentives, behavior, and feedback loops. With such an understanding, it should be possible to design a workable system that rewards people and organizations for making the changes that will lead to a reduction in the economic causes and consequences of health problems. Furthermore, it appears that such a goal is attainable.

SUMMARY

This book has presented an empirical analysis of the interrelationships between poverty and health. Identifying the causes and consequences of health problems is of major importance. Over the last decade, people have become concerned about the rapidly rising cost of medical care, the handicapped, and environmental and lifestyle factors that cause health problems. Although there are causal relationships in both directions, it is possible to separate the primary influences.

The magnitude of the problem is large and growing. A seventh of the noninstitutionalized working age population is disabled. As the population ages, this fraction is likely to grow. The disabled suffer substantial losses. Many are impoverished, and the available transfer payments are only partially sufficient. The social costs of being disabled and unable to fulfill one's social role, although largely unmeasured in this study, are not offset by transfers. Thus, while more can and should be done to offset income losses, the primary focus of my policy suggestions are to prevent health problems and to reduce their severity.

My underlying assumption in offering these policies is that while direct intervention and regulation may be necessary in some instances, it is too easily subverted and too cumbersome to be the predominate strategy. Instead, I have tried to outline policies establishing financial and other incentives for behavior change in the context of a system that internalizes the costs of health problems. Thus, the agency that pays for medical care and income transfers will have the incentive and power to pass some of those costs on to the responsible polluters and hazard creators. In some cases, taxes and insurance premiums can be used to have the costs borne by the appropriate party. In other cases, rather than having the consumer bear the brunt of both health problems and taxes, more direct measures may be taken, such as counteradvertising. In spite of all reasonable preventive measures, people will still become disabled. The system must then provide not only income support, but also incentives for rehabilitation and reintegration into society.

The proposals in this chapter are ambitious, but large problems require large solutions. Hopefully, this book will lead to more comprehensive and effective thinking and policies.

Bibliography

Acton, Jan Paul. 1973. *Evaluating Public Programs to Save Lives: The Case of Heart Attacks.* Santa Monica, Ca.: The Rand Corporation, R–950–RC (January).

Aday, Lu Ann. 1975. "Economic and Non-Economic Barriers to the Use of Needed Medical Services." *Medical Care* 13:6 (June): 447–56.

Alford, Robert R. 1972. "The Political Economy of Health Care: Dynamics Without Change." *Politics and Society* 2 (Winter): 127–64.

American Rheumatism Association. 1964. "Primer on the Rheumatic Diseases." *Journal of the American Medical Association* 190 (October 12): 127–40; (November 2): 425–44; (November 9): 509–30; (November 23): 741–51.

Andersen, Ronald; Joanna Lion; and Odin W. Anderson. 1976. *Two Decades of Health Services: Social Survey Trends in Use and Expenditures.* Cambridge, Ma.: Ballinger Publishing Company.

Anderson, James G. 1973. "Health Services Utilization: Framework and Review." *Health Services Research* 8:3 (Fall): 184–99.

Antonovsky, Aaron. 1967A. "Social Class and Illness: A Reconsideration." *Sociological Inquiry* 37 (Spring): 311–22.

_____ . 1967B. "Social Class, Life Expectancy, and Overall Mortality." *Milbank Memorial Fund Quarterly* 45, pt. 1 (April): 31–73.

Arrow, Kenneth J. 1963. "Uncertainty and the Welfare Economics of Medical Care." *American Economic Review* 53:5 (December): 941–73.

_____ . 1974. "Government Decision Making and the Preciousness of Life." In Laurence R. Tancredi, ed., *Ethics of Health Care*, pp. 33–47. Washington, D.C.: National Academy of Sciences, Institute of Medicine.

Ashford, Nicholas Askounes. 1975. *Crisis in the Workplace: Occupational Disease and Injury.* Cambridge, Ma.: The MIT Press.

Associated Press. 1977. "Drug-Sterility Link Told." *Palo Alto Times,* August 25.

243

Bailey, Richard M. 1970. "Economic and Social Costs of Death." In Orville G. Brim, Jr., Howard E. Freeman, Sol Levine, and Norman A. Scotch, eds., *The Dying Patient*. New York: Russell Sage Foundation.

Bauer, Katharine G. 1974. "Averting the Self-Inflicted Nemeses (Sins) From Dangerous Driving, Smoking, and Drinking." In Selma J. Mushkin, ed., *Consumer Incentives for Health Care*, pp. 3–33. New York: Prodist.

Benham, Lee. 1974. "Benefits of Women's Education within Marriage." *Journal of Political Economy* 82:2, II (March): S57–71.

Berg, Robert L., ed. 1973. *Health Status Indexes*. Chicago: Hospital Research and Education Trust.

Berkowitz, Monroe, and William G. Johnson. 1971. *The Causes of Disability*. New Brunswick, N.J.: Bureau of Economic Research, Rutgers—The State University of New Jersey. Pp. 5–65.

Bice, Thomas W.; Robert L. Eichhorn; and Peter D. Fox. 1972. "Socioeconomic Status and Use of Physician Services: A Reconsideration." *Medical Care* 10:3 (May–June): 261–71.

Bowen, William G., and T. Aldrich Finegan. 1969. *The Economics of Labor Force Participation*. Princeton, N.J.: Princeton University Press.

Braunwald, Eugene. 1977. "Coronary-Artery Surgery at the Crossroads." *The New England Journal of Medicine* 297:12 (September 22): 661–63.

Brenner, M. Harvey. 1973. *Mental Illness and the Economy*. Cambridge, Ma.: Harvard University Press.

———. 1975A. "Effects of National Economic Trends on Utilization of General Hospitals." Paper presented at the 103rd Annual Meeting of the American Public Health Association, Chicago, Illinois, November 16–20.

———. 1975B. "Trends in Alcohol Consumption and Associated Illnesses: Some Effects of Economic Changes." *American Journal of Public Health* 65:12 (December): 1279–92.

———. 1976. "Reply to Mr. Eyer." *International Journal of Health Services* 6(1): 149–55.

Brody, Wendyce H. 1975. "Economic Value of a Housewife." *Research and Statistics Note* 9–1975. Washington, D.C.: U.S. Social Security Administration, Office of Research and Statistics, DHEW pub. no. (SSA)75–11701 (August 28).

Bunker, John P. 1970. "A Comparison of Operations and Surgeons in the United States and in England and Wales." *The New England Journal of Medicine* 282:3 (January 15): 135–44.

Burdette, Mary Ellen. 1975. "Changes in Personal Care Needs and Living Arrangements of the Noninstitutionalized Disabled, 1966–69." *Disability Survey 69, Follow-up of Disabled Adults*, Report No. 1. Washington, D.C.: Social Security Administration, Office of Research and Statistics, DHEW pub. no. (SSA)76–11715 (October).

Burger, Edward J. 1974. "Health and Health Services in the U.S.: Perspectives and Discussion of Some Issues." *Annals of Internal Medicine* 80:5 (May): 645–50.

California Medical Association, Bureau of Research and Planning. 1975. "A Survey of Physician Participation in the Medi-Cal Program." *Socioeconomic Report* 15:2 (February–March).

Caplan, Robert; John French; R. Van Harrison; et al. 1975. "Job Stress, Strain and Health." Paper presented at the 103rd Annual Meeting of the American Public Health Association, Chicago, November 16–20, 1975.

Caplovitz, David. 1967. *The Poor Pay More: Consumer Practices of Low Income Families.* New York: The Free Press.

Cassel, John. 1974. "Psychosocial Factors in the Genesis of Disease." In Robert L. Kane, ed., *The Challenges of Community Medicine.* New York: Springer Publishing Company.

Center for Human Resource Research. 1977. *NLS Newsletter.* Columbus: College of Administrative Science, The Ohio State University.

Chen, Martin K. 1975. "Health Status Indexes—Work in Progress." *Health Services Research* 11:4 (Winter).

Cobb, Stanley. 1971. *The Frequency of the Rheumatic Diseases.* Cambridge, Ma.: Harvard University Press.

Cochrane, Archibald L. 1972. *Effectiveness and Efficiency: Random Reflections on Health Services.* London: Nuffield Provincial Hospitals Trust.

Cochrane, Archibald L., and P. Elwood. 1969. "Screening: The Case Against It." *Medical Officer* 121:5 (January 31): 53–57.

Cohen, Alexander; Michael Smith; and H. Harvey Cohen. 1975. "Safety Program Practices in High Versus Low Accident Rate Companies—An Interim Report (Questionnaire Phase)." Washington, D.C.: U.S. National Institute for Occupational Safety and Health (June), DHEW pub. no. (NIOSH)75–185.

Conley, Ronald W. 1965. *Economics of Vocational Rehabilitation.* Baltimore: Johns Hopkins Press.

_____. 1969. "A Benefit-Cost Analysis of the Vocational Rehabilitation Program." *Journal of Human Resources* 4:2 (Spring): 226–52.

Cooper, Barbara S., and Dorothy P. Rice. 1976. "The Economic Cost of Illness Revisited." *Social Security Bulletin* 39:2 (February): 21–36.

Corning, Peter A. 1969. *"The Evolution of Medicare: From Idea to Law.* Washington, D.C.: Social Security Administration, Office of Research and Statistics, Report no. 29.

Covell, Ruth. 1967. *Delivery of Health Services for the Poor.* Program Analysis. Washington, D.C.: U.S. Department of Health, Education, and Welfare, Office of the Assistant Secretary (Planning and Evaluation).

Davis, Karen, and Roger Reynolds. 1976. "The Impact of Medicare and Medicaid on Access to Medical Care." In Richard N. Rosett, ed., *The Role of Health Insurance in the Health Services Sector.* New York: National Bureau of Economic Research.

DeBusk, Robert F.; Lee Domanico; Harold S. Luft; and Donald C. Harrison. 1977. "Return to Work Following Myocardial Infarction: A Medical and Economic Critique of the Work Evaluation Unit." *Journal of Chronic Diseases* 30:6 (June): 325–30.

Doeringer, Peter B., and Michael J. Piore. 1971. *Internal Labor Markets and Manpower Analysis.* Lexington, Ma.: D.C. Heath and Company.

Dohrenwend, Barbara S., and Bruce P. Dohrenwend. 1973. *Life Events: Their Nature and Effects.* New York: Wiley-Interscience.

Dubos, Rene. 1959. *Mirage of Health: Utopias, Progress and Biological Change*. New York: Harper and Row.

Dutton, Diana B. 1977. *A Causal Model of Health Status Determinants*. Final Report for PHS Grant 7 R21 HS02565−01 HSR (March), Stanford, Ca.: Stanford University Health Services Research Program.

Elinson, Jack, and Ray E. Trussell. 1957. "Some Factors Relating to Degree of Correspondence for Diagnostic Information Obtained by Household Interviews and Clinical Examinations." *American Journal of Public Health* 47 (March): 311−21.

Enthoven, Alain. 1977. "Consumer Choice Health Plan." Memorandum to Joseph A. Califano, Secretary of Health, Education, and Welfare (September). Stanford, Ca.: Stanford University Graduate School of Business.

Eyer, Joseph. 1976A. "Review of Mental Illness and the Economy." *International Journal of Health Services* 6(1): 139−48.

_____. 1976B. "Rejoinder to Dr. Brenner." *International Journal of Health Services* 6(1): 157−68.

Farquhar, John W. et al. 1977. "Community Education for Cardiovascular Health." *The Lancet* 1:8023 (June 4): 1192−95.

Feldstein, Martin S. 1971. "A New Approach to National Health Insurance." *The Public Interest* 23 (Spring): 93−105.

Flaim, Paul O. 1969. "Persons Not in the Labor Force." *Monthly Labor Review* 92 (July): 3−14.

Fogarty International Center. 1976. *Preventive Medicine USA*. New York: Prodist.

Fraumeni, Joseph F., Jr., ed. 1975. *Persons at High Risk of Cancer: An Approach to Cancer Etiology and Control*. New York: Academic Press.

Friedman, Milton. 1957. *A Theory of the Consumption Function*. Princeton, N.J.: Princeton University Press.

Frohlich, Philip. 1971. "Demographic Characteristics of Institutionalized Adults." *Social Security Survey of Institutionalized Adults: 1967*. Report no. 1. Washington, D.C.: Social Security Administration, Office of Research and Statistics (July).

Fuchs, Victor R. 1974. *Who Shall Live? Health, Economics, and Social Choice*. New York: Basic Books.

_____. 1976. "A More Effective, Efficient and Equitable System." *The Western Journal of Medicine* 125:1 (July): 3−5.

Goodwin, Leonard. 1972. *Do the Poor Want to Work? A Social-Psychological Study of Work Orientations*. Washington, D.C.: The Brookings Institution.

Graham, Saxon, and Leo G. Reeder. 1972. "Social Factors in the Chronic Diseases." In Howard E. Freeman, Sol Levine, and Leo G. Reeder, eds., *Handbook of Medical Sociology*, pp. 63−107. Englewood Cliffs, N.J.: Prentice-Hall.

Grossman, Michael. 1972. *The Demand for Health: A Theoretical and Empirical Investigation*. New York: Columbia University Press for the National Bureau of Economic Research.

Gruenberg, Ernest M. 1977. "The Failures of Success." *Milbank Memorial Fund Quarterly/Health and Society* 55:1 (Winter): 3−24.

Gulledge, Z.L. 1963. "Vocational Rehabilitation of Industrially Injured Workers." In Earl F. Cheit and Margaret S. Gordon, *Occupational Disability and Public Policy*. New York: John Wiley and Sons.

Haber, Lawrence D. 1967. "Identifying the Disabled: Concepts and Methods in the Measurement of Disability." *Social Security Survey of the Disabled: 1966.* Report no. 1 (December). Reprinted from *Social Security Bulletin* 30. Washington, D.C.: Social Security Administration.

_____. 1968. "Disability, Work, and Income Maintenance: Prevalence of Disability, 1966." *Social Security Survey of the Disabled, 1966*. Report no. 2 (May). Reprinted from the *Social Security Bulletin* 31. Washington, D.C.: Social Security Administration.

_____. 1970. "The Epidemiology of Disability: II. The Measurement of Functional Capacity Limitations." *Social Security Survey of the Disabled: 1966.* Report no. 10 (July). Washington, D.C.: Social Security Administration.

_____. 1973. "Social Planning for Disability." *Journal of Human Resources* 8 (Supplement): 33–55.

Hambor, John C. 1975. *Unemployment and Disability: An Econometric Analysis with Time Series Data.* Staff Paper no. 20 (January). Washington, D.C.: Social Security Administration, Office of Research and Statistics, DHEW pub. no. (SSA)75–11855.

Harris, Richard. 1966. *A Sacred Trust.* New York: New American Library.

Haveman, Robert H. 1975. "Earnings Supplementation as an Income Maintenance Strategy: Issues of Program Structure and Integration." In Irene Lurie, ed., *Integrating Income Maintenance Programs*. New York: Academic Press.

Hinkle, Lawrence E., Jr. 1973. "The Concept of Stress in the Biological and Social Sciences." *Science, Medicine, and Man* 1(1): 31–48.

Holmes, Thomas H., and Minoro Masuda. 1972. "Psychosomatic Syndrome." *Psychology Today* 5 (April): 71.

Illich, Ivan. 1976. *Medical Nemesis: The Expropriation of Health.* New York: Pantheon-Random House.

Kadushin, Charles. 1964. "Social Class and the Experience of Ill Health." *Sociological Inquiry* 34 (Winter): 67–80.

Kelman, Sander. 1971. "Toward the Political Economy of Medical Care." *Inquiry* 8:3 (September): 30–38.

Kessner, David M., and Carolyn E. Kalk. 1973. *A Strategy for Evaluating Health Services.* Washington, D.C.: Institute of Medicine of the National Academy of Science.

King, Stanley H. 1972. "Social-Psychological Factors in Illness." In Howard E. Freeman, Sol Levine, and Leo G. Reeder, eds., *Handbook of Medical Sociology*, pp. 129–47. Englewood Cliffs, N.J.: Prentice-Hall.

Knowles, John H. 1966. "Chronic Obstructive Pulmonary Disease: Bronchitis and Emphysema." In T.R. Harrison et al., *Principles of Internal Medicine*, pp. 904–10. New York: McGraw-Hill (Blakiston Division).

Koris, Sally. 1977. "Industrial Hygienists in Strong Demand as U.S. Widens Role in Workplace Safety." *Wall Street Journal* (August 2).

Kosa, John, and Irving Kenneth Zola, eds. 1975. *Poverty and Health: A Sociological Analysis.* Rev. ed. Cambridge, Ma.: Harvard University Press.

Kubler-Ross, Elisabeth. 1969. *On Death and Dying.* New York: Macmillan.

Kwitney, Jonathan. 1976. "Patients Who Recover Often Can't Regain Spot in Work Force." *Wall Street Journal* (July 20): 1.

LaDou, Joseph; John Sherwood; and Lewis Hughes. 1975. "Health Hazard Appraisal in Patient Counseling." *The Western Journal of Medicine* 122:2 (February): 177−80.

Lave, Judith R., and Lester B. Lave. 1977. "Measuring the Effectiveness of Prevention: I." *Health and Society/Milbank Memorial Fund Quarterly* 55:2 (Spring): 273−89.

Lefcowitz, Myron J. 1973. "Poverty and Health: A Reexamination." *Inquiry* 10:1 (March): 3−13.

Lerner, Monroe. 1975. "Social Differences in Physical Health." In John Kosa and Irving Kenneth Zola, eds., *Poverty and Health: A Sociological Analysis.* Rev. ed. Cambridge, Ma.: Harvard University Press.

Lerner, Monroe, and Odin Anderson. 1963. *Health Progress in the United States, 1900−1960.* Chicago: University of Chicago Press.

Lerner, Monroe, and Richard N. Stutz. 1977. "Have We Narrowed the Gaps Between the Poor and the Nonpoor? Part II—Narrowing the Gaps, 1959−1961 to 1969−1971: Mortality." *Medical Care* 15:8 (August): 620−35.

Leveson, Irving. 1972. "The Challenge of Health Services for the Poor." *Annals of the American Academy of Political and Social Sciences* 399 (January): 22−29.

Levitan, Sar A., and William B. Johnson. 1973. *Work is Here to Stay, Alas.* Salt Lake City: Olympus Publishing Company.

Levitan, Sar A., and Robert Taggart. 1977. "Employment Problems of Disabled Persons." *Monthly Labor Review* 100:3 (March): 3−13.

Lloyd, J. William. 1971. "Long-Term Mortality Study of Steelworkers: V. Respiratory Cancer in Coke Plant Workers." *Journal of Occupational Medicine* 13 (February): 53−68.

Lloyd, J. William; Frank E. Lundin, Jr.; Carol K. Redmond, and Patricia B. Geiser. 1970. "Long-Term Mortality Study of Steelworkers, IV. Mortality by Work Area." *Journal of Occupational Medicine* 12 (May): 151−57.

Louria, Donald B.; Allyn P. Kidwell; Marvin A. Lavenhar et al. 1976. "Primary and Secondary Prevention Among Adults—Screening and Health Education." *Preventive Medicine* 5:4 (December): 549−72.

Luft, Harold S. 1972. "Poverty and Health: An Empirical Investigation of the Economic Interactions." Ph.D. Dissertation, Harvard University.

———. 1974. "Education, Activity Limitations, and Labor Force Participation: A Source of Bias in Human Capital Analysis." Research Paper Series 74−7, Stanford University Health Services Administration Program, Stanford, Ca. (December).

———. 1975. "The Impact of Poor Health on Earnings." *Review of Economics and Statistics* 57:1 (February): 43−57.

———. 1976. "Benefit-Cost Analysis and Public Policy Implementation: From Normative to Positive Analysis." *Public Policy* 24:4 (Fall).

———. 1977. "Why Do HMOs Seem to Provide More Health Maintenance Services?" Paper presented at the 105th Annual American Public Health Association Meeting (November).

McKeown, Thomas, and C.R. Lowe. 1974. *An Introduction to Social Medicine.* 2nd ed. Oxford: Blackwell Scientific Publications.

McKinlay, John B. 1972. "Some Approaches and Problems in the Study of the Use of Services—An Overview." *Journal of Health and Social Behavior* 13:2 (June): 115–52.

———. 1975. "The Help-Seeking Behavior of the Poor." In John Kosa and Irving Kenneth Zola, eds., *Poverty and Health: A Sociological Analysis.* Rev. ed. Cambridge, Ma.: Harvard University Press.

MacLeod, Dan. 1975. "UAW Safety and Health Representatives: Occupational Helath Manpower in the Ranks of Labor." Paper presented to the Occupational Health Manpower Session of American Industrial Hygiene Conference, Minneapolis, Minnesota (June 5).

McQuade, Walter. 1977. "Those Annual Physicals Are Worth the Trouble." *Fortune* (January): 164–73.

Margolis, Bruce L.; William H. Kroes; and Robert P. Quinn. 1974. "Job Stress: An Unlisted Hazard." *Journal of Occupational Medicine* 16:10 (October): 659–61.

Marmor, Theodore R.; Donald A. Wittman; and Thomas C. Heagy. 1976. "The Politics of Medical Inflation." *Journal of Health Politics, Policy, and Law* 1:1 (Spring): 69–84.

Mason, Thomas J.; Frank W. McKay; Robert Hoover et al. 1975. *Atlas of Cancer Mortality for U.S. Counties: 1950–1969.* Washington, D.C.: U.S. Government Printing Office.

———. 1976. *Atlas of Cancer Mortality Among U.S. Nonwhites: 1950–1969.* National Cancer Institute, U.S. DHEW pub. no. (NIH)76–1204. Washington, D.C.: U.S. Government Printing Office.

Mather, H.G. et al. 1971. "Acute Myocardial Infarction: Home and Hospital Treatment." *British Medical Journal* 3:5770 (August 7): 334–38.

Mechanic, David. 1968. "The Study of Social Stress and Its Relationship to Disease." In David Mechanic, *Medical Sociology.* New York: The Free Press.

Mid-Peninsula Health Service, Inc. 1977. "Don't Miss New Member Seminar." *MHS Newsletter* 2:1 (February): 5.

Mincer, Jacob. 1962. "Labor Force Participation of Married Women: A Study of Labor Supply." In *Aspects of Labor Economics*, Universities-National Bureau of Economic Research, pp. 63–97. Princeton, N.J.: Princeton University Press.

Morgan, James N.; Martin H. David; Wilbur J. Cohen; and Harvey E. Brazer. 1962. *Income and Welfare in the United States.* New York: McGraw-Hill.

Morison, Robert S. 1973. "Dying." *Scientific American* 229:3 (September): 55–62.

Mossberg, Walter. 1974. "More Unions Devote Efforts to Eliminating Hazards in Workplace." *Wall Street Journal* (August 19): 1.

Mueller, Marjorie Smith, and Robert M. Gibson. 1976. "National Health Expenditures, Fiscal Year 1975." *Social Security Bulletin* 39:2 (February): 3–20, 48.

Murphy, Marvin L. et al. 1977. "Treatment of Chronic Stable Angina: A Preliminary Report of Survival Data of the Randomized Veterans Administration Cooperative Study." *New England Journal of Medicine* 297:12 (September 22): 621–27.

Nagi, Saad Z. 1969A. "Congruency in Medical and Self-Assessment of Disability." *Industrial Medicine and Surgery* 38:3 (March): 27–36.

———. 1969B. *Disability and Rehabilitation: Legal, Clinical and Self-Concepts and Measurement.* Columbus: Ohio State University Press.

Nagi, Saad Z., and Linda W. Hadley. 1972. "Disability Behavior: Income Change and Motivation to Work." *Industrial and Labor Relations Review* 25:2 (January): 223–33.

Nelson, Richard. 1974. "Intellectualizing About the Moon-Ghetto Metaphor: A Study of the Current Malaise of Rational Analysis of Social Problems." *Policy Sciences* 5:4 (December): 375–414.

New Zealand, Accident Compensation Commission. 1976. *A Brief Description of the Accident Compensation Scheme Operating in New Zealand.* Wellington: Accident Compensation Commission.

Noll, Roger G. 1971. *Reforming Regulation: An Evaluation of the Ash Council Proposals.* Washington, D.C.: Brookings Institution.

Oil, Chemical and Atomic Workers. 1973. *To Eliminate Industrial Health Hazards.*

Orshansky, Mollie. 1965. "Who's Who Among the Poor: A Demographic View of Poverty." *Social Security Bulletin* 28:1 (July): 3–29.

———. 1967. "Counting the Poor: Before and After Federal Income-Support Programs." *Old Age Income Assurance, Part II: The Aged Population and Retirement Income Programs.* U.S. Congress, Joint Economic Committee Print. Washington, D.C.: U.S. Government Printing Office (December).

Parnes, Herbert S. et al. 1970A. *The Pre-Retirement Years: A Longitudinal Study of the Labor Market Experience of Men.* Vol. I. Manpower Research Monograph 15. Washington, D.C.: U.S. Department of Labor, Manpower Administration.

———. 1970B. *The Pre-Retirement Years: A Longitudinal Study of the Labor Market Experience of Men.* Vol. II. Manpower Research Monograph 15. Washington, D.C.: U.S. Department of Labor, Manpower Administration.

———. 1974. *The Pre-Retirement Years: Five Years in the Work Lives of Middle-Aged Men.* Vol. 4. Columbus: Center for Human Resource Research, Ohio State University (December).

Parnes, Herbert S.; Gilbert Nestel; and Paul Andrisani. 1972. *The Pre-Retirement Years: A Longitudinal Study of the Labor Market Experience of Men.* Vol. III. Columbus: Center for Human Resource Research, Ohio State University (August).

Parnes, Herbert S., and Jack Meyer. 1971. "Withdrawal from the Labor Force by Middle Aged Men, 1966–67." Columbus: Center for Human Resource Research, Ohio State University (January). Mimeo.

Parnes, Herbert S., and Gilbert Nestel. 1974A. "Early Retirement." In Parnes et al., *The Pre-Retirement Years: Five Years in the Work Lives of Middle-Aged Men.* Vol. 4. Columbus: Center for Human Resource Research, Ohio State University (December).

———. 1974B. "Middle Aged Job Changers." In Parnes et al., *The Pre-Retirement Years: Five Years in the Work Lives of Middle Aged Men.* Vol. 4. Columbus: Center for Human Resource Research, Ohio State University (December).

Phillips, Ronald L. 1975. "Role of Life-style and Dietary Habits in Risk of Cancer Among Seventh-Day Adventists." *Cancer Research* 35 (November): 3513–22.

Poirier, Dale J. 1977. "Econometric Methodology in Radical Economics." *American Economic Review* 67:1 (February): 393–399.

Powles, John. 1973. "On the Limitations of Modern Medicine." *Science, Medicine and Man* 1(1): 1–30.

Rahe, Richard H.; Jack L. Mahan; and Ransom J. Arthur. 1970. "Prediction of Near-Future Health Change from Subjects' Preceding Life Changes." *Journal of Psychosomatic Research* 14: 401–406.

Reynolds, Roger A. 1976. "Improving Access to Health Care Among the Poor—The Neighborhood Health Center Experience." *Milbank Memorial Fund Quarterly/Health and Society* 54:1 (Winter): 47–82.

Rice, Dorothy P. 1966. *Estimating the Cost of Illness.* Health Economics Series no. 6. Washington, D.C.: U.S. Government Printing Office, 947–6.

Riley, Vernon. 1975. "Mouse Mammary Tumors: Alteration of Incidence as Apparent Function of Stress." *Science* 189 (August 8): 465–67.

Rosenblatt, Daniel, and Edward A. Suchman. 1964. "Blue Collar Attitudes and Information Toward Health and Illness." In Arthur B. Shostak and William Gomberg, *Blue Collar Worker*, pp. 324–33. Englewood Cliffs, N.J.: Prentice-Hall.

Rosett, Richard N. 1958. "Working Wives: An Econometric Study." In Thomas F. Dernberg, *Studies in Household Economic Behavior.* New Haven: Yale University Press.

Russell, Louise B. 1974. "Safety Incentives in Workmen's Compensation Insurance." *Journal of Human Resources* 9:3 (Summer): 361–75.

Safilios-Rothschild, Constantina. 1970. *The Sociology and Social Psychology of Disability and Rehabilitation.* New York: Random House.

Scheffler, Richard M., and George Iden. 1974. "The Effect of Disability on Labor Supply." *Industrial and Labor Relations Review* 28:1 (October): 122–32.

Schelling, Thomas C. 1968. "The Life You Save May be Your Own." In Samuel B. Chase, ed., *Problems in Public Expenditure Analysis*, pp. 127–62. Washington, D.C.: Brookings Institution.

———. 1971. "On the Ecology of Micromotives." *The Public Interest* 25 (Fall): 59–98.

Schifrin, Leonard G. 1978. "The Economics and Epidemiology of Drug Use." In Kenneth L. Melmon and H.F. Morrelli, eds., *Clinical Pharmacology: Basic Principles and Therapeutics*, 2nd ed., ch. 26. New York: Macmillian Publishing Company.

Schultz, Theodore W. 1975. "The Value of the Ability to Deal with Disequilibria." *Journal of Economic Literature* 13:3 (September): 827–46.

Schultze, Charles L. 1977. *The Public Use of Private Interest.* Washington, D.C.: Brookings Institution.

Sinai, Nathan. 1967. *Disability Insurance and Vocational Rehabilitation.* Bureau of Public Health Economics Research Series No. 13. Ann Arbor: University of Michigan School of Public Health.

Smith, Richard T., and Abraham M. Lilienfeld. 1971. *The Social Security Disability Program: An Evaluation Study.* Social Security Administration, Office of Research and Statistics, Research Report No. 39, DHEW pub. no. (SSA)72–11801. Washington, D.C.: U.S. Government Printing Office.

Spodick, David H. 1975. "On Experts and Expertise: The Effect of Variability in Observer Performance." *The American Journal of Cardiology* 36 (October): 592–96.

Stamler, Jeremiah. 1975. "The Recent Decline in Death Rates from Premature Coronary Heart Disease in the United States: Is It Real? If So, What Are Its Possible Causes." Paper presented at the American Heart Association Second Science Writers Forum, Marco Island, Florida, (January 19–22).

Stanley, Gertrude L. 1971. "Work and Earnings of the Disabled." *Social Security Survey of the Disabled, 1966.* Report no. 17 (November). Washington, D.C.: Social Security Administration.

Stigler, George J. 1971. "The Theory of Economic Regulation." *Bell Journal of Economics and Management Science* 2:1 (Spring): 3–21.

Swartz, Harold M., and Barbara A. Reichling. 1977. "The Risks of Mammograms." *Journal of the American Medical Association* 237:10 (March 7): pp. 965–66.

Swisher, Idella G. 1970. "Family Income of the Disabled." *Social Security Survey of the Disabled: 1966.* Report no. 13 (October). Washington, D.C.: Social Security Administration.

——. 1971. "Sources and Size of Income of the Disabled." *Social Security Survey of the Disabled: 1966.* Report no. 16 (June). Washington, D.C.: Social Security Administration.

Thaler, Richard, and Sherwin Rosen. 1975. "The Value of Saving a Life: Evidence from the Labor Market." In Nestor J. Terleckyj, ed., *Household Production and Consumption.* New York: National Bureau of Economic Research.

The Travelers Insurance Company. 1977. "The Travelers Thinks That Staying Alive Shouldn't Be An Optional Extra On Your Car." *Newsweek* (September 16): 106.

Urban Planning Aid. 1976. *Survival Kit.* Cambridge, Ma.: Urban Planning Aid.

U.S. Bureau of the Census. 1966. "Median Family Income Up About 5 Percent in 1965." *Current Population Reports.* Series P–60, no. 49 (August 10). Washington, D.C.: U.S. Government Printing Office.

——. 1967A. "Income in 1965 of Families and Persons in the United States." *Current Population Reports.* Series P–60, no. 51. Washington, D.C.: U.S. Government Printing Office.

——. 1967B. *Statistical Abstract of the United States: 1967.* Washington, D.C.: U.S. Government Printing Office.

U.S. Bureau of Labor Statistics. 1971. *Handbook of Labor Statistics, 1971.* Bulletin no. 1705. Washington, D.C.: U.S. Government Printing Office.

U.S. Center for Disease Control. 1977. "Adult and Teenage Cigarette Smoking Patterns—United States." *Morbidity and Mortality Weekly Report* 26:19 (May 13): 160.

U.S., Congress, House. 1977. *Health Security Act, H.R. 21.* 95th Cong. 1st sess. (January 4). Washington, D.C.: U.S. Government Printing Office.

U.S., Congress, House. Committee on Ways and Means. 1974. *Committee Staff Report on the Disability Insurance Program* (July). Washington, D.C.: U.S. Government Printing Office.

U.S. Department of Labor, and U.S. Department of Health, Education, and Welfare. 1975. *Manpower Report of the President, 1975.* Washington, D.C.: U.S. Government Printing Office.

U.S. Employment Service. 1965. *Dictionary of Occupational Titles, 1965.* Vol. II, Occupational Titles. 3rd ed. Washington, D.C.: U.S. Government Printing Office.

———. 1966. *Dictionary of Occupational Titles, Third Edition Supplement: Selected Characteristics of Occupations (Physical Demands, Working Conditions, Training Time.* Washington, D.C.: U.S. Government Printing Office.

U.S. National Cancer Institute Ad Hoc Working Groups on Mammography Screening for Breast Cancer. 1977. *Final Report and Summary Report of Their Joint Findings and Recommendations.* National Institutes of Health, DHEW pub. no. (NIH)77–1400 (March). Washington, D.C.: U.S. Government Printing Office.

U.S. National Center for Health Statistics (USNCHS). 1977. "Advance Report, Final Mortality Statistics, 1975." *Monthly Vital Statistics Report* 25:11 (Supplement, February 11). Washington, D.C.: U.S. Government Printing Office.

———. 1977. *Clearinghouse on Health Indexes, 1974–77.* Supplement to (HRA)77–1225. Washington, D.C.: U.S. Government Printing Office.

———. 1976. *Health, United States, 1975.* DHEW pub. no. (HRA)76–1232. Washington, D.C.: U.S. Government Printing Office.

USNCHS. *Vital and Health Statistics.* Washington, D.C.: U.S. Government Printing Office:

1965. Series 1, no. 4. "Plan and Initial Program of the Health Examination Survey" (July).

1967. Series 1, no. 5. "Plan, Operation, and Response Results of a Program of Children's Examinations" (October).

1969. Series 1, no. 8. "Plan and Operation of a Health Examination Survey of U.S. Youths 12–17 Years of Age" (September).

1975. Series 1, no. 11. "Health Interview Survey Procedure 1957–74" DHEW pub. no. (HRA)75–1311 (April).

1965. Series 2, no. 7. "Health Interview Responses Compared with Medical Records" Pub. no. 1000 (July).

1965. Series 2, no. 9. "Cooperation in Health Examination Surveys" Pub. no. 1000 (July).

1967. Series 2, no. 23. "Interview Data on Chronic Conditions Compared with Information Derived from Medical Records" Pub. no. 1000 (May).

1969. Series 2, no. 36. "Factors Related to Response in a Health Examination Survey, U.S. 1960–62" Pub. no. 1000 (August).

1973. Series 2, no. 43. "Sample Design and Estimation Procedures for a National Health Examination Survey of Children" DHEW pub. no. (HRA)74–1005 (August).

1972. Series 2, no. 48. "Interviewing Methods in the Health Interview Survey" (HSM)72–1048 (April).

1972. Series 2, no. 49. "Reporting Health Events in Household Interviews: Effects of an Extensive Questionnaire and a Diary Procedure" (HSM)72–1049 (April).

1973. Series 2, no. 57. "Net Differences in Interview Data on Chronic Conditions and Information Derived from Medical Records" (HSM)73–1331 (June).

1977. Series 2, no. 69. "A Summary of Studies of Interviewing Methodology" (HRA)77–1343 (March).

1965. Series 10, no. 21. "Selected Health Characteristics by Occupation, U.S. July 1961–June 1963" (August).

1967. Series 10, no. 37. "Current Estimates from the Health Interview Survey, U.S. July 1965–June 1966" (May).

1967. Series 10, no. 38. "Acute Conditions: Incidence and Associated Disability, U.S. July 1965–June 1966" (June).

1967. Series 10, no. 42. "Family Hospital and Surgical Insurance Coverage, U.S. July 1962–June 1963" (November).

1968. Series 10, no. 43. "Current Estimates from the Health Interview Survey, U.S. July 1966–June 1967" (January).

1968. Series 10, no. 44. "Acute Conditions: Incidence and Associated Disability, U.S. July 1966–June 1967" (March).

1970. Series 10, no. 58. "Persons Injured and Disability Days Due to Injury, U.S. July 1965–June 1967" (March).

1970. Series 10, no. 60. "Current Estimates from the Health Interview Survey, U.S. 1968" (June).

1971. Series 10, no. 61. "Chronic Conditions and Limitations of Activity and Mobility, U.S. July 1965–June 1967" (January).

1972. Series 10, no. 68. "Work Injuries Among Blue-Collar Workers and Disability Days, U.S. July 1966–June 1967" (HSM)72–1035 (February).

1973. Series 10, no. 83. "Prevalence of Selected Chronic Digestive Conditions, U.S. July–December 1968" (HRA)74–1510 (September).

1973. Series 10, no. 84. "Prevalence of Selected Chronic Respiratory Conditions, U.S. 1970" (HRA)74–1511 (September).

1973. Series 10, no. 87. "Impairments Due to Injury, U.S. 1971" (HRA) 74–1514 (December).

1974. Series 10, no. 92. "Prevalence of Chronic Skin and Musculoskeletal Conditions, U.S. 1969" (HRA)75–1519 (August).

1974. Series 10, no. 94. "Prevalence of Chronic Circulatory Conditions, U.S. 1972" (HRA)75–1521 (September).

1974. Series 10, no. 95. "Current Estimates from the Health Interview Survey, U.S. 1973" (HRA)75–1522 (October).

1974. Series 10, no. 96. "Limitation of Activity and Mobility Due to Chronic Conditions, U.S. 1972" (HRA)75–1523 (November).

1975. Series 10, no. 97. "Physician Visits: Volume and Interval Since Last Visit, U.S. 1971" (HRA)75–1524 (March).

1975. Series 10, no. 99. "Prevalence of Selected Impairments, U.S. 1971" (HRA)75–1526 (May).

1975. Series 10, no. 100. "Current Estimates from the Health Interview Survey, U.S. 1974" (HRA)76–1527 (September).

1976. Series 10, no. 105. "Persons Injured and Disability Days by Detailed Type and Class of Accidents, U.S. 1971–1972" (HRA)76–1532 (January).

1964. Series 11, no. 1. "Cycle I of the Health Examination Survey: Sample and Response, U.S. 1960–1962" Pub. no. 1000 (April).

1965. Series 11, no. 9. "Findings on the Serologic Test for Syphilis in Adults, U.S. 1960–1962" Pub. no. 1000 (June).

1965. Series 11, no. 10. "Coronary Heart Disease in Adults, U.S. 1960–1962" Pub. no. 1000 (September).

1965. Series 11, no. 12. "Periodontal Disease in Adults, U.S. 1960–1962" Pub. no. 1000 (November).

1966. Series 11, no. 13. "Hypertension and Hypertensive Heart Disease in Adults, U.S. 1960–1962" Pub. no. 1000 (May).

1966. Series 11, no. 16. "Oral Hygiene in Adults, U.S. 1960–1962" Pub. no. 1000 (June).

1966. Series 11, no. 17. "Rheumatoid Arthritis in Adults, U.S. 1960–1962" Pub. no. 1000 (September).

1966. Series 11, no. 18. "Blood Glucose Levels in Adults, U.S. 1960–1962" Pub. no. 1000 (September).

1966. Series 11, no. 20. "Osteoarthritis in Adults by Selected Demographic Characteristics, U.S. 1960–1962" Pub. no. 1000 (November).

1967. Series 11, no. 22. "Serum Cholesterol Levels of Adults, U.S. 1960–1962" Pub. no. 1000 (March).

1967. Series 11, no. 23. "Decayed, Missing and Filled Teeth in Adults, U.S. 1960–1962" Pub. no. 1000 (February).

1967. Series 11, no. 24. "Mean Blood Hematocrit of Adults, U.S. 1960–1962" Pub. no. 1000 (April).

1967. Series 11, no. 25. "Binocular Visual Acuity of Adults, by Region and Selected Demographic Characteristics, U.S. 1960–1962" Pub. no. 1000 (June).

1967. Series 11, no. 27. "Total Loss of Teeth in Adults, U.S. 1960–1962" Pub. no. 1000 (October).

1968. Series 11, no. 31. "Hearing Levels of Adults by Education, Income, and Occupation, U.S. 1960–1962" Pub. no. 1000 (May).

1970. Series 11, no. 36. "Need for Dental Care Among Adults, U.S. 1960–1962" Pub. no. 1000 (March).

1970. Series 11, no. 37. "Selected Symptoms of Psychological Distress, U.S." Pub. no. 1000 (August).

1971. Series 11, no. 106. "Decayed, Missing, and Filled Teeth Among Children, U.S." DHEW pub. no. (HSM)72–1003 (August).

1972. Series 11, no. 111. "Hearing Levels of Children by Demographic and Socioeconomic Characteristics, U.S." (HSM)72–1025 (February).

1972. Series 11, no. 112. "Binocular Visual Acuity of Children: Demographic and Socioeconomic Characteristics, U.S." (HSM)72–1031 (February).

1972. Series 11, no. 117. "Periodontal Disease and Oral Hygiene Among Children, U.S." (HSM)72–1060 (June).

1972. Series 11, no. 118. "Color Vision Deficiencies in Children, U.S." (HSM)73–1600 (August).

1972. Series 11, no. 119. "Height and Weight of Children: Socioeconomic Status, U.S." (HSM)73–1601 (October).

1972. Series 11, no. 122. "Hearing and Related Medical Findings Among Children: Race, Area, and Socioeconomic Differentials, U.S." (HSM)73–1604 (October).

1973. Series 11, no. 127. "Visual Acuity of Youths 12–17 Years, U.S." (HSM)73–1609 (May).

1973. Series 11, no. 129. "Examination and Health History Findings Among Children and Youths, 6–17 Years, U.S." (HRA)74–1611 (November).

1973. Series 11, no. 130. "An Assessment of the Occlusion of the Teeth of Children 6–11 Years, U.S." (HRA)74–1612 (November).

1974. Series 11, no. 134. "Color Vision Deficiencies in Youths 12–17 Years of Age, U.S." (HRA)74–1616 (January).

1973. Series 11, no. 135. "Blood Pressure Levels of Children 6–11 Years: Relationship to Age, Sex, Race, and Socioeconomic Status, U.S." (HRA)74–1617 (December).

1974. Series 11, no. 141. "Periodontal Disease Among Youths 12–17 Years, U.S." (HRA)74–1623 (June).

1974. Series 11, no. 144. "Decayed, Missing, and Filled Teeth Among Youths 12–17 Years, U.S." (HRA)75–1626 (October).

1975. Series 11, no. 145. "Hearing Levels of Youths 12–17 Years—U.S." (HRA)75–1627 (January).

1974. Series 11, no. 146. "Hematocrit Values of Youths 12–17 Years, U.S." (HRA)75–1628 (December).

1974. Series 11, no. 148. "Refraction Status of Youths 12–17 Years, U.S." (HRA)75–1630 (December).

1975. Series 11, no. 149. "Skeletal Maturity of Children 6–11 Years: Racial, Geographic Area, and Socioeconomic Differentials, U.S." (HRA)76–1631 (October).

1975. Series 11, no. 151. "Oral Hygiene Among Youths 12–17 Years, U.S." (HRA)76–1633 (September).

1975. Series 11, no. 152. "Serum Uric Acid Values of Youths 12–17 Years, U.S." (HRA)76–1634 (August).

1975. Series 11, no. 155. "Eye Examination Findings Among Youths Aged 12–17 Years, U.S." (HRA)76–1637 (November).

1974. Series 20, no. 16. "Mortality Trends for Leading Causes of Death, U.S. 1950–69" (HRA)74–1853 (March).

U.S., Office of Economic Opportunity. 1970. *Guide to the Documentation and Data Files of the 1966 and 1967 Survey of Economic Opportunity.* Washington, D.C.: U.S. Government Printing Office.

U.S., Office of the President. 1972. *President's Report on Occupational Safety and Health.* Washington, D.C.: U.S. Government Printing Office.

U.S. Vocational Rehabilitation Administration. 1967. *An Exploratory Cost-Benefit Analysis of Vocational Rehabilitation.* Division of Statistics and Studies. Washington, D.C.: U.S. Government Printing Office.

Vickery, Donald M., and James F. Fries. 1976. *Take Care of Yourself: A Consumer's Guide to Medical Care.* Reading, Ma.: Addison-Wesley.

Vogel, Ronald, and Roger Blair. 1975. "Health Insurance Administrative Costs." *Staff Paper No. 21.* Washington, D.C.: U.S. Social Security Administration, Office of Research and Statistics, DHEW pub. no. (SSA)76–11856 (October).

Walker, Weldon J. 1977. "Changing United States Life-Style and Declining Vascular Mortality: Cause or Coincidence?" *The New England Journal of Medicine* 297:3 (July 21): 163–65.

Wall Street Journal Staff Reporter. 1977. "Breast Cancer Screening Project Finds Some Women Had Unnecessary Surgery." *The Wall Street Journal* (September 19).

Warner, Kenneth E. 1977. "The Effects of the Anti-Smoking Campaign on Cigarette Consumption." *American Journal of Public Health* 67:7 (July): 645–50.

Warner, Kenneth E., and Joseph M. Chadwick. 1976. "Health Maintenance Insurance: Toward An Optimal HMO." Draft, unpublished.

Watts, Harold W. et al. 1974. "The Labor Supply Response of Husbands." *Journal of Human Resources* 9:2 (Spring): 181–200.

Weiss, Randall D. 1970. "The Effect of Education on the Earnings of Blacks and Whites." *Review of Economics and Statistics* 52:2 (May): 150–59.

Weiss, Robert J., and Bernard J. Bergen. 1968. "Social Supports and the Reduction of Psychiatric Disability." *Psychiatry: Journal for the Study of Interpersonal Processes* 31:2 (May): 107–15.

Wennberg, John, and Alan Gittelsohn. 1973. "Small Area Variations in Health Care Delivery." *Science* 182:4117 (December 14): 1102–08.

————. 1975. "Health Care Delivery in Maine I: Patterns of Use of Common Surgical Procedures." *Journal of the Maine Medical Association* 66:5 (May): 123–30, 149.

Wilson, Ronald W., and Elijah L. White. 1977. "Changes in Morbidity, Disability, and Utilization Differentials between the Poor and the Nonpoor: Data from the Health Interview Survey: 1964 and 1973." *Medical Care* 15:8 (August): 636–46.

Winick, Myron. 1969. "Malnutrition and Brain Development." *Journal of Pediatrics* 74:5 (May): 667–79.

Wray, Joe D. 1974. "The Malnutrition-Morbidity-Mortality Complex in Children Under Five." In A.R. Omran, ed., *Community Medicine in Developing Countries: Theory and Practice.* New York: Springer Publishing Company.

Wynder, Ernest L., and Dietrich Hoffmann. 1976. "Tobacco and Tobacco Smoke." *Seminars in Oncology* 3:1 (March): 5–15.

Wynder, E.L.; F. Lemon; and I. Bross. 1959. "Cancer and Coronary Artery Disease Among Seventh-Day Adventists." *Cancer* (New York) 12: 1016.

Zeckhauser, Richard J. 1973. "Coverage for Catastrophic Illness." *Public Policy* 21:2 (Spring): 149–72.

Zola, Irving Kenneth. 1966. "Culture and Symptoms—An Analysis of Patients' Presenting Complaints." *American Sociological Review* 31: 615–30. Reprinted in Eliot Freidson and Judith Lorber, eds., *Medical Men and Their Work*, pp. 390–13. Chicago: Aldine-Atherton, 1972.

Index

nonoccupational, 222; nutrition and, 207; policy questions concerning, 9-11; prevention of, 4; psychosocial stresses and, 208, 209-10; reducing impact of, 11; reducing incidence of, 9-10; reducing severity of, 10-11; socioeconomic factors as a cause of, 31-72
Health, socioeconomic factors and, model, 20-27
Health, socioeconomic status and, 15-16
Health status, definitions of, 17-20
Hearing impairments, 56, 62t, 63t
Hearing levels: adults, 45t, 50t; children, 46t, 51t; youths, 48t, 52t
HEART, 130, 136
Heart attack, obesity and, 20
Heart disease: coronary, 43t, 50t, 60t, 61t, 64t; death and, 5-6; hypertensive, 43t, 49, 50t, 60t, 61t, 64t; reduction of, 5
Heart rhythm, disorders of, 60t, 61t, 64t
Height, children, 46t, 51t, 53
Hematocrit values: adults, 44t, 50t; youths, 48t, 52t
Hemorrhoids, 60t, 61t, 64f
Heredity, disease and, 6, 208
Hernia, 60t, 61t, 66f
HOURWAGE, 156, 160
Household heads (HHEAD), 102
HRSWRKED, 156, 160, 166
Hypertension, 42, 43t, 49, 50t; obesity and, 20
Hypertensive heart disease. *See* Heart disease, hypertensive

Illness, defined, 18-19
Impairment: defined, 19; prevalence of, 53-59; socioeconomic factors and, 22-23, 24, 28
Incentives, health problems and, 221-22, 223-25, 227-28; economic, 235-40; insurance, 223-25; rehabilitation, 228-30, 235; wage subsidy, 232-33; workers' compensation, 221-22
INCOME, 103
Income; disability problems and, 88t, 90; health and, 15-16, 53-54; reducing impact of disability on, 233-35
Income, effects of disability of, 183-96; extended family, 185-87; nuclear family, 183-85

Industrial pollution, health problems and, 20
Influenza, 5, 16
Injuries, 57-59
Insurance incentives, health problems and, 223-25
Interventionist strategy, public policy, 213-14, 215, 217

Job stresses, health problems and, 20
JOBYRLIM, 126, 145
Jogging, 224

Kidney transplants, 3

Labor market, improving for the disabled, 230-33
Labor market behavior, disabled and, 152-67
Lacto-vegetarian diet, health and, 223
Lefcowitz, Myron J., 42
LFPYEAR, 155
Life, prolonging of, 6
Lifestyle, health problems and, 209-10
LIFTS, 102
LIFTS*HVYLABOR, 103
Lower extremity/hip impairments, 56, 62t, 63t
LUNGS, 130, 136

Malnutrition, 20
Market strategy, public policy and, 214-15, 216, 217
Medicaid, 2,, 3, 4
Medical care: increased expenditure on, 1960s and 1970s, 5; value of, at margin, 4-6
Medicare, 2, 3, 4, 18n
Mental illness, 28; economic fluctuations and, 197-98
Methodology, 15-29
MOBILITY, 130, 136
Monthly Labor Survey, 26
Morbidity, 18n
Morgan, James, et al., 164, 165, 166, 167
Mortality, 18n
Mortality rates, poor, 16
Musculoskeletal condition, chronic, 62t, 67f
Myocardial infarction, 42, 43t, 49, 50t

About the Author

Harold S. Luft received his doctorate in economics at Harvard University, specializing in public finance and health economics. His current research interests are in health and medical care, with special emphases on the behavior of medical care providers in various organizational and competitive settings, and the role of the consumer in health care decisions. He is presently writing *Health Maintenance Organizations: Theory, Rhetoric and Evidence.* At Stanford University he is assistant professor of health economics in the Health Services Research Program of the School of Medicine.